Georgia
FLIGHT
The History of Aviation in Georgia
1907 - 2007

Georgia Flight: The History Of Aviation In Georgia

Published by Wm. Robb Group, LLC

Editor: Phillip Rob Bellury
Copy Editor: Mandy Templeton Wilson
Image Editor: Susan Gemmill

Editorial Contributors:
Marty Steiner: Chapters 1-4 and 6, The Fowler Transcontinental Flight, Eugene Jacques
Bullard, Lindbergh In Georgia, Doug Davis, Atlanta: Candler Field, The Bell Bomber Plant
Susan Gemmill: Chapter 5, Vic Hewes, Agricultural Aviation In Georgia, Women In Georgia
Aviation, African American Aviators In Georgia
Walter Knapp: Ben T. Epps, E. Patrick Epps, Greenland Expedition
Russell Still: Brig. General Robert L. Scott

Georgia's Next Century of Flight:
Dave Hirschman: Looking Forward
Dr. Deborah J. Huffman: What's Next For Aviation Education?
Lt. Governor Casey Cagle: Roadmap For The Future

Book Design: Mabry-Green Studios - Mike Green, Art Director; Sue Mabry, Production Manager

Inquiries:
Wm. Robb Group, LLC
Randy Hasty, randy@wmrobbgroup.com

Book Development: The Storyline Group, Inc.

Library of Congress Cataloging-in-Publication Data

Wm. Robb Group, LLC
Georgia flight: the history of aviation in Georgia/ by Wm. Robb Group, LLC
Includes biographical references.
ISBN 978-0-9791115-0-1
1. Aviation—History—Georgia. 2. Flight in Georgia.

The field of aviation has a rich and dynamic history in Georgia. Gulfstream Aerospace Corporation is proud to have been part of Georgia's aviation heritage for the past 40 years, and looks forward to continuing to be a part of the future.

Gulfstream®

A GENERAL DYNAMICS COMPANY

Georgia Flight
The History Of Aviation In Georgia

Message from Governor Sonny Perdue

The history of aviation in Georgia is one of our state's most fascinating and important stories. Ever since Ben Epps built his airplane and made his historic flight in Athens just a few years after Kitty Hawk in 1903, aviation has played a vital role in Georgia's growth and economic development. Commercial and general aviation are integral parts of this state's transportation network, and the aviation industry – including a number of major aircraft manufacturers and military bases – contributes billions of dollars annually to Georgia's economy.

During the 2007 hundred-year anniversary of powered flight in Georgia, all citizens of this state, especially our young people, should come to know and appreciate aviation's contributions to our growth and prosperity. *Georgia Flight* is indeed a valuable tool for documenting the rich history of a great industry in Georgia.

As Governor of Georgia and as a pilot, I commend the many people and organizations who have contributed to the publication of this book.

Sincerely,

Sonny Perdue

FOREWORD

The clouds were pink – just like cotton candy. Sometimes at sunset, you'll find them like that. Today, we had lucked out. I was 12 years old and next to me in the back seat of a J-3 Piper Cub was my best friend, Willie. Brother Doug, the pilot, 17, was flying in and out of the clouds, executing loops and wingovers and just plain having fun. We loved it! Later, Willie's mother made it clear that she didn't think a 17-year-old should be taking her baby boy flying. No whipping, but a few big frowns.

Those thrills in the clouds are still available – you just need to pay more attention to the regulations. Take off from a dark, rain-soaked runway on an instrument clearance, climb for 10 minutes and then break out on top – clouds below and a magnificent, clear blue sky above. A spiritual experience. All is right with the world.

Today, Georgia has 103 paved public airports, and there are many more private grass strips all over the state. The future of aviation is bright. The next 5, 10 or 20 years promise to see continued growth for pilots, mechanics and many other aviation-related jobs and careers.

This book on the history of 100 years of Georgia aviation chronicles the origins of an industry and the foundation laid by many individuals and companies mentioned in the chapters to follow. We owe them all a debt of gratitude for their contributions. They have left us a great legacy to continue to build on for the next century of flight in Georgia.

Pat Epps
Epps Aviation

INTRODUCTION

Less than four years after the Wright Brothers flew across the sand dunes at Kitty Hawk, Georgia aviation pioneer Ben T. Epps piloted his own aircraft about 100 yards across a cow pasture near Athens, Georgia. The significance of that flight in 1907 cannot be overestimated, especially by anyone remotely connected to the field of aviation. And most of us are. Epps set the stage for an industry that today ranks among the leading economic generators in the state and touches all Georgians in one way or another.

Much of aviation history is about firsts, as this book will demonstrate. That Ben Epps made the first documented powered flight in Georgia is undisputed, but not everyone agrees that Orville Wright's 1903 flight at Kitty Hawk was the first powered flight in the world. More than one historian credits Georgia's own aviation pioneer, Augustus Herring, as the first to fly a "motorized machine" about 73 feet along the sand dunes of Lake Michigan's Silver Beach in October of 1899. It was an event that might have been deemed the first flight, but the press did not give it coverage. They were distracted by an event taking place just down the road in Three Oaks, Michigan. President McKinley was visiting the small town to dedicate a cannon captured during the Spanish-American War by Admiral Dewey. The people of Three Oaks had won the cannon in a national competition to raise money for the war effort, and Edward K. Warren, city father and founder of The Warren Featherbone Company, was a master promoter who garnered all the attention away from Herring. An interesting side note to that story is that The Warren Featherbone Company eventually moved its operations to Gainesville, Georgia in the mid-1950s.

While Ben Epps was the first Georgia aviator to fly a powered aircraft, he was not the first in the state to take to the air. Balloon flights took place as early as 1835 and actually played a role as field observation aircraft during the War Between the States, but aviation as an industry really got wind under its wings with the advent of controlled, engine-powered flight. The prospect of flying machines that could transport people, goods and mail led to giant leaps in technology, aided in large part by branches of the military working with aircraft manufacturers in a scramble to develop the best aircraft as fast as possible, a race that continues today.

The economic impact from the four primary areas involved in Georgia aviation – military, manufacturing, general and commercial aviation – measures in the billions of dollars. Aircraft manufacturers, airports, military bases and dozens of other businesses related to aviation offer jobs, pay taxes, contribute to charities and generally contribute to the economies of communities all over the state. In almost every case, the relationship between the aviation community and the community at large is a happy one. It is a relationship that has stood the test of time.

Few states in the U.S. can claim to have the depth of aviation history that Georgia does. The list of distinctions by Georgia people and organizations in the field of aviation are many and include:

- One of the earliest American balloon ascensions
- One of the first U.S. military aviation training fields
- The first black military pilot in the world
- The first U.S. Marine pilot
- The site of Charles Lindbergh's first solo flight

- The winner of the first National Air Races
- The training site of thousands of RAF pilots for WWII
- The home of the Mighty Eighth Air Force
- The first U.S. Presidential pilot
- The world's most highly-regarded corporate jet
- The world's most advanced manned military aircraft
- The world's most highly-regarded STOL aircraft
- The world's busiest airport (passengers boarded)
- The aircraft with the longest production run in aviation history
- The designer and commander of the Berlin Airlift

The idea for publication of *Georgia Flight: The History of Aviation in Georgia* grew out of a collective spirit that pervades the aviation community in Georgia. That spirit is as old as humankind's centuries-old dreams to fly like birds, and that community has its roots with the early pioneers such as Ben Epps, Doug Davis and others who followed. They all contributed to a statewide industry that today has global significance, with manufacturers who build aircraft sold around the world and airlines that travel the globe.

To that end, the publishers of this first centennial history of powered flight in Georgia would like to express their gratitude to all those in the Georgia aviation community who supported this challenging undertaking. They are far too numerous to mention in a paragraph so we have dedicated an entire section to them at the end of this book. That said, however, special thanks must be given to Epps Aviation for their initial support and Gulfstream Aerospace Corporation for their immediate recognition of the importance of producing this historical record. Both of these great Georgia companies have built long-standing reputations that reach far beyond the borders of this state and legacies that will reach far beyond this first 100 years.

Finally, recognition should be granted to the researchers, writers, editors, photographers, designers and other publishing professionals who labored to bring this story to light. Their determination to capture the essence of Georgia's aviation history led them to libraries, museums, businesses and private collections in every corner of the state.

No history of aviation in Georgia can include every story of every individual, event or location, and this book makes no claims to do so. Given the limitations of time and space, *Georgia Flight* is as comprehensive and accurate as possible, and perhaps our greatest challenge as publishers was making the hard decisions about whether a particular story would remain in the book or not. Every city or town, every airport and military base has its own unique history, and each story deserves to be told. Our goal with this book was to include as many individual stories as possible while we made certain that the story of a great industry was adequately conveyed.

Going forward, it is our hope as publishers that this book will stand the test of time and be a source of enlightenment for all those who find the field of aviation as fascinating and intriguing as we do. Furthermore, it is hoped that young people who read and study these pages will be inspired to consider aviation as their chosen field.

And… may the next century of aviation in Georgia be as rewarding as the first.

Early Flight
&
Early Birds

Above: Augustus Moore Herring – early aviation engineer/designer and test pilot.

Facing Page: Herring tests the Chanute biplane glider over Indiana Dunes, near Lake Michigan, 1896.

National Air & Space Museum

PRE-POWERED FLIGHT – Early manned flight includes all efforts to remain aloft for more than an instant. Centuries before successful manned flight, men who were fascinated by the flight of birds would fashion flapping wings only to fail miserably in their attempts to get off the ground. By the mid-1800s, however, the development of lighter-than-air aircraft, specifically hot air and captive gas balloons, became the standard for becoming airborne. During the latter half of the 19th Century, balloon flights became a common sight at fairs and other public gatherings.

The War Between the States saw both sides utilizing balloons, primarily for observation. Georgians were involved in the most significant efforts by the Confederacy.

THE BALLOON

Long before Georgia's aviation pioneers mastered powered flight, earlier aspirants set the stage with lighter-than-air aircraft. Indeed, Georgia's first aircraft was the balloon; Georgia's first aircraft designer and manufacturer was noted balloonist, Charles Cevor; and Georgia's first military pilot, Major Edward Porter Alexander, C.S.A., used a balloon to observe movement of Union troops.

Evidence of balloon ascensions in Georgia appears in Georgia newspapers as early as 1835. One particularly well-documented flight occurred on March 8, 1860. Charles Cevor of Savannah launched his balloon, *Montpelier*, into a heavy gale. The balloon, Cevor, and a paying passenger, Mr. Dalton, were carried out to sea, but Cevor managed to successfully bring the balloon down along the coast, some forty miles from Savannah.

A year later in April of 1861, Cevor volunteered the services of his current balloon, *Forest City*, to the Confederate government, but the offer was refused. However, General Thomas Drayton, C.S.A., of South Carolina had for some time shown interest in the potential use of balloons for field observation. He authorized Capt. Langdon Cheves, C.S.A., to contract with Charles Cevor to construct a balloon, providing that gas and materials could be procured. With help from another Confederate officer, Capt. Pratt, Cevor successfully developed a hydrogen gas-generating process, and General Drayton authorized construction of the balloon.

Construction began on the *Gazelle* at St. Andrews Hall in Savannah. Frequently referred to as the "Silk Dress" or "Petticoat" balloon, the *Gazelle* was created from every yard of fine silk fabric available in Savannah and Charleston. The Confederate financial records of Capt. Langdon Cheves reveal "eight pieces of colored silk totaling over 110 yards were purchased at $1.50 per yard." Witnesses to the construction noted black, white, yellow, and green strips were utilized. The often-recorded romantic story of Southern ladies donating their fine silk dresses for the

Above: Realizing the utility of the Federal balloons, Confederates wanted one of their own. They requisitioned all of the silk dresses in Savannah and sewed them together into a balloon, which was oiled and varnished and inflated at the Richmond Illuminating Gas Works. The balloon made one ascension before it was captured by Union forces. Thaddeus S.C. Lowe found the balloon unfit for military use and cut it up.

National Air & Space Museum

Facing Page: A depiction of a Civil War-era observation balloon.

Illustration: Sue Mabry

construction of this balloon and for the cause of the Confederacy is undocumented, although a number of otherwise authoritative sources repeat this tale.

Silk was selected due to its light weight and tight weave. Even so, the seal was not tight enough to hold air or gas. A coating was developed by dissolving worn rubber rail car springs in naphtha, a flexible, varnish-like substance that was both airtight and lightweight.

The *Gazelle* was offered as ready for service around May 22, 1862. Initially considered for use in the defense of Savannah, there is no evidence that it was ever put to such use. (There were reports of a Union balloon near Fort Pulaski at that time, however.) The *Gazelle* was being inflated for ascension near Charleston when it was ordered to Richmond instead. Carried on a specially scheduled train, it was to be used as part of Gen. Robert E. Lee's defense of Richmond against Union Gen. George McClellan.

Since efforts to develop a hydrogen gas generator for field use had not yet been successful, the *Gazelle* was filled with illuminating gas (used for street lights) at the Richmond Gas Works. The aircraft was then moved to the front on a cable tethered to a train locomotive.

Major Edward Porter Alexander was responsible for the operations of this balloon for observation at the Battle of Gaines Mill (near Richmond) from June 27-29, 1862. He ascended to an altitude of about one thousand feet and reported, by semaphore signals, the location and strength of the enemy troops. Alexander, in fact, had developed this semaphore system which was the basis for the formation of the Army Signal Corps. All U.S. Army aviation operations remained under the Signal Corps through the First World War.

While the initial operations of this balloon were quite successful, the battle lines eventually moved away from the rail line and closer to the nearby James River. At that point, the balloon was transferred to a small Confederate gun boat, the *CSS Teaser*, to be towed upriver. The *Teaser* ran aground and was captured, with the balloon, by the Union gunboat *Maratanza*. Major Alexander escaped by swimming to the woods along the banks of the James.

Charles Cevor did construct a replacement balloon in Savannah which was completed in late August of 1862. By then the threat to Richmond was over, so the new balloon was used in the Charleston, South Carolina area. Orders were issued directing Cevor and his balloon to Charleston and authority was issued to reimburse Cevor for his expenses in maintaining and deploying it. Records indicate that a number of successful reconnaissance flights were performed in the Charleston area. During such a flight in 1863, a high wind carried the balloon over Union lines and it was captured. That balloon was sent to the U.S. Patent Office where it was cut into pieces and distributed to many locations, including the Smithsonian Institution.

Later promoted to General, Alexander has been claimed by many cities. His *Fighting for the Confederacy*, a voluminous work finally assembled and published within the last twenty years, describes his early life in Washington, Georgia. His previous highly-regarded work, *Military Memoirs of a Confederate*, was published in 1907.

After the war General Alexander had a very successful career in business. He was Professor of Engineering at the University of South Carolina and served as President of the Columbia Oil Company, the Georgia Railroad and Banking Company, and the Central Georgia Railroad Company. Cevor returned to Savannah and is known to have produced and promoted a variety of special events. He later moved to Valdosta sometime prior to 1868.

The two Georgians responsible for these historic balloon flights, General Edward Porter Alexander and Charles Cevor, later commissioned Captain, were enshrined in the Georgia Aviation Hall of Fame in April 2006. They are among the first American military aviators.

Other attempts at manned flight involved a variety of kites and gliders. While no known glider experiments or flights occurred in Georgia prior to 1900, a Georgia-born inventor and flyer did participate in this phase. Augustus Moore Herring may be the most elusive of America's early aeronauts. This shadowy figure was the only individual who actually worked with every American early aviation experimenter including Chanute, Langley, Curtiss and, of course, the Wright Brothers.

AUGUSTUS MOORE HERRING: GEORGIA AVIATION PIONEER
The names of America's most prominent early aviation experimenters are well known: Langley, Chanute, Curtiss, and the Wright Brothers. Others who worked diligently in groups associated with these early pioneers are somewhat less known. One such unknown, Georgia-born Augustus Moore Herring, is the only one to have participated with every one of these pioneers. His story is vague and shifting, perhaps intentionally distorted by Herring himself.

Tom D. Crouch, Senior Curator, Aeronautics, National Air and Space Museum, identifies Herring as "born in Somersville, Georgia, the son of a wealthy cotton broker." Of the two Summerville, Georgia communities, the defunct town near Augusta is most likely Herring's birthplace. Herring attended Stevens Institute in Hoboken, New Jersey, studying mechanical engineering. He claimed that he failed to graduate in 1888 because the faculty rejected his thesis on mechanical flight, although Institute records indicate that his thesis actually was for a marine steam engine.

In 1894, Herring built and tested two different Lilienthal-style (birdlike) gliders. One was fitted with a spring-loaded movable tail that would lessen, or damper, the effect of wind gusts. Like the other pioneers, he was addressing the problem of flight control.

Based on his experience with these gliders, Herring was hired by Samuel Langley to assist with aeronautical experiments at the Smithsonian Institution. Herring resigned seven months later in a "fit of temperament."

The next documented appearance of Herring was as one of three assistants to Octave Chanute's glider experiments in 1896. Chanute, who might be regarded as the grandfather of American aviation, was a highly successful civil engineer. He had earlier put aside a lifelong passion for the possibility of manned flight until he felt financially secure enough to risk his reputation on aerial navigation.

Chanute had authored a series of articles on man's attempts to fly for *The Railroad and Engineering Journal*, which were published from October 1891 to December 1893. He was the Chairman of the "International Conference on Aerial Navigation" at Chicago's Columbian Exposition (World's Fair) in 1893. Chanute's articles were collected into a book, *Progress on Flying Machines*, in 1894. This book established Chanute as the elder statesman of American aviation.

Chanute had been informed by Langley that Herring's "reliability was as questionable as his discretion." In spite of that warning, Chanute designated Herring as supervisor for construction of a movable wing glider. Herring was also to reconstruct his Lilienthal glider for further testing under Chanute's guidance.

In June of 1896, Chanute and his three assistants showed up at the dunes of

Below: The gentleman in the jaunty straw boater, leaning against the wing of the Curtiss-B1, is probably A.M. Herring.

National Air & Space Museum

A.M. HERRING. C.M. MANLY A.R. HAWLEY J.A.D. McCUROY.

Indiana to experiment with these two gliders. With experiences remarkably similar to the later Wright Brothers' at Kitty Hawk, a camp was established, flights made, and Chanute compiled a diary of it all. Most of the flights were by Herring.

The group established a new camp in August, after rebuilding the Chanute glider and adding two new gliders to the fleet. Like the Wrights, they sought privacy for their experiments. The most successful glider was a biplane design with a variation of Herring's movable tail. Some referred to this glider as the Chanute-Herring machine.

A few weeks later, Herring invited the press, and had a showdown with Chanute. He also claimed to have made impressive flights without the observation of anyone on the Chanute team.

In December 1896, Herring applied for a patent on a powered glider similar to the successful Chanute-Herring machine. This patent application was rejected in 1898 as theoretical and unprovable. Herring set about actually building the machine.

Herring, a self-professed expert in lightweight engines, was unable to produce what he needed for this aircraft. He mounted a compressed air motor with a 30-second endurance and claimed success in October of 1898. Chanute was invited to witness a demonstration of a powered flight, but the craft did not fly.

Herring essentially disappears until 1902, when news of a large prize for a flying machine to be awarded at the 1904 St. Louis Exposition gets his attention. First he approaches Chanute, then American Hiram Maxim in London, with intention to assist in building a prize-winning aircraft.

Below: Camp Chanute, Indiana. Octave Chanute (seated fifth from the right) and Augustus Moore Herring (probably seated second from right).

National Air & Space Museum

Above:
As Augustus Moore
Herring prepares to
launch himself in his
1897 biplane glider,
Octave Chanute's dogs,
Rags and Tatters, stand
ready to witness the
event. An unidentified
man supports the lower
wing of the craft. Indiana
Dunes, 1897.

Letters between Chanute and Maxim describe Herring as "possessing considerable ability, knowledge, and mechanical instinct ... but he cannot be easily managed."

Chanute, well along in years, offered to donate his gliders to the Wright Brothers for testing at Kitty Hawk in 1902. Part of the deal was for Herring, knowledgeable about the Chanute machines, to join the Wrights in North Carolina. Wilbur Wright wrote Chanute, "several things I had heard about Mr. Herring's relations with Mr. Langley ... indicate a jealous disposition."

Chanute, Herring and two gliders arrived at the Wright Brothers' Kitty Hawk camp. While this was the flight control breakthrough year for the Wrights, neither Chanute glider ever performed well in their few flights.

The Chanute party left for Washington, the Smithsonian and specifically Langley. Chanute was planning to pay a courtesy call but it appeared that Herring was attempting to gain employment with Langley by offering information about the latest Wright developments. This early version of industrial espionage was fairly obvious and after Langley spent a few minutes with his friend Chanute, he refused to see Herring at all.

Well over a year later, following the Wright Brothers' successful first flight, a congratulatory letter from Herring reached the Wrights. Herring apparently had filed a patent request for a machine remarkably similar to the Wright 1903 Flyer. In "consideration for the brothers … and to avoid litigation and competition…," Herring proposed a joint company to market the Flyer. That company would provide one-third ownership to three participants, Wilbur, Orville, and Herring.

Below: The Octave Chanute 1896 biplane glider in flight down the Indiana Dunes near Lake Michigan.

National Air & Space Museum

Above: The 1896 Chanute biplane glider in low level flight, probably piloted by A. M. Herring. Here the biplane glides down the side of a dune at Camp Chanute on the shores of Lake Michigan near Gary, Indiana, in late summer, 1896.

National Air & Space Museum

This offer fueled a number of letters among the Wrights, the Smithsonian and Chanute. It was the final straw for Chanute, who never communicated with Herring again.

The first Aero Club of America show in 1904 did include Herring's two propellers that had been utilized on his 1898 compressed-air-driven "first flight" machine.

Again, Herring fades away.

In December of 1907, the U.S. Army Signal Corps advertised for bids for a "Heavier-Than-Air Flying Machine." This was regarded as merely a formality to ordering a Wright Flyer. Instead, forty-one bids were received. Only two bids met all the legal requirements – the Wrights and the elusive Herring.

In spite of giving every evidence of establishing a shop and constructing a flying machine, Herring continued to receive extensions for delivery to the Fort Myer trials in 1908. He "delivered" some suitcases that purported to hold much of his radical machine. It was never assembled or flown at Fort Myer. Herring received permission from the Signal Corps to demonstrate his craft

(continued on page 14)

BEN T. EPPS –
Georgia's First Airplane Pilot
(February 1888 – October 1937)

Among the sand dunes of Kitty Hawk, North Carolina in 1903, Wilbur and Orville Wright proved to the world that flight in a heavier-than-air apparatus was possible. Papers all over the world heralded the feat as one of man's great accomplishments, and one young reader from Athens, Georgia took the news particularly to heart. In 1904, inspired to study engineering, 16-year-old Ben T. Epps headed off to Georgia Tech. Unfortunately, the cost of living in Atlanta was too high and Ben returned to Athens to set up shop as an electrical contractor.

In short time, Ben expanded the small business on Washington Street to include automobile and motorcycle service. Business was good, but Ben's interest was aviation. He tinkered with different ideas about how to build a flying machine. If he worked from drawings, none have survived. Finally, in 1907, four years after the Wright Brothers' first flight, 19-year-old Ben Epps wheeled his prototype out of the garage to the edge of town and prepared for flight. (Unlike the Wrights' aircraft, Ben's flying machine had wheels.)

There were many differences between the Epps aircraft and the Wrights'. Most obvious was that the Epps plane was a monoplane (one wing). It also had one engine but the pilot sat upright, not prone. Similarities included a pusher propeller located behind the wing that "pushed" the airplane. Epps also employed a large canard up front which acted as the elevator and allowed up and down movement and wing warping to facilitate turning.

With townspeople looking on, Ben began the first takeoff roll ever in the state of Georgia. To everyone's amazement, the contraption lifted off the ground, albeit for only about fifteen feet before it crashed. Undaunted, Epps made a few adjustments and corrections and tried it again. On the second takeoff roll ever in Georgia, Ben T. Epps flew over one hundred yards and reached an altitude of nearly fifty feet. The flight lasted at least as long as the Wrights' first flight, and the 1907 Epps flyer and its pilot inaugurated Georgia's aviation history.

Ben Epps went on to design, build and fly eight different airplanes. The question always lingers, "Why isn't he better known?" The answer speaks volumes about the man. For one, Ben was a loner. When others were battling for the aviation limelight and constantly looking for financial backing, he went it alone. There are no records that he ever corresponded with the other aviation pioneers or ever solicited any individuals or corporations for assistance. His automobile, motorcycle and bicycle service and repair business financed the fledgling aviation enterprise until it could finance itself through barnstorming flights on the weekends.

Family members attest to the fact that he would work on a new idea during the week and on the weekend put the idea into play. If it worked, it was incorporated into a new design. If it didn't, it frequently resulted in a crash. Research and development during the first few decades of aviation were straightforward; it either worked and the airplane flew higher, faster, farther, or it didn't and the airplane crashed. Of the eight airplanes Ben Epps designed, built and flew, he crashed every one of them. Being an aviation pioneer was a risky and dangerous pursuit.

By the time Ben met and married Omie Williams in 1913, he had already built and flown four airplanes and incorporated some significant design changes. Photographs of his 1909 monoplane show the removal of the canard and the establishment of the elevator on the tail assembly. This action was necessary so that he could mount a tractor propeller on the front, making it the first airplane to fly in the United States with the propeller in the front.

In his first three designs, fabric covered only the bottom half of the wing and struts, while cables and wire flapped noisily in the breeze passing over the top. Aerodynamics had not yet progressed far enough for inventors to understand the significance of the curved upper wing. It was not until Ben's 1912 monoplane that he radically re-designed the wing. The 1912 airplane incorporated fully covered wings as well as his first use of ailerons. Ben did not invent any of these features for the 1912 airplane, nor did he collaborate with other inventors or designers. He was an avid reader of scientific and aviation magazines and kept abreast of advances and accomplishments. He then incorporated those ideas into his own designs and constructions.

Facing Page: Ben Epps, from a photograph taken in 1931.

Illustration: Sue Mabry

Right: A drawing of the 1907 Epps Flyer.

Ben T. Epps Monoplane
1907

Epps Family Archives

Daughter Evelyn was born prior to the outbreak of World War I and Ben's status as husband and father exempted him from military service. Now twenty-six, he had begun the family he wanted, and he also maintained a successful auto business. However, his love for aviation could not be quelled. With the full support of Omie, Ben bought a commercially built biplane with a passenger cockpit and continued flying.

This particular airplane incorporated many technological advances of the day, and Ben's interest was simply to learn how they worked. He flew the plane regularly for over a year before building his first biplane in 1916. Instead of connecting the ailerons to the trailing edge of the wings for this design, he deployed them between the upper and lower wings as a separate airfoil. The design worked very well for at least six flights and finally nosed over on takeoff and crashed. Ben never rebuilt the airplane. It would be nine more years before another Epps design flew.

With the war over, there was no shortage of surplus airplanes on the market, and Ben kept his aviation interest alive by buying, refurbishing, flying and selling surplus Jenny aircraft. Ben became acquainted with a French war veteran named L. M. "Monte" Rolfe who happened into town, and they soon became friends and business partners in The Rolfe-Epps Flying Service. The enterprise specialized in passenger service, aerial photography, flight training and sales. Ben's relationship with Rolfe was the closest thing to collaboration he had experienced in his career, and the knowledge he gained from listening to Rolfe's experiences and their joint tests on surplus aircraft led Ben to design and build a controllable pitch propeller, the mainstay for his 1924 light monoplane.

Weighing in at 340 pounds with a 2-cylinder motorcycle engine for power, the 1924 light monoplane could sustain 60 miles per hour and averaged 25 miles per gallon. Ben believed that this plane was ready for mass production and began advertising it for $1,000.00. As good as the airplane was, records indicate that only one was ever sold.

The last Epps-designed airplane was a light biplane finished in 1930. It was technologically and aerodynamically equal to any production airplane of the time, and was the primary trainer for the oldest Epps children. Ben came from a family of ten children, and he fathered ten of his own. Nine survived to adulthood and eight became pilots and/or involved in the aviation business. Eldest son, Ben, Jr., soloed at 13 and gained some notoriety being introduced to President Hoover as America's youngest aviator.

In 1935, Ben took two young people for a ride over Athens. No one knows exactly what, but something happened and the flight controls became stuck. The airplane plummeted to the ground, critically injuring Ben and fatally injuring a female passenger. Ben was hospitalized with a broken hip and other injuries. He was unable to make the rent payment on his automobile business and was evicted from the building. Responsibility for cleaning out the shop fell to Ben, Jr., age 16. Although he survived the crash, Ben Epps, Sr. was unable to continue in the automobile business. He eventually took a job with the University of Georgia, but as soon as he was able, he went back to flying.

Two years later, October, 1937, late in the afternoon, Ben, age 49, and a student took off from the field later to be named in his honor. The engine quit and the airplane stalled then spun into the ground, taking the life of Georgia's first airplane pilot. Ben's twelve-year-old son, Charles, was at the field and witnessed the crash. He was one of the first people on the scene and helped as his father was removed from the wreckage.

Ben T. Epps dedicated three decades to the history of aviation personally, but he also left behind a legacy of three generations of aviators who have become legends in their own right. Sons Ben, Jr., Harry, Charles, George, Douglas and Pat all went on to military and/or civilian flying careers. Two daughters, Evelyn and Virginia taught instrument ground training to Navy pilots via the link trainer at NAS Atlanta.

Facing Page: Ben Epps preparing to pilot daughter Evelyn for a wreath-laying flyover ceremony honoring the dead of WWI, circa 1924.

Right, Top: Ben Epps, Sr. and Jr., in front of his WACO in 1929. Several of the kids were already pilots.

Right, Bottom: Ben T. Epps, Sr., with wife Omie and children Douglas, Evelyn, Ben, Jr., Mary Virginia, James, Charles and George.

Epps Family Archives

(continued from page 9)

elsewhere. He was purported to have done so at Hempstead, Long Island, although there were no witnesses.

All through this period, Herring had courted and won the support of the leadership of the Aero Club of America. It would be through this alliance that Herring would be most successful.

The other significant American aviation inventor, Glenn Curtiss, had moved his operations to the Alexander Graham Bell laboratory in Nova Scotia. There, organized as the Aerial Experiment Association (AEA), Curtiss avoided the constant patent battles with the Wrights and was successful with a number of powered aircraft.

At this point, Herring and many of the Aero Club leaders approached Curtiss to create the first American company to build and sell airplanes. The Herring-Curtiss Company was incorporated in 1909.

Later that year, Curtiss traveled to Rheims, France to participate in the world's first aviation event. His "Rheims Racer" was the star of the event. Herring made the most of this success by renting the airplane for display at Wanamaker's Department Store. This action deprived Curtiss of his best mount for the Hudson-Fulton celebration. This celebration was to be the first direct flying confrontation between the Wright and Curtiss aircraft in America. That never occurred, as Curtiss' backup aircraft failed to perform.

The confrontation that did take place, however, was the beginning of the patent wars. At this point the Aero Club and Curtiss discovered that Herring had grossly misled both about his patents, developments, and other matters. Eventually, Herring was confronted by the Herring-Curtiss board of directors and forced out of the company.

Over the years that immediately followed, Herring was involved with the Herring-Burgess Airplane Company. He also continued to hold stock in Curtiss, which had thrived after reforming without Herring. This stock became the object of a legal fight, which was only resolved after Herring and Curtiss had both died.

No Herring designs, aircraft or other significant artifacts have ever been seen.

Augustus Herring partnered with several early airplane manufacturers, among them, Glenn Curtiss. This 1909 advertisement uses a "special incentive" to encourage orders of Herring-Curtiss aeroplanes deliverable in January 1910.

M. Steiner Archives

AT WANAMAKER'S, TO-DAY, WE SAW THE HERRING-CURTISS FLYING
MACHINE THAT WON THE CHAMPIONSHIP.

POWERED FLIGHT AND THE SEEDS OF AN INDUSTRY

Most early airplane flights in America had only one purpose – to sell
aeroplanes, as they were so named at that time. The earliest Georgia flights
were no exception. The two major manufacturers, Wright Exhibition
Company and Curtiss Aeroplane Company, both trained teams of
demonstration pilots and launched traveling exhibition teams equipped with
demonstration aircraft. The strategies of these two companies were somewhat
different, however, with Curtiss inclined to more public demonstrations than
the Wrights, who were notorious for protecting the secrets of their inventions.

Georgia had significant experiences with both of these exhibition groups.
In September 1908, the Wright Brothers demonstrated an aeroplane to the
Army's Aeronautical Board at Fort Myer, Virginia, just outside Washington
D.C. Beset with delays and the first fatal crash, these tests were continued into
1909. Once the aircraft was accepted by the Army's Signal Corps, the need
for an army pilot training site became obvious. The first such training field
was established near College Park, Maryland, but its use was marginal due to
winter rain, cold and soft earth. Clearly, a location with a more moderate year-
round climate was needed, and the city of Augusta, Georgia proposed a site
then known as the "Barnes Farm," which seemed to fit the bill.

The Signal Corps Aviation School at Augusta served as the winter
quarters for the entire Army aviation fleet. This fleet of five Wright Model Bs
and one Curtiss aircraft converged in Georgia during December of 1911, but
operations proved to be only slightly better than College Park. In February,
weather conditions worsened and all flight operations ceased. December of
1912 was no better and only the Wright aircraft moved to Georgia since the
Curtiss Aeroplane Company had by then established its own school at North
Island near San Diego, California.

WRIGHT EXHIBITION COMPANY

The Wright Exhibition Company was determined to set new speed, altitude and distance records, and those marks were continually eclipsed. The distance goal drew the interest of publisher William Randolph Hearst, who established a prize of $50,000 for the first transcontinental flight completed in 30 days.

In 1911, three Wright Exhibition Company pilots attempted this flight. The first effort failed almost immediately. The Wrights' second aircraft was the well-known *Vin Fiz* flying from Sheepshead Bay, New York to Los Angeles with Cal Rodgers as pilot. The *Vin Fiz* was a highly modified Wright "B" essentially built for racing. Its name was derived from the sponsor, a soft drink bearing that name. The least known third effort was another Wright "B" piloted by Robert M. Fowler who left Los Angeles bound for Jacksonville, Florida. In early 1912, this aircraft traveled through South Georgia, making several stops in small towns along the way.

Both the *Vin Fiz* and the Fowler aircraft ultimately completed their flights, but neither did so in the prescribed 30 days. With no established airfields, landing sites were a significant part of the challenge. Telegraph messages frequently alerted local townspeople in advance of intended landings and probable landing sites became a sea of spectators.

CURTISS AEROPLANE COMPANY

The other major American contender for business/sales was the Curtiss Aeroplane Company. Unlike the Wrights', the Curtiss demonstrations were more like today's air shows. Usually scheduled on weekends, these events took advantage of sites where spectator facilities, such as bleachers, were already in place. Automobile or horse race tracks, baseball fields and fairgrounds were the norm. Most of these were on rail lines which provided transportation for the spectators.

The Curtiss team usually shipped their disassembled and crated aircraft from location to location, rather than flying over any distance. The same railroad that brought spectators also delivered the plane, pilot and support team. Curtiss pilots also performed experimental "air mail" flights at most of these stops.

THE PIONEER PERIOD

The period from 1910 through 1916 is generally known as the "Pioneer Period." During this time, early aircraft builders and pilots experimented with possible uses for airplanes, including transporting of mail. Many of these early mail flights were authorized by postal authorities in Washington and assigned official postal route numbers. Others were sanctioned by the local

Lincoln Beachey, seated at the controls of a Curtiss pusher, hands an air mail bag to First Asst. Postmaster General Dr. C.P. Grandfield in conjunction with the November 16-18, 1911 air mail flights in Atlanta.

National Air & Space Museum

16

postmaster but were acknowledged by the Post Office Department. Less than one hundred "Pioneer Flights" took place during this period. All five of the Georgia mail flights were authorized, more than any other state during this period. Four took place late in 1911 at Atlanta, Savannah, Columbus, and Albany. All mail carried during these events was specially cancelled and is highly collectible today.

The Atlanta flights were on November 16 - 18, 1911 and also included a race between the airplane and an automobile, since the site was the Candler Automobile Race Track. To demonstrate the potential of airplane-carried mail, each day a bag of mail with special cancellations was carried halfway to downtown Atlanta, dropped to a waiting Post Office truck that then carried it to the main post office. Quickly sorted, some mail was handed to motorcycle express riders and delivered to the addressee. Reports reveal that express delivery occurred within four hours of mailing. Approximately 3,500 letters were carried as well as a small number of advertising cards.

Savannah's flights took place a week later at the Athletic Park from November 25 - 28, 1911. Mail was only carried on the first and last days of the "Athletic Park Aviation Meet."

The Columbus Ledger sponsored the "Driving Park Aviation Meet" December 12 – 13, 1911. Like Atlanta, mail was carried part way to downtown Columbus, dropped to a waiting truck and transported to the main post office for sorting and delivery.

Albany was to repeat this procedure December 28 – 29, 1911, at the "South Atlantic League Aviation Meet." Pilot Thornwall Andrews made a "spectacular flight over the city, dropped the mail within view of the spectators and later crashed." The meet ended with only one day's air mail demonstration as this was the only airplane authorized to carry the mail.

Nearly a year later, October 31 – November 2, 1912, the Randolph County Fair Association held an air meet at their fair grounds in Cuthbert. A small quantity of mail (about a hundred pieces) was carried on the first day and dropped directly onto the roof of the Gay Hotel in downtown Cuthbert.

The novelty of aviation created other opportunities. On December 10, 1912, a Valdosta couple were married in front of a visiting airplane. Another modern invention, the camera, recorded the event.

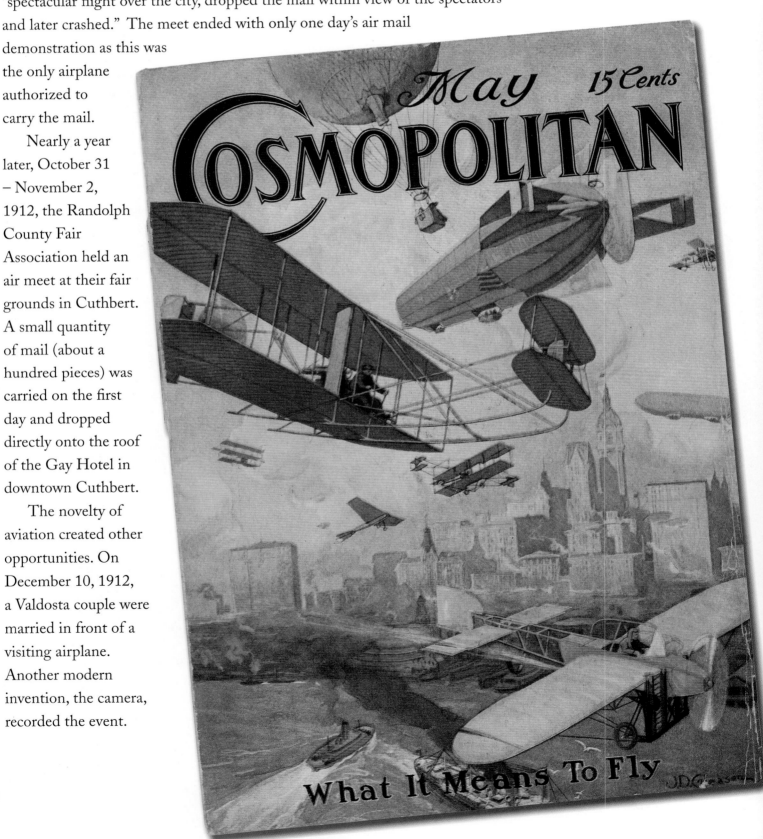

Birthday cards and postcards of the era reflected the public's growing fascination with all things flight-related.

M. Steiner Archives

A BIRTHDAY WISH

May your spirits "FLY HIGH"

SMITH BROTHERS
BLACK
COUGH
DROPS

Like the WRIGHT BROTHERS brave—

Ho! See the man-bird in the air,
Taking his bride to Hartman's, where
He'll "Feather their Nest"
With Feathers new.
On the Hartman plan
As wise men do.
Ho! For the men-bird in the air,
He's going right when he's going There.

RULES REGULATION
HOW TO FLY A
MONO- PLANE

· OUR · FIRST · LESSON ·

19

The Fowler Transcontinental Flight

Hansell Watt Collection, Thomas County Historical Society, Thomasville, Georgia.

An entire book has been written and published about the transcontinental flight of the *Vin Fiz*. Piloted by Cal Rodgers, it left Sheepshead Bay, New York, on September 17, 1911, bound for Long Beach, California. Rodger's journey was finally completed on December 10, 1911, after a number of crashes. The *Vin Fiz* was just one of five long distance flights launched in late 1911, including four transcontinental efforts. These flights were all attempted by members of the Wright Exhibition Company, which was essentially the marketing arm of the Wright Aeroplane Company. All of the pilots were trained at the Wright's Huffman Prairie field near Dayton, Ohio.

The first effort, with pilot Harry Atwood, covered *only* 1,300 miles from St. Louis to Boston. Robert Fowler, the first civilian pilot trained at the Wright flying school, was the next to embark on a transcontinental flight, leaving San Francisco on September 11, 1911. His attempt ended within the week when the aircraft was unable to fly over the Sierra Nevada Mountains to Denver and crashed.

Jimmy Ward left Governor's Island, New York, on September 13 and only reached Addisson, New York, a distance of about

300 miles, where he crashed and quit. This was quickly followed by Cal Rodgers in the *Vin Fiz*. Fowler, undaunted by his failure from San Fransisco, shipped his damaged plane, the *Cole Flyer*, to Los Angeles. After repairs, he would attempt a southern route with lower mountain passes to traverse. His intended destination was Jacksonville, Florida.

All four efforts were attempts to win a $50,000 prize offered by publisher William Randolph Hearst. The Hearst prize was for the first transcontinental flight completed within thirty days. None were completed within the deadline.

The author of *Cal Rodgers and the Vin Fiz, the First Transcontinental Flight*, Eileen E. Lebow, laments that the Rodgers flight is little known or remembered even within the aviation community. Second successes, like second children, sometimes get even less notice, and the Fowler flight has certainly suffered that very fate.

Flying a relatively standard Wright Model B, Fowler eventually flew across much of South Georgia. As was the rule in most early distance flights, his route followed the rail lines. Fowler's arrival in Georgia was a near-spiritual event. A fouled spark plug caused an unscheduled stop in Jakin, near the Georgia-Alabama state line. This event was recalled by Mrs. Jo Smith Webb at Jakin's Centennial celebration on May 27, 1995. Her account was published in *Jakin Remembers, A Salute to Jakin:*

"The plane developed trouble on the way to Bainbridge and had to land in Grandmother Merritt's field at Jakin. Shade and Deanna Hicks, a beloved black couple, lived across the road from the field and were the first ones to reach the plane, something that nobody in the parts had ever seen. Upon their arrival the pilot was stepping out of the open cockpit all dressed in leather, headcap fastened under the chin, huge eye goggles, and his long white duster, gloves, etc. Shade, seeing this person coming from the sky, said, 'Good morning, Mr. Jesus, how is your Pa?' Then the pilot had to explain he too was only a man and not Jesus. It was also reported that the school principal was exhausted at the end of the day from whipping the students he had told not to leave school. Obviously they had!"

Delays and unscheduled stops were the order of the day. Fowler was originally scheduled to arrive in Bainbridge from Brantley, Alabama, on January 23, 1912. Articles in *The Bainbridge Post Searchlight* fill in the details. On January 19, 1912, this then weekly newspaper had a brief front page item headlined, "Flying Machine for Bainbridge." The following week's article (January 26) stated "Airship Had Accident." It describes the accident in Brantley, Alabama: "In starting to ascend the machine struck a stump..." A telegram from Brantley stated that after repairs the aviator would fly from Dothan to Donalsonville and then on to Bainbridge.

An extensive article on February 2, 1912 provides some insight into Fowler's experiences in Georgia, including confirmation of the stop at Jakin. Headlined "Airship Was Here Tuesday," it starts, "The airship that was looked for two weeks ago landed here Tuesday afternoon, and most of the population of Bainbridge witnessed the thrilling sight for the first time. There never was a prettier sight nor a sight more wonderful to those who had not seen the flight of an airship." The article specifically stated that the "machine is a Wright biplane and weighs 1,000 pounds...is a two-cylinder thirty-five horse power and cost $5,000."

Thomasville provides the best documentation of Fowler's flight in Georgia. On February 7 or 8, 1912, local photographers Hansell Watt and Mr. Moller recorded the visit with excellent views of both the aircraft and pilot, Fowler. Thomasville's records also suggest that Fowler left for Quitman that same day.

The rail line being used by Fowler runs on from Quitman to Valdosta before turning south and entering Florida. A 1913 Valdosta newspaper report mentions a previous "box kite like flying machine...last year." Could this have been Fowler? Fowler finally made it to Jacksonville 112 days after leaving Los Angeles.

World War I: Georgians Get Involved

It was referred to quite simply as "the Great War," a term still in use as late as 1939, on the very brink of the Second World War. With a strong opposition to direct involvement by the United States, America was late in joining World War I. In April 1917, however, nearly three years after Germany declared war on Russia and France, President Wilson declared that "the world must be made safe for democracy" and asked Congress for a declaration of war.

World War I was the first conflict to employ aviation in its many forms and helped to define the many possible roles of airpower in all future conflicts. Lighter-than-air aircraft included balloons, blimps and zeppelins. Heavier-than-air aircraft (aeroplanes) were used for scouting (observation), bombing, aerial battles, and even early transport and medical evacuation.

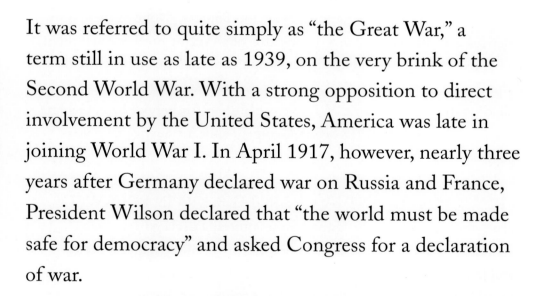

World War I was a wake-up call to American air power. A report by the British Minister of War in the spring of 1916, two years into the war, counted 1,149 aircraft. These included Farman, Voisin, Caudron, Nieuport, Caproni, Breguet, Morane Saulnier, Spad and Ponnier. None of them were American aircraft. More than a decade after the Wright Brothers' first flight, the United States produced no airplanes that compared favorably with any of the European manufacturers. We had fewer trained pilots and very few airfields worthy of that name. With no established Air Service base, Georgia was typical. It would be 1917 before Georgia's only Air Service field was established near Americus.

EARLY INVOLVEMENT BY GEORGIANS: KIFFIN ROCKWELL

During the years before the United States officially declared war, many individual Americans found ways to become involved. Perhaps no better example can be found than Kiffin Rockwell, a Georgia resident who felt compelled to enter the war the same year it started. Rockwell had moved to Atlanta in 1911 to take a position with an advertising agency. In 1914, he and his brother Paul joined the French Foreign Legion infantry. Later, after recovering from serious wounds suffered in trench warfare, they were invited to join the Escadrille Americaine, which was renamed the Lafayette Escadrille to satisfy neutral and isolationist American politicians. The Lafayette Escadrille was a squadron of the French Air Service made up primarily of American volunteers. Kiffin Rockwell was one of the seven founding members of this group. Four of them, including Rockwell, would not survive the war.

On May 18, 1916, Corporal Kiffin Yates Rockwell flew his first combat mission with the French Squadron 124, the Lafayette Escadrille. He fired his first shots at an enemy aircraft, which resulted in his first downed German airplane. His signature technique was both daring and effective. He would aim his plane at the target aircraft, ignore enemy fire until within a hundred feet, fire a short burst, and climb away just in time to avoid colliding with his adversary.

Although idealism was tempered by the loss of each pilot, this was a time of chivalry in the air, an exhilarating experience shared with like-minded men. Rockwell wrote his mother, "If I die, you will know that I died as every man should … for the cause of humanity, the most noble of all causes." Although officially credited with only two victories, Rockwell was recognized by his peers as an outstanding leader and strategist. He was shot down on September 23, 1916, and buried in France.

THE UNITED STATES ENTERS THE WAR
Georgia Aviators Get Involved
When the United States finally entered the war in 1917, the Aviation Section of the Signal Corps owned 55 airplanes, mostly trainers, and had only 35 pilots with about 2,000 other personnel. The Americans in the Escadrille and in other French flying units were absorbed into the United States Air Service on February 18, 1918 as the 103rd Pursuit Squadron.

LT. FRANK O'DRISCOLL HUNTER
Native son Lt. Frank O'Driscoll Hunter, a pilot with the 103rd Squadron, may be the best known World War I aviator to Georgians. He was awarded the Distinguished Service Cross (DSC) and France's Croix de Guerre for his actions. Born in Savannah, Lt. Hunter was alone on patrol on September 13, 1918, when he came upon two German biplanes. He attacked, downed one, and caused the other to flee. Hunter was wounded in this action and his aircraft damaged, but he was able to return to his aerodrome. Four days later, he and an accompanying aircraft attacked a flight of six enemy aircraft. Hunter shot down one and the others fled behind enemy lines.

On October 4, 1918, Hunter's patrol of three airplanes encountered eight enemy planes. Hunter bagged two of the four victories in that action. Two days later, Hunter became separated from his patrol group and came upon an allied group of seven Breguets engaged with ten Fokkers. Hunter joined the fray focusing on a pair of German craft that were chasing a single Breguet. Hunter downed one, but was immediately jumped by five others. He managed to down one of his attackers and the others retired. His last victory also came in an uneven match. Hunter destroyed one of six monoplanes and drove the

The U.S. sent American aircraft to France in parts, where they were reassembled, flight-tested and had tail markings applied.

M. Steiner Archives

others away. Hunter Field in Savannah was named for him in May of 1940. Hunter retired to Savannah as a Major General, having been an active fighter pilot through World War II. He passed away in 1988.

Hunter was not the only Georgia aviator awarded the DSC. Others included Captain Walter R. Lawson. Lawson was an aerial observer with the 91st Aero Squadron. Observers were certainly not immune to risk. Captain Lawson had been wounded by anti-aircraft fire but completed his mission. While still recovering he volunteered for another high risk mission, this one in poor weather. Forced to fly low, deep behind the enemy lines, he took heavy fire but succeeded in gathering valuable information.

LT. PATRICK H. MELL

Athens-born and Augusta resident, 1st Lt. Patrick H. Mell of the 213th Aero Squadron, volunteered for a patrol on October 28, 1918. His group of six allied aircraft had engaged four enemy when an additional nine enemy craft

(continued on page 30)

Eugene Jacques
Bullard

The First Black Military Pilot in the World

Like many of the early WWI American flyers, Eugene Jacques Bullard began action in the trenches, and like the Rockwell brothers, it was only after he was wounded on the ground that air service became an option. Perhaps the American pilot with the most unique story, Bullard had not gone to Europe with just a patriotic fervor. He was also seeking a land of equal opportunity.

Born in Columbus, Georgia, on October 9, 1895, Bullard was descended from a former slave family in Haiti. That family had been transported to Martinique by their French owners following the uprising of the Haitian slaves that ended French rule in Haiti. Years later and now free, the descendents lived in Georgia. This background brought French as a culture and a language into the Bullard family experience.

Jacques was the seventh of ten children born to William Bullard, a former slave, and Josephine Thomas, who was part Creek Indian. Jacques attended the 28th Street School in Columbus and was intelligent, literate and bilingual. He was not content with the second-class existence of blacks in Georgia. Some sources suggest that he witnessed a lynching attempt on his father in 1903. In spite of this, his father encouraged him to "maintain dignity and self-respect" in the face of prejudice.

When he was still in his teens, he ran away "to join the circus," which was actually a group of gypsies from England who were touring America. Later he found work in Dawson, Georgia working with horses owned by Zachariah Turner, and in 1911 was on record as a jockey at the Terrell County Fair.

Hearing of a more accepting and inclusive racial attitude in Europe, Bullard stowed away on a ship to Scotland, then later made his way through England to the continent. During that time, he became a professional boxer and also appeared in vaudeville with a black group that first performed in Paris in November of 1913.

Illustration: Sue Mabry

When the war began in 1914, Eugene enlisted in the French Foreign Legion, was assigned to the Moroccan Division of the Infantry, and was later seriously wounded in action at Verdun. He was awarded the Croix de Guerre, the French equivalent of the Medal of Honor. No longer fit for infantry service, he was offered an assignment in the French Flying Corps.

Bullard started flight school on May 5, 1917, and after successfully completing training on August 17, was assigned to the 93rd Spad Squadron. He was credited with two victories, flying twenty missions with this squadron. He was the first black military pilot in the world.

After the war, Jacques Bullard remained in France and owned and managed jazz nightclubs, which frequently featured American performers like Louis Armstrong. Many of these clubs drew an international and diplomatic clientele.

In July of 1939, Bullard joined the French counter-intelligence. He already was a fixture in the world of international intrigue through his night clubs. When Paris fell to the Germans, Bullard and his two daughters were evacuated to Orleans, France. There he was wounded in defense of that city. He was smuggled into Spain and eventually on to New York City for medical treatment. He settled into relative obscurity in a small apartment in Harlem. His last employment was as an elevator operator in Rockefeller Center.

The French never forgot their American friend. In 1954, Bullard was invited to Paris to rekindle the Eternal Flame at the French Unknown Soldier's Tomb. He was named a Knight of the Legion of Honor in 1959, after which he gave a rare interview on the Dave Garroway television show. He tried to describe his feelings about the two countries in his life: "The United States is my mother and I love my mother. France is my mistress and you love your mistress more than your mother…but in a different way!"

In 1960, French President Charles DeGaulle visited New York and publicly honored Bullard. Bullard died in New York City on October 12, 1961, in poverty and still virtually unknown to Americans. The French government awarded him one last honor. He was buried with full military honors by French War Officers in the French War Veteran's section of the Flushing Cemetery on Long Island, New York.

In their December 1967 issue, *Ebony* magazine published a feature article about Bullard, the first one published in this country since an obscure piece during World War I in the *Saturday Evening Post*. Today, Americans are rediscovering Eugene Bullard. He is featured in an exhibit in the Air Force Museum in Dayton, Ohio. He was inducted into the Georgia Aviation Hall of Fame in 1989.

On August 23, 1994, thirty-three years after his death, and seventy-seven years to the day after his rejection by the U. S. Air Service, Bullard was posthumously commissioned as a 2nd Lt. in the U.S. Air Force.

Georgia Aviation Hall Of Fame

(continued from page 27)
joined the fight. Mell brought down one and safely returned to his base. A week later, Mell and his wingman engaged three aircraft behind the enemy lines. Mell downed one and lost contact with another in dense fog at very low altitude. This action earned Mell his DSC.

LT. DACHE M. REEVES

Atlanta resident, 1st Lt. Dache M. Reeves, may have set a record for number of parachute jumps. Reeves, with the 9th Aero Squadron, was an observer in the suspended basket of an observation balloon near Avocourt, France when his balloon was attacked by enemy aircraft. He jumped after his hydrogen gas-filled balloon burst into flames. He immediately re-ascended when another balloon was inflated. Two weeks later the scene was repeated, except Reeves' balloon was attacked by fifteen enemy aircraft and his second balloon also was shot down, forcing another jump. Reeves finished the day in yet his third observation balloon. These actions earned him the DSC.

THOMAS LOUIS SPENCE, Jr.

Lt. Thomas Spence may have the distinction of being the last air

Above: Frank O'Driscoll "Monk" Hunter, World War I flying ace.

Georgia Aviation Hall Of Fame

Below: Rows of American aircraft would have been a familiar sight to Lt. Spence while stationed in France.

M. Steiner Archives

U. S. AVIATION TRAINING FIELD.

SERIES NO. 12   222670

Above: An observation balloon such as this was the perch for 1st Lt. Dache Reeves.

M. Steiner Archives

service casualty of World War I. He died in a crash that occurred almost two weeks after the armistice.

After his death in France, Spence was widely described as a hero, but he had already been a hometown hero in Thomasville when he enlisted. Perceived as a future community leader, he had been the outstanding high school athlete in every major sport. The baseball catcher with the best hitting record, the team leader and forward on the basketball team and the winner of all nine events at the regional track meet could do no wrong in the eyes of the community. His enlistment and request for air service only enhanced his image as a hero.

Spence volunteered for war service in July, 1917. He was enlisted into the Aviation Department at Atlanta, one of three Georgia locations that accepted enlistments for aviation. He finished ground school at Georgia Tech on November 11, 1917 and was shipped to France by the end of the year. He joined other Americans at the French Flying School at Chateauroux, and after receiving his commission as 2nd Lt., was assigned as a flight instructor.

The fatal accident was described in a letter from Lt. Ray Traxler, Commander of the 257th Aero Squadron, to Frank Park, then the U.S. Congressman representing Thomasville:

"Lt. Spence left Field Nine, 3rd Aviation Instruction Center, Issoudun, Indre, France, to take a message to a friend at St. Floren, about twelve miles away. We later learned from witnesses that he was doing some acrobatics over the town for the benefit of the inhabitants. It seems that either something happened to the motor or that Lt. Spence lost control of the machine and crashed to the ground. We believe that he was killed instantly, as he was dead when reached by the onlookers."

The letter closed, "Lt. Spence had many friends and was liked by all officers and enlisted men wherever he was known. He was an ideal American and every inch a man!"

Spence was initially honored by having an early airfield in Thomasville named after him. Later, an Army Air Corps training field was established at nearby Moultrie and was designated Spence Field in 1942. Spence Field was one of the many training bases built in anticipation and preparation for America's entry into WWII.

M. Steiner Archives

NAVY AND MARINE AVIATORS

The involvement of the United States Navy and Marine Corps in World War I was on a much smaller scale than the Army's Air Service. Georgians were among the most notable of the few naval and marine aviators. From the time of the army air trials at Ft. Myer, Virginia, the U.S. Navy was searching for possible uses of aviation.

ADMIRAL JOHN H. TOWERS

Future Admiral, John H. Towers, was among the few U.S. Naval aviators present in the war zone during World War I. A native of Rome, Georgia, Lt. Towers was assigned to the battleship *USS Tennessee* as its radio officer. The *Tennessee* was dispatched to England and Europe in August of 1914, officially to render aid to Americans caught in the confusion of war activities. The unofficial mission for the *Tennessee* was to observe and report on the Royal Navy's activities. Towers was specifically charged with observing the recently formed Royal Navy Aeronautical Service (RNAS). His observation efforts were frequently thwarted because of England's reaction to America's continued neutrality.

No one was more qualified for this assignment. Towers had trained with Glenn Curtiss at his factory in Hammondsport, New York. In the company of Lt. Theodore Ellyson and John Rodgers, Towers earned Aviator #3 in September, 1911. He also flew the U.S. Navy's first airplane, the Curtiss Seaplane A-1. Carrying extra fuel, he established the Navy's first world record with an endurance flight exceeding six hours. In 1912, he commanded the Naval Academy's pilot training program, and in 1914, he established and commanded the first Naval Air Station at Pensacola, Florida.

Many of the RNAS's operations were similar to the U.S. Navy's first

Below: Towers fought for, and won, recognition of aviation as a vital part of naval doctrine.

Georgia Aviation Hall Of Fame

Above: Towers established the first naval aviation unit at Annapolis, Maryland, in the fall of 1911 and in 1916, he supervised the establishment of the Naval Air Corps.

Georgia Aviation Hall Of Fame

Right: Alfred Austell Cunningham – first Marine Corps aviator and first Director, Marine Corps Aviation.

Georgia Aviation Hall Of Fame

experiments in 1911 with Glenn Curtiss and the cruiser, *USS Pennsylvania*. Seaplanes were carried on board warships to launch points, lowered into the water and took off for their missions. Upon return, they made water landings and were hoisted back aboard their mother ships. This crude aircraft carrier concept would become integral to development of U.S. naval aviation. The RNAS also employed dirigibles to locate German submarines, and Towers' observations of this activity would significantly impact future U.S. Navy operations.

Towers flew one combat mission as an observer on September 7, 1916. This was in clear violation of U.S. neutrality. This "unofficial" mission and his other observations were the seed of America's aircraft carrier strategy that would lead to victory in the Pacific during the next world war.

Admiral Towers was inducted into the National Aviation Hall of Fame, the Naval Aviation Hall of Fame, the International Aerospace Hall of Fame and the Georgia Aviation Hall of Fame.

ALFRED CUNNINGHAM
The First U.S. Marine Pilot

In many ways, the career and impact of Marine Corps pilot, Alfred Austell Cunningham, parallel that of Admiral John Towers. Born in Atlanta, Alfred Cunningham trained at the Burgess Aircraft Company and soloed in August of 1912 with less than three hours of instruction, becoming Naval Aviator #5 and Marine Pilot #1. He was then assigned to the Naval Aviation Camp at the Naval Academy in Annapolis. This camp was staffed with navy Lieutenants Ellyson, Rodgers, and Towers – Naval Aviators #1, #2, and #3, respectively.

Over the next few months, Cunningham made over 400 flights in a Curtiss B-1. Serving on a board charged with developing a naval and marine aeronautical plan, he, like Towers, was involved in the establishment of NAS Pensacola. Like Towers, Cunningham was dispatched to observe aviation activity in Europe.

One significant difference from Towers' involvement, however, was Cunningham's actual combat flight experience during the war. He traveled to England and France after the United States had declared

war on Germany. His personal diary provides a direct account of his activities and covers the ten weeks from his departure in the United States until just prior to his return. In the diary he describes his visits to French, English, and American (Lafayette Escadrille) bases in France. He intentionally visited a variety of primary, gunnery, maintenance and forward operational fields.

After a combat mission on December 18, 1917, he entered this report: *"Got up frozen stiff. The weather fairly clear. Persuaded a French pilot of a biplane fighting Spad to take me over the lines. We went up like an elevator and talk about speed! We were over the lines in no time and I was all eyes."* After describing ground fire he continues, *"We sighted a boche 2 seater just below us. We made for him. It was the finest excitement I ever had. I got my machine gun ready."*

After he returned from Europe, Cunningham was involved in site selection for naval air stations and the formation of a Marine aviation company. He became the *de facto* head of Marine aviation.

Cunningham has been inducted into the National Aviation Hall of Fame and the Georgia Aviation Hall of Fame.

Above: Between October 1912 and July 1913, Cunningham made some 400 flights in the Curtiss B-1, conducting training and testing tactics and aircraft capabilities.

Georgia Aviation Hall Of Fame

OTHER GEORGIANS IN WWI AVIATION

Other Georgians served in aviation units, but were not as recognized for their efforts. In fact, many lost their lives while in the service and are hardly remembered. Lt. Robert James Cochran, 8th Aero Squadron, from Camilla, died in action on October 10, 1918. There are many unanswered questions about others. For example, a Private Hugh M. Willett died during surgery on February 17, 1918, intended to "make him fit for air service." Exactly what that surgery was intended to accomplish is not explained.

Also among these were the flight instructors who never even left the states. With training fields at Kelly, Randolph and Ellington in Texas and elsewhere, it was inevitable that accidents and disease would take their toll.

Then, as now, the maintenance of the aircraft was essential to any action whatsoever. Many Georgians also served in this capacity. Records indicate that more than thirty Georgians died serving in some capacity with an aviation unit. This includes members of the French Air Force, the Royal Air Force (England) and the Royal Canadian Air Force.

Many of these instructors and mechanics did survive the war, returned to Georgia and lived full lives. Most of these men are gone now, their gravesites modestly mentioning their involvement in The Great War.

ARMISTICE AND CELEBRATIONS

America's response time improved dramatically with the celebration of the Armistice. In Moultrie, the news of the end of the war coincided with the first Colquitt County Fair. The local paper, *The Daily Observer*, of November 12, 1918, noted "Big Fleet of Airships Will Come Here for Demonstration." This was only one day after the end of the war. The "fleet" that was coming from Souther Field would feature "Dare devil stunts in the air by the flyers from Americus." Another front page article stated, "This morning two airplanes from Americus came down and it helped to furnish entertainment. Hundreds who had never seen a battleplane turned their eyes skyward when they heard the purr of the motor high in the air. The ships gave some exhibition flying before returning to Souther Field this afternoon." In fact, these were hardly "battleplanes" but trainers.

In Thomasville, the Armistice was celebrated with a parade, recognition of local heroes (the wounded that had returned home), and speeches by politicians and veterans of the Civil War and the Spanish-American War. Celebrations of this nature took place all across the state.

Many of these celebrations included the appearance of aircraft from Souther Field. Few could foresee the prophetic nature of aircraft able to visit almost any community in the state.

SOUTHER FIELD, AMERICUS
Georgia's Only World War I Air Base

In 1917, Sumter County purchased a peach orchard four miles northeast of Americus and leased it to the United States military for development of a "landing" field. The field was located on a large, flat site ideal for flight operations. Early in 1918 the orchard was cleared, the site was graded, and an "all-directions" landing field was established. Contractors built hangars, barracks and a variety of military post buildings, including a hospital. Designated a "one-unit field," it was capable of providing the primary training of hundreds of student pilots. The Air Service Flying School and the Americus Aviation Depot were initially combined as a single command but were later separated into entirely separate commands.

This new base was named after Major Henry Souther, an army aviation pioneer. The first recorded military flight to Souther was in May of 1918 when Major Carlyle Wash landed and took off in a Standard biplane. This signaled that the new training base was "open for business." Aero Service training squadrons began to arrive from existing bases at Fort Sam Houston and Kelly Field, both in Texas, and were formed into a single Flying School Detachment.

The very latest American military trainer, the Curtiss JN-4, known as the "Jenny," arrived by rail to the depot portion of the base. There, the crated machines were assembled, flight-tested and turned over to the flying school. Classes of twenty-five cadets each trained for about two months with these Jennies. Over 500 cadets earned their wings at Souther by the end of World War I, on November 11, 1918. Most of these pilots never shipped out or saw any action.

This view shows three Jennies in a Souther Field World War I hangar, giving some idea of the size of the structure. These hangars were still in use during the World War II training role of the base.

South Georgia Technical
College Library

Curtiss preferred V-type liquid-cooled engines. The Souther engine shop not only maintained these engines it also trained the mechanics.

South Georgia Technical College Library

Souther Field had been leased with a fixed-price option to purchase it, and after the Armistice, Souther was recommended for purchase by the U.S. government. The general aviation depot function would serve the southeast and eventually become one of three sites for the sale of war surplus aircraft and engines. Through government auctions and private sales of the surplus aircraft, Souther had a significant impact on aviation during the post-war years, an impact that extended beyond Georgia.

Souther was discontinued as a government flying field in 1922. The last military personnel vacated in April 1923. Souther had been the only World War I military air field in Georgia and one of the first "official" landing fields in the state.

Souther Field again saw service during World War II as a Contract Flight School operated by Graham Aviation. The military designation was the 56th Army Air Forces Flying Training Detachment.

Part of a "yard-long" class graduation picture. The entire class poses in front of their venerable Curtiss Jennies.

M. Steiner Archives

Douglas Davis –
Atlanta's Premier Pilot

Doug Davis seldom looked like a pilot. He usually flew in a business suit and tie. Just prior to takeoff, his hat was replaced with his flying helmet and his coat with a flight jacket. Immediately after landing, he would swap back into his business attire.

In an interview, his wife said, "My husband had a very different style than a showman like Roscoe Turner. He looked like any other very ordinary business person. That's what he wanted people to think. He wanted them to accept aviation as a common, ordinary, average means of transportation, rather than merely a stunt machine for heroic persons."

Douglas H. Davis quit high school during his senior year in Barnesville, Georgia to enlist in the Army Air Service. He was just eighteen years old at the time. Within a few months he was a 2nd Lt. and the youngest military pilot in the country. Dreaming of aerial combat, he became an instructor and check pilot instead.

Upon his discharge in 1919 he bought a Curtiss JN-4 Jenny, named it *Glenna Mae* for his sweetheart, and began an air service from Atlanta to Montgomery, Alabama. An encounter with a fence near Griffin, Georgia left him with a wrecked plane. The rebuild cost a lot, so he joined the Mabel Cody Flying Circus in Florida to supplement his other earnings.

In a later movie-making venture, Doug Davis and his Jenny were used in a daring pickup of a person from a speeding train. Survey teams had missed one low telegraph wire above the tracks, but Doug didn't. He miraculously crash-landed into a ditch when one wing suddenly left the aircraft.

The Curtiss Candy Company contracted with Davis to promote their Baby Ruth candy bars. Like other pilots across the country, he dropped candy bars attached to little parachutes from his airplane which was painted to look like a giant Baby Ruth candy bar. He became an overnight sensation. This success allowed him to acquire a new WACO airplane, establish the Douglas Davis Flying Service, and become the distributor for the WACO aircraft.

In 1925, Davis and his wife settled in Atlanta. He built the first hangar at Candler Field, which later was used by Charles Lindbergh during his famous 1927 tour of forty-eight states. As much as anyone, Davis wanted Atlanta to have an airport, and during numerous flights around Atlanta with Mayor Hartsfield, he provided convincing arguments that aviation would help the city grow and that Candler was the best location for an airport.

Illustration: Sue Mabry

A popular feature in the Sunday newspapers of the late 1920s was the photogravure, a section complete with sepia tone photographs of both news and human interest subjects. Davis had frequently been pictured in the Atlanta Journal Constitution photogravure. In yet another innovative air service, he became the pilot that carried an Atlanta newspaper photographer around the state to take aerial photos of many of the county courthouses and their squares.

In 1928, Davis made a switch and became the distributor for Travel Air aircraft. Flying a Travel Air in races at Atlanta's Candler Field, Davis placed either first or second in every event. He was a pilot's pilot. Glenna Mae, who had become Mrs. Davis, remembers, "Once Doug won a transcontinental race, and the young man who came in second said that Doug had spent the entire night before the race helping him with his maps. He had given him many tips as well. This competitor said that without Doug's help he simply wouldn't have made it!"

His racing performances, coupled with being the top sales distributor for Travel Air, brought Doug Davis and Walter Beech together. In 1929, Beech contacted Davis to fly the Wright Whirlwind-powered Travel Air R Model. Arriving in Wichita only days before the races, Davis made a series of short test flights. His departure for the Cleveland races was almost catastrophic. Making a low-level, high-speed pass to thrill the spectators, he misjudged his shallow dive and his wheels contacted the runway. Although it appeared that no damage was done, he discovered upon landing in Cleveland that he had collapsed the wheels.

Davis was very busy at the Cleveland 1929 National Air Races. He performed with the Travel Air stunt team. He piloted the Chevrolet-powered "R" Model to a first place in the "Experimental" event, and he flew a Curtiss OX-5-powered Travel Air to first place in a relay race. His crowning achievement, however, was Event No. 26, the Fifty Mile Free-For-All. Seven

Doug Davis is acknowledged as the first pilot for Eastern Air Transport, predecessor to Eastern Air Lines. He signed and carried this letter on the first West Palm Beach to Atlanta flight on February 9, 1931.

M. Steiner Archives

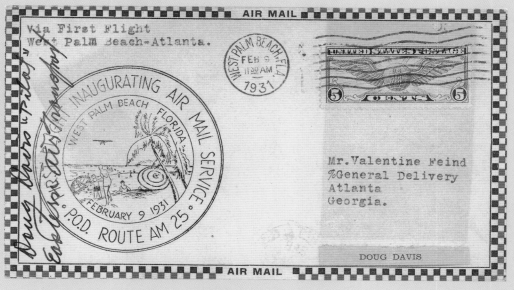

aircraft were entered – two military and five civilian. Davis quickly took the lead and began to run away from the field. As he began the third of the five laps, he failed to go around a pylon. Reacting quickly, he banked back around the pylon at high speed. The high "G" forces caused a brief blackout, and he was unsure if he had successfully cleared the pylon. So he recircled it. Now behind the entire field he managed to pass everyone and finish thirty seconds ahead of the Army's best pursuit plane.

Returning to Atlanta to continue his various aviation ventures, he became the Curtiss Wright (Travel Air) distributor. A Davis Air Line was formed using his name (with permission), but he was not part of that venture.

In 1930, Eastern Air Transport decided to begin passenger service along with their air mail contract. Eastern utilized the Curtiss Kingbird aircraft, and Davis became the first Eastern Captain. He later flew the large (for its time) Curtiss Condor commercial biplane airliner.

In 1934, Jimmy Wedell, another famous racing pilot, was killed in a crash while instructing a student. Wedell's partner asked Doug Davis to fly their Wedell-Williams racer at the National Air Races. Flying the racer from Burbank to Cleveland, he won the 1934 Bendix Trophy. An even more powerful engine and special cowling were installed at Cleveland, and Davis won a preliminary event with the fastest speed of the meet. One lap of that race produced a speed over 325 mph.

The feature event, the Thompson Trophy race was a twelve-lap event. To facilitate spectator viewing, the course was changed at the last minute from a ten-mile lap to only 8½ miles. Davis warned that, "Someone is going to get killed this afternoon, if that course isn't lengthened!" On the eighth lap Davis' Wedell-Williams racer started to go into a spin, momentarily recovered and then plunged into the ground killing Davis upon impact. Fellow pilots, including greats like Jimmy Haizlip and Jimmy Doolittle, were stunned. One summed it up, "Mister, that one made a lot of grown men cry!" It was later discovered that the horizontal stabilizer had failed under the stress of the tighter turns on the shorter course.

Today a street near the Atlanta airport is named "Doug Davis Drive" and very few know why. Doug Davis was inducted into the Georgia Aviation Hall of Fame in 1991.

Pictured in the September 15, 1929 Atlanta Photogravure *was Doug Davis after winning the National Air Races feature event. "Atlanta's Speed King...noted Atlanta Air Pilot" was the caption. The child is not identified.*

M. Steiner Archives

Lindbergh In Georgia

Charles Augustus Lindbergh made his first solo flight at Souther Field in Georgia. Souther Field, near Americus, had been an air depot during World War I and was one of only three sites in the country selling surplus Curtiss JN-4 Jennies. Lindbergh, too young for air service in World War I, wanted to learn to fly, and in early 1923, he rode his motorcycle to Florida to visit the Curtiss Flying School. He planned to return through Americus, Georgia to possibly purchase a Jenny.

Lindbergh recounts that trip and the purpose of the Georgia stop in his 1927 book, *We.* He wrote the book to correct the press distortions and sensationalism that followed his historic trans-Atlantic flight. In his account, he mentions sleeping in the abandoned hangars and climbing the old base water tower in Americus while his airplane was assembled. He also mentions, specifically, that his first solo flight occurred there.

Lindbergh's career after Souther Field is generally well-known. He was hired as an air mail pilot on the St. Louis-to-Chicago route (CAM 2) by the Robertson Aircraft Corp. of St. Louis. Through this contact, sponsorship funding was secured from the St. Louis business community to build and buy a custom Ryan monoplane for the trans-Atlantic attempt. The plane was named the *Spirit of St. Louis* in appreciation of this community sponsorship.

The successful trans-Atlantic flight made Lindbergh a super-celebrity. He was besieged with offers, mostly from promoters seeking to "cash in" on his success. He refused all offers until he finally signed on with the Guggenheim Fund, which had been established to promote and extend commercial aeronautics in the United States. The fund had already sponsored the Byrd Polar Plane Tour in 1926. The project interested Lindbergh, and he trusted the Guggenheims.

In spite of many local Atlanta reports that Lindbergh came to Atlanta and spent the night because of City Alderman William Hartsfield's persuasiveness, the stop was only one of 82 cities visited on a carefully planned tour. Lindbergh also planned to spend at least one night in each of the forty-eight states, and Atlanta was the only stop in Georgia planned by the Guggenheim Fund. The flight to Atlanta from Jacksonville included "over-flights" of McRae, Vidalia, and Millen, Georgia. Commemorative streamers were dropped at each of these over-flight sites.

The official program for "Lindbergh Day" in Atlanta, October 11, 1927, was developed by a committee headed by Henderson Hallman and included bands, appearances with politicians, a parade and the placing of a wreath at the World War I memorial at Pershing Point. There was also a visit with patients at the Veteran's Hospital and an official party at the Biltmore Hotel in the late afternoon. The next morning, he left promptly for Candler Field at 9:15 AM (as scheduled), and was soon airborne to Spartanburg, South Carolina. Days later, Mayson Avenue, a short road that ran from Peachtree Road to Piedmont Road past the old Mayson homeplace, was renamed Lindbergh Drive.

Lindbergh visited Atlanta a number of times over the years. Some of these visits were as a consultant on aviation matters. He once served as the test pilot for an Atlanta-built, all-metal transport plane, produced by the Atlanta Airplane Company. Little is known about this aircraft as it apparently never went into production.

Commercial Aviation & Passenger Airlines

PASSENGER AIRLINES

There have been four distinct generations of passenger airlines in the United States. The first, beginning in 1926, was based on the Kelly Act establishing commercial air mail and the Air Commerce Act establishing registration and certification processes. The second generation, the period at and shortly after the end of World War II, saw unprecedented growth as air travel gained acceptance with the general public. Deregulation in 1978, the third generation, created both chaos and opportunity in the industry. The last and most recent generation, the partner (or connection) airlines, are typically independent carriers that operate under contract to a major airline.

MAIL ROUTES

The first official U.S. air mail was inaugurated on May 15, 1918, nearly seven years after the Curtiss air mail demonstration flights of 1911-12. Four of these demonstration flights took place in Georgia. The official U.S. air mail was carried by postal employees flying post office planes on routes that were limited to Washington, D.C., Philadelphia and New York City. Chicago was added in December 1918. These limited routes made air mail irrelevant to most of the country.

In 1926, the U.S. Post Office Department decided to expand air mail service by contracting with private operators for the transport of mail. These Contract Air Mail (CAM) flights were awarded for specified routes through competitive bidding. Many aviation visionaries, mostly World War I aviators who were looking for ways to fly for a living, saw this as a great opportunity and scrambled for contracts.

Atlanta, Georgia was served by three of the original thirty-four designated (CAM) routes. Like the pioneer flights, many of these routes followed the major rail lines. Rail hubs such as Atlanta became destinations for air mail service. The major north-south route from New York City to Atlanta was awarded to Philadelphia-based Pitcairn Airways. This was referred to as the "eastern route." New Orleans-based St. Tammany and Gulf Coast Airways served New Orleans to Atlanta, via Mobile. Although a route from Jacksonville to Miami was initially awarded to Florida Airways, it was isolated from any other air mail routes. An Atlanta-to-Miami route award to Pitcairn soon replaced the Florida Airways contract and thereby established a through route from New York to Miami.

In 1934, early in the first presidential term of Franklin D. Roosevelt, the air mail contracts awarded under President Herbert Hoover's Postmaster General, Walter Brown, were investigated by a U.S. Senate committee. Early

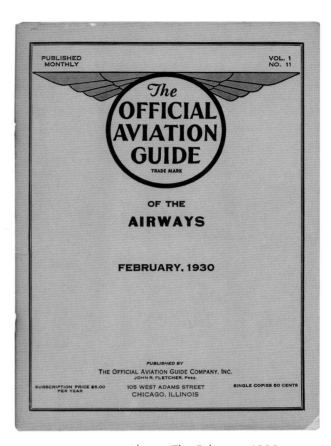

Above: The February 1930 Official Aviation Guide (OAG) had only a single route for many of the listed airlines.

Left: Passenger service in early 1930 was reliant on the air mail routes. This Air Mail map was published as part of the February 1930 OAG.

M. Steiner Archives

testimony suggested that numbers of small but highly qualified operators' bids had been ignored. Roosevelt's Postmaster General, James Farley, reacted quickly by cancelling all existing air mail contracts. Interim air mail service was provided by the Army Air Corps until new contracts could be awarded. None of the old route holders would be allowed to bid on these new contracts.

In an innovative move, most carriers that had held contracts simply reincorporated with new names and bid on the new contracts. Eastern Air Transport became Eastern Air Lines; American Airways became American Airlines, etc. While some new corporations did retain their old routes, some established lines lost their air mail contracts (routes) to upstarts. Among these was the award of the Dallas-to-Atlanta route to Delta Air Lines.

Through most of these early years, fewer than one million passengers were carried each year by all carriers. Then came the introduction of aircraft designed specifically for passenger service. The Boeing 247 debuted in 1933, the DC-2 and Lockheed Electra in 1934, the legendary DC-3 in 1936, and Lockheed Lodestar in 1937. By 1941, passenger boardings grew to four million per year.

WORLD WAR II

Possibly the least recognized, most significant event in U.S. commercial airline history was the naming of Col. Edgar S. Gorrell as the first president of the Air Transport Association of America (ATA). Col. Gorrell was one of Gen. "Billy" Mitchell's disciples, having served as Mitchell's Chief of Air Staff. Under Gorrell's guidance, a commercial aviation "war preparedness plan" was developed in 1936. As the United States entered World War II, Col. Gorrell, accompanied by Gen. "Hap" Arnold, took this plan to Washington. Convinced, President Roosevelt literally tore up his Executive Order that would have nationalized the airlines. Under the plan, all existing air carriers would remain private corporations, operating both civilian and

Right: The carrying of air mail by U.S. Army pilots started off with great excitement and special flight covers. The operation quickly became a disaster and was ended.

Fly EASTERN'S *Great New* SILVER FALCON
The world's <u>most advanced</u> twin-engine airliner

military operations. Many, including Atlanta-based Delta, converted their maintenance shops into military production and modification centers.

World War II had a significant impact on commercial aviation. Commercial aircraft production was diverted to military use, as were airline-owned aircraft. Vastly increased production capacity, establishment of numerous military airfields, advances in technology, and vast training of all types of aviation skills all contributed to increased awareness about aviation by the general public. However, since all commercial airlines were involved in the war effort, the net result was that passenger boardings were essentially flat until late in 1944.

POST-WAR GROWTH

After World War II, a number of positive factors converged to facilitate rapid expansion of existing airlines and the forming of many new carriers. These factors included the return of loaned airline equipment, the availability of large fleets of military surplus transport aircraft, and the manufacturing capacity for many more. The newer technologies and manufacturing methods made future airliners available within a short period of time. A trained and experienced pool of aviation personnel had come home from the war and were anxious to go to work in aviation-related fields. The federal government was closing much of the network of military aviation bases, many of which provided instant operational commercial airports. An economic boom provided expendable, discretionary income that was available for travel. Many Americans had experienced air travel and seen exotic places; they were now anxious to visit these with their families.

The introduction of DC-4 and Lockheed 1049 Constellation aircraft boosted boardings to 14 million in 1946. The first DC-6, 749 Constellations, and Boeing 377 aircraft in 1947 and 1948 began an upsurge in capacity and boardings. By 1951, when the DC-6B and 1049

SKYSWEEP BROOMS

A fascination with flying fueled the advertising world. Even cigar box labels reflected the interest in air travel.

"Connies" appeared, boardings had already reached 25 million. The last years of new, piston-powered airliners continued this growth. The year 1953 and the DC-7 saw 32 million boardings, the DC-7B and "G" Model Connies in 1955 reached 42 million, and the DC-7C in 1956 peaked at 46 million passengers for the year. Georgia-based and Georgia-serving airlines all participated in this growth.

Shortly after the war, a number of new airlines were formed across the country. Among these were Piedmont Airlines, Georgia-based Southern Airways, and World Airways. Southern provided scheduled passenger service with DC-3 aircraft. Southern's highly experienced staff had operated military contract schools in a number of locations, including Bainbridge and Atlanta. World Airways was a non-scheduled charter operator whose initial route was from New York to San Juan, Puerto Rico.

Many of the small regional carriers crossed over to become national and international airlines. Among these was Delta Air Lines.

DEREGULATION

Deregulation in November of 1978 spawned a flurry of new airlines. Among these were Georgia-based Air Atlanta and ValuJet. Air Atlanta was service focused, seeking business clientele. ValuJet offered bargain fares and no frills. Other such startups served the Georgia market. Among these was Kiwi Airlines which was formed and operated primarily by former Eastern Air Lines personnel.

Most of these deregulation airlines utilized leased aircraft that had been retired from the fleets of the major airlines. They also outsourced everything

The tobacco industry used airplane images to sell cigarettes. The WINGS brand included a collectible card in each cigarette pack and published small albums to hold sets of these cards.

M. Steiner Archives

from maintenance to ticket counter personnel. Gate positions at many major airports were not available, so many of these airlines provided service to alternate airports.

As many major (legacy) carriers encountered financial difficulties, another generation of airlines came into existence. These partner carriers operated entirely with the major airlines' outward appearances. Flight numbers, aircraft livery, and ticket jackets all carried the major carriers' logos and identities. Most of the Delta Connection family fell into this category. They included Chautauqua, Freedom, Shuttle America, SkyWest, Atlantic Southeast (ASA), and Comair.

The following pages present the history of those carriers that have been headquartered or based in Georgia, as well as those whose history is significant to the development of Georgia aviation.

The major airlines flew increasingly large aircraft on the profitable long haul routes. The McDonnell Douglas MD-11 was a later version of the Douglas DC-10 concept.

AIR FREIGHT AIRLINES

Almost all passenger service airlines carry freight, or cargo. Some operate separate air cargo fleets. United Parcel Service (UPS) Airlines is an all-cargo airline with corporate headquarters in Atlanta, Georgia.

AGRICULTURAL SERVICES

Agriculture is Georgia's largest business. The use of aircraft for agricultural services is varied, but generally is still referred to as "crop dusting." The history of this important aviation activity in Georgia is closely tied to the history of Delta Air Lines.

EASTERN AIR LINES

Eastern Air Lines could easily claim to be Atlanta's first airline. The airline and its predecessors probably had more Atlanta "firsts" than any other single carrier.

Among the early commercial aviation visionaries was Harold F. Pitcairn. A graduate of the Wharton School of Business, Pitcairn had a passion for designing airplanes, and his dream was to create a market for the airplanes that he would design and produce. He decided to utilize those aircraft. In 1925, with World War I experience in the Army Air Service behind him and using family money, Pitcairn established Pitcairn Aviation outside of Philadelphia, Pennsylvania. He built a small factory and an adjacent airfield and began production of the PA-1 Fleetwing. The standard model, already a sleek biplane powered with a 90 HP Curtiss OX-5 engine, was modified with a 200 HP engine and entered in the 1925 Mitchell Field Air Races.

Above: Significant expansion of Eastern's routes included a Gulf Coast line (Mobile to Brownsville) and a Chicago-to-Mobile route. "Reducing travel time to a minimum and offering every travel comfort" was the company pitch.

Right: The Pitcairn Mailwing was designed for one purpose – to haul air mail. The pilot sat well to the rear behind a large mail compartment.

M. Steiner Archives

His entry, renamed the Fleet Aero, won the race, giving Pitcairn Aviation immediate credibility.

Pitcairn visited Europe to learn more about their airline industry. Airlines in Europe began to develop almost immediately after World War I and were already operating aircraft built specifically for passenger service. To further sharpen his focus on his airline vision, Pitcairn also observed a comprehensive air mail service in operation. Up to that point, the U.S. Post Office Department had operated a limited air mail service from Washington, D.C. to New York.

In February of 1925, the Kelly Act, which established Contract Air Mail and allowed private contractors to bid on specific air mail routes, became the basis of almost all American commercial aviation. The first CAM routes had been awarded and began operations in 1926. Reed Chambers, who headed Florida Airways, had served as an ace in World War I and subsequently became part of an aerial survey company with Captain Eddie Rickenbacker from 1918 to 1921. Chambers had also encouraged Pitcairn to bid on the New York-to-Atlanta route in order to link his isolated Florida Airways operation with the Northeast U.S. by air mail. Pitcairn successfully bid for CAM 19 with service from New York to Atlanta with numerous intermediate stops. The contract was awarded in November of 1927 and initially flown in May 1928. This route also provided a vital link through the Florida Airways connection with Pan American Airways' international flights out of Miami. The route from New York to Miami became known as the "eastern" route.

On December 1, 1928, Pitcairn took over the Florida Airways route from Atlanta to Miami, providing a continuous service from New York to Miami and beyond to South America. A number of stops were added during 1929,

but Harold Pitcairn yearned to concentrate on his aircraft design and manufacturing. Even as his airline began serving the Florida route, he was negotiating with Juan de la Cierva for production of the autogiro in the United States. On July 10, 1929, Pitcairn sold out to North American Aviation, then a conglomerate of many aviation interests. North American was headed by Clement Melville Keys, who also was Chairman of National Air Transport (NAT). The conglomerate also owned Curtiss Aircraft, Sperry Gyroscope, and Transcontinental Air Transport (TAT).

The name was changed to Eastern Air Transport on January 15, 1930, and passenger service from New York to Atlanta began on August 18, 1930. By this time the fleet included Ford Tri-Motors, Curtiss Kingbirds, and leased Fokker Trimotors. This passenger service was so successful that six Curtiss Condor aircraft were ordered and put into service. On New Years Day 1931, the passenger service was extended from Atlanta to Miami. The beginning of the winter snowbird arrival in south Florida, by air, had begun. Later, an alternative coastal route, bypassing Atlanta via Augusta and Savannah, was also inaugurated.

Above: Inaugural air mail flights were celebrated by the local post master, mayor and other town dignitaries. Envelopes were stamped "First Flight" to commemorate the event.

This was the era of huge conglomerates, of which North American was the most vulnerable. On February 28, 1933, in a frenzy of wheeling and dealing, an outside conglomerate, General Motors, bought that part of North American known as Eastern Air Transport. Initially engaged as a consultant, Captain Eddie Rickenbacker would in June of 1933 be named a vice president of Eastern.

The beginnings of modern air service were introduced by Eastern. Condor sleeper service, between New York and Atlanta, offered Pullman-like beds. Thirteen-hour New York-to-Miami service was introduced.

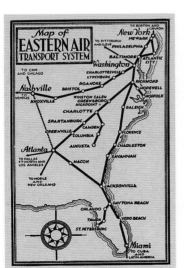

A small airline on the verge of bankruptcy, the Ludington Line, was acquired by Eastern. An eager Hearst newspaper reporter began investigating the air mail contract awards by President Hoover's Post Master General, Walter Brown. In the process, he discovered that Eastern had received a mail contract with a bid over three times that of Ludington's. The Eastern-Ludington deal was the trigger for the U.S. Senate investigation that resulted in cancellation of all air mail contracts.

Left: Eastern Air Transport's 1933 route map shows the original mainline from New York to Miami via Atlanta. New "shortcut routes" that serve Augusta and Savannah are also shown on the map. No meals were provided but meal stops were scheduled at select cities.

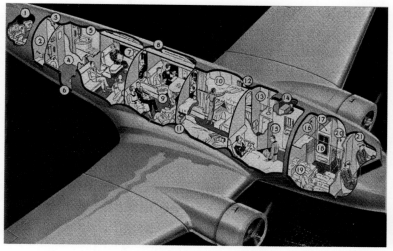

Above: A cutaway view of a Douglas Sleeper Transport (DST).

Above: This Eastern Air Lines Atlanta letterhead carries the earliest logo with a red duckhawk – also known as a falcon. The Silver Fleet logo had not yet been created.

Right: Eastern's newly built fleet of Douglas DC-3 airliners await delivery at the Douglas Santa Monica plant.

M. Steiner Archives

After the disastrous attempt by the Army Air Service to fly the mail, temporary air mail contracts were awarded, pending a full round of new contracts. Eastern, as well as other carriers, got by the best that they could.

On January 1, 1935, "Captain Eddie" Rickenbacker became General Manager of Eastern Air Lines, Inc., the new corporation. His goal was to make Eastern self-sufficient, without reliance on any government subsidies such as air mail. Eastern moved their operations and maintenance facilities from Atlanta to Miami. Though he had lost some of his "Ace of Aces" image when Lindbergh crossed the Atlantic, Rickenbacker was still an American icon. He ran Eastern with a discipline of rigid cost control, hard work, and efficiency – a practical management approach versus a romantic endeavor.

In a dramatic duel for ownership of Eastern Air Lines, Rickenbacker's contacts and reputation enabled him to buy the airline from General Motors for $3.5 million. At one point during the negotiations he told a friend, "I was about 3,450,000 dollars short!" An investment firm advanced the money and arranged a public subscription for repayment. April 22, 1938, was the start of Captain Eddie's Eastern Air Lines.

Confirmation of Rickenbacker's vision of an airline that would be profitable with passenger service alone came in the form of Congressional action. The Civil Aeronautics Authority was established in 1938, and the post office no longer was involved in routes and contracts. At this point, Eastern's fleet was ten DC-2s, ten DC-3s, and two Stinson Reliants. Eastern had the best safety record of any U.S. carrier: eight years (1930-1937) with no fatalities.

Atlanta would be the sight of one of Rickenbacker's most memorable survival miracles. He had left his New York office the night of February 26, 1940, bound for Birmingham, to speak to Birmingham's Aviation Committee. Eastern Flight 21, known as the *Mexico Flyer*, was one of Eastern's new Douglas Sleeper Transports (DST), a DC-3 with sleeping berths. It also had a small private compartment, the "Sky Lounge," which Rickenbacker booked so he could work on his speech notes. Flight 21 had made its Washington, D.C., stop and was attempting to land in Atlanta, when the plane clipped some trees and flipped onto its back. With a smashed pelvis, shattered hip, broken ribs, and an eye out of its socket, Captain Eddie was taken to Atlanta's Piedmont hospital. A triage intern had skipped over Rickenbacker when he was brought in, to "work on the live ones." He spent over four months at Piedmont and left with only a limp and a slight stoop.

Rickenbacker spent little time at the office while enduring his long and painful convalescence. He stayed in touch by phone and gained pleasure from his airline's successes, including Eastern making the first flight into the new, state-of-the-art Washington National Airport. American Airlines would have had that honor, but a delay on their part and an aggressive Eastern pilot brought all the attention to Eastern.

Reprinted from MARCH APRIL 1953

THE GREAT SILVER FLEET News

EASTERN AIR LINES

Above: "Captain Eddie" was a great communicator. Here he graces the cover of the company newsletter, "The Great Silver Fleet News" commemorating Eastern's 25th anniversary.

Georgia Aviation Hall Of Fame

World War II potentially placed Rickenbacker in a difficult position. He was an isolationist, and much like Lindbergh, had predicted the German threat and had preached on the need for a strong air force. Also like Lindbergh, as history has since revealed, he stood ready to be a patriot. Eastern, like the other Air Transport Association (ATA) member airlines,

EASTERN *Air Lines*
FLY THE GREAT SILVER FLEET

Left: Eastern dominated airline service to cities in the East: Boston, Detroit, Chicago, and St. Louis formed the outer ring of the sixty-five cities served.

M. Steiner Archives

Colorful ticket jackets displayed the Silver Falcon Martin 404, the New Type Constellation and the Super C Constellation.

The Spring 1947 issue of "The Great Silver Fleet News" announced the new standardized Eastern Air Lines insignia. Note the block lettering and the more graceful duckhawk.

M. Steiner Archives

gave up aircraft, flight crews and ground crews for military airlift duty. Eastern established its Military Transport Division (MTD), which was christened the "Great Chocolate Fleet" for its strange chocolate-hued paint scheme.

Eastern's MTD flew the supply route for the African campaign. This route started in Miami with stops in San Juan, Trinidad, Brazil and Ascension Island, ending in Africa. The return trips brought wounded back to Miami area hospitals. Rickenbacker declined offers to be commissioned a general, but did agree to visit air bases and was sent to England to do so. Following that mission, he left for New Guinea with a message for General MacArthur. They never made it. Lost at sea, the B-17 carrying Rickenbacker ditched, and yet another survival miracle took place. The occupants of the B-17 were rescued after more than twenty days in a life raft.

Following the war, most of Eastern's aircraft were returned from military service. Additional aircraft were placed on order to service new routes that were being awarded. These included Douglas DC-4s and Lockheed Constellations. Both of these aircraft had been designed as airliners, but all production had been routed to the military. In 1946, the Douglas DC-4s joined the fleet, and San Juan was added to the Eastern routes. The first Connies were received in 1947.

The 1950s were growth years. New aircraft included newer versions of the Constellation (the Super Constellation), DC-6 and DC-7Bs. The two-tiered designations of "Golden Falcon" and "Silver Falcon" were applied to specific aircraft to highlight the newest and fastest offered. The new Martin 404 twin-engine transport was designated the "Silver Falcon."

In late 1953, Super-C Constellations continued the expansion and upgrading of the fleet. Eastern developed an interchange with Braniff to provide service to South and Central America. Eastern bought out Colonial

Airlines in 1956 to gain routes to Canada, Bermuda and New England. There was a bitter feud over Colonial with upstart, Miami-based National Airlines. National and Delta had both been winning new routes, and this competition was taking its toll on Eastern.

The first jets were ordered, and Lockheed Electra turboprops were placed in service prior to receiving those jets. The idea was to bridge the gap in flight time between piston and jet service on longer routes. Unfortunately, there had been two fatal crashes of Electras with other airlines due to structural failure. The FAA ordered a reduced cruise speed for all users, and the Electra no longer offered any advantage over the piston aircraft then in service with Eastern. Consumer confidence in the Electra also had suffered.

In 1959, Eastern posted its twenty-third consecutive profitable year. The Sixties saw jet service beginning with the Douglas DC-8 in 1960. The Boeing 720 arrived a year later, offering an advantage in the short range market.

Eastern now had surplus, fully depreciated prop aircraft, and created the "Air-Shuttle" concept in the high density Northeast corridor: Boston, New York, Philadelphia and Washington. Announced on April 30, 1961, the Shuttle flew every hour and guaranteed a seat to anyone who showed up on time, even if an additional aircraft would be required to fly only one passenger.

No reservations were made, no tickets were sold and fares were paid on board. This concept would appear years later on many of the startups after deregulation.

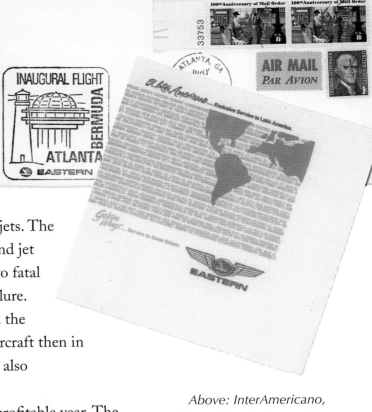

Above: InterAmericano, Eastern's exclusive service to Latin America, flew many of the old Braniff Airways routes. Previously, Eastern and Braniff had enjoyed an interchange agreement on these same routes. On May 1, 1973, Eastern expanded its international routes with Atlanta to Bermuda service.

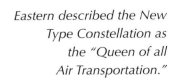

Eastern described the New Type Constellation as the "Queen of all Air Transportation."

Above: "The Wings of Man" registered the name "WhisperLiner" for its Lockheed 1011 TriStars introduced in 1972.

M. Steiner Archives

Another, equally unconventional service was offered in an earlier experiment in October of 1960. The "Air-Bus" utilized piston aircraft from mid-western cities to Florida at Greyhound fares. These various experiments were designed to increase sagging sales.

On December 16, 1963, Floyd Hall became President of Eastern. He built a "New Team," which included the first obvious defectors from Delta. Todd Cole, credited with being the financial wizard of Delta, went over to Eastern. He took with him a team which drew heavily from the management of the computer department. This was the beginning of the age of computerization and Eastern was anxious to take a lead.

Floyd Hall also changed the image of Eastern. His team introduced the "hockey stick" logo with a new color scheme. Aircraft took on new names like "WhisperJet" for the Boeing 727, put in service in 1963. Much later, in 1972, the Lockheed 1011 TriStar would be designated the "WhisperLiner." Eastern would be the first airline to utilize the 1011.

The 1970s started off with more growth and additional routes. The purchase of Puerto Rico-based Caribair added West Indies vacation destinations. Frank Borman, former astronaut, had served as an advisor to the airline since 1969. In 1975 he was elected president and CEO. Borman set about building a newer fleet. Among these purchases was an order for thirty-four Airbus 300s. Those purchases of new aircraft, coupled with deregulation and resulting fare wars, took Eastern into a $2.2 billion debt by the end of the decade.

In spite of even deeper debt, Eastern bought Braniff's South American routes in 1982, and was the launch (first) customer for Boeing's 757 in 1983. Douglas DC-10s were added for long range routes to Europe and South America. Eastern was heavily unionized and conflicts between management and the unions had escalated, especially on the issue of concessions.

In 1986, the Eastern board of directors accepted an offer from Texas Air Corp., headed by Frank Lorenzo. Lorenzo was known as a union-buster and confirmed it by rejecting all union demands. Charlie Bryan and the International Association of Machinists (IAM) walked out on March 4, 1989, joined by pilots and flight attendants. The pilots and attendants would later return, but many had been replaced. Eastern filed bankruptcy on March 9th, started hiring replacements and resumed flying. Day by day, the number of flights increased, especially at Atlanta, Eastern's largest hub.

The Federal bankruptcy judge found irregularities with Lorenzo's actions and in April of 1990 named Martin Shugrue, an airline veteran, as the court's trustee. Frank Lorenzo sold his stock in Continental Holding, and was replaced by a former Delta executive, Hollis Harris. As late as January 15, 1991, Shugrue, speaking at the International Aviation Club in Washington, said discussions with two potential partners "would change the economics and operations...allowing the airline to become profitable this year."

"Eastern Air Lines Quits" was the headline on the January 24, 1991 issue of *ATL,* the Atlanta Airport Newspaper. The agony finally had ended at midnight on January 18, 1991, with the official end of all operations. This article was accompanied by a photo of a portion of the ninety aircraft that were being repositioned to the Eastern maintenance hangar at Hartsfield Atlanta International Airport. Other articles in that same newspaper speculated on the future of Eastern's eighteen gates in Atlanta and facilities elsewhere. Ivan Allen III, chair of the Atlanta Chamber of Commerce Aviation Committee, commented on the economic impact on Atlanta of Eastern's shutdown.

Eventually, sales of Eastern equipment and supplies would be conducted at the Eastern flight kitchen near Hartsfield. The flight kitchen had only been opened in December of 1988 with much

Below: The combination of logo changes – and variations on each – created a number of different baggage decal designs over the years.

M. Steiner Archives

fanfare and comments by Joseph Leonard, Eastern Executive Vice President. Many of the buyers were displaced Eastern personnel who wanted to salvage a tangible heirloom of their careers with a legendary airline. For many, it was difficult to accept Eastern's demise. For years, the familiar "hockey stick" logo remained on one of the fuel storage tanks at Hartsfield Atlanta Airport and was visible to passengers on airplanes of other carriers as they taxied out for takeoff.

Former Eastern personnel were involved in various airline startups that were almost entirely staffed by former Eastern employees. One such carrier, Kiwi Airlines, would serve Atlanta.

Many believe that Delta, without Eastern as a competitor, had taken advantage of Eastern's failure to the detriment of the traveling public. This, it is argued, laid the groundwork for carriers like ValuJet (now AirTran) to thrive on customer dissatisfaction with Delta's service and air fares. And Joe Leonard, who opened the Eastern flight kitchen, later became Chairman and CEO of AirTran.

To date, no other airline has tried again to be "The Wings of Man."

DELTA AIR LINES

For many years, Delta Air Lines has been an integral part of the Georgia community, especially Atlanta. The names Delta and Atlanta seem synonymous today. That has not always been true. In fact, the annual stockholders meetings were still being held in Monroe, Louisiana long after the headquarters had moved to Atlanta. Delta Air Lines started as a crop dusting operation and takes its name from the Mississippi Delta agricultural area of Louisiana. That is where Collett Everman (C.E.) Woolman, Delta's founder, started his career in 1912 as an entomologist/county agricultural agent in Monroe. As agent and later a supervisor of other agents, Woolman dealt with the scourge of the boll weevil that was all but destroying the cotton growing industry.

Delta founder C.E. Woolman, circa 1940.

Delta Air Transport Heritage Museum

A new, powdered chemical agent, calcium arsenate, had shown effectiveness against the boll weevil. One of the United States Department of Agriculture entomologists in Louisiana, Dr. Bert Coad, secured a grant to experiment with aerial distribution against the boll weevil, otherwise known as crop dusting. Although there had been some experiments of "crop dusting" as early as 1918, no successful marriage of the airplane and calcium arsenate had yet been made.

World War I brought on the advent of improved and somewhat practical airplanes. One of the many aspiring aircraft manufacturers during the war was a New York firm, the Huff-Daland Company. Only moderately successful during the war years, Huff-Daland was still trying to sell airplanes to the military when by coincidence a Huff-Daland demonstration plane happened to stop at Dr. Coad's airfield in Tallulah, Louisiana. Conversation led to understanding, and the Huff-Daland Dusters, Inc. came into being.

What was lacking was a knowledgeable salesman, but Dr. Coad had the man, C.E. Woolman. Macon, Georgia, had offered an airfield as a base for operations, a location that had the advantage of being able to service other crops in addition to cotton. In 1924, Huff-Daland Dusters set up shop in Macon, but even with all of these advantages, the company did not stay

in Macon very long. C.E. knew Monroe, Louisiana, well, and Dr. Coad's lab facilities were not too far away. Monroe also was more central to the expanding crop dusting territory, which now included Arkansas and Texas. Dusting in Mexico had also begun, and the fleet had grown to over twenty "dusters."

The off-season still was not producing much revenue in the south, so Woolman, the salesman, looked further south – to South America. Aviation is one of the few businesses that can move its entire operation in a matter of days. Peru became the new off-season territory.

It was 1925 and the business leaders of Monroe had provided an airfield and a hangar, built specifically to Huff-Daland's needs. They saw a marriage that would continue for decades, not knowing that it would go well beyond crop dusting.

For all of the early airlines, air mail was an essential source of revenue, but Huff-Daland did not receive any mail contracts. In late 1928, the owners of Huff-Daland Dusters sold the corporation to its operators. The new owners then incorporated a new company, Delta Air Service, Inc. Delta took over the dusting, and a flight school, then added an Army Corps of Engineers survey contract. Using their stock, Delta purchased a Louisiana flying service for its sole passenger aircraft. The first passenger flight, from Dallas to Monroe, took off on June 17, 1929. Delta had become an airline.

Delta took over management of Monroe's airport, Selman Field. The revenues from the field kept Delta alive through the Great Depression. They failed to get any of the additional mail contracts that were let in 1930. The circumstances of being bypassed led to the award of a revised route after the cancellation of all air mail routes. On June 8, 1934, Delta finally got the contract from Ft. Worth to Atlanta. The next month it was extended to Charleston, and this would become Delta's main route for decades to come.

Ironically, Delta had no aircraft to serve this route. American Airlines, however, now had five surplus Stinson "Ts", the Tri-Motor, that they had used on this very same route. Delta bought them for about a quarter on the dollar. These were followed by Stinson As, Lockheed Electra 10s and Douglas DC-2s. In the summer of 1940, Delta made the decision to replace its limited and aging fleet with the popular and proven Douglas DC-3. This aircraft would be used for the next two decades, and in fact, one DC-3 was still flying cargo into the 1960s.

"Welcome to Southern Skies" was Delta's seat pocket reading in the early 1940s.

In 1941, Delta moved its headquarters to Atlanta, but the annual meeting remained in Monroe well into the 1970s. The last of these years the meeting was held in a large tent, because there was no facility large enough for the crowd of stockholders.

If ever a relatively obscure event would significantly impact Delta's future, it was the awarding of Air Mail route 54, from Atlanta to Cincinnati. Service,

M. Steiner Archives

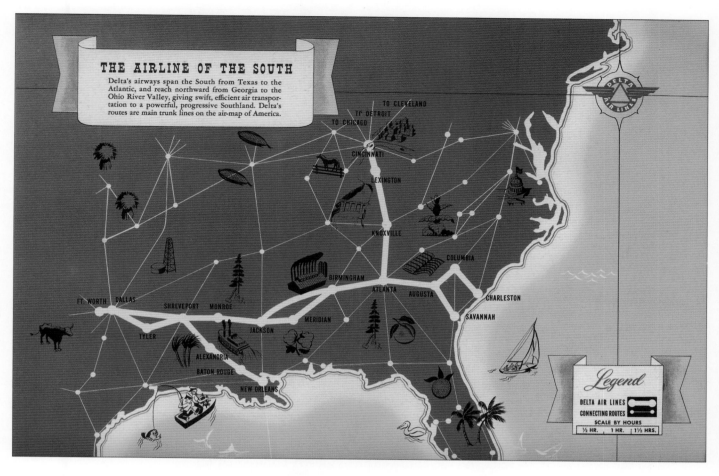

THE AIRLINE OF THE SOUTH

Delta's airways span the South from Texas to the Atlantic, and reach northward from Georgia to the Ohio River Valley, giving swift, efficient air transportation to a powerful, progressive Southland. Delta's routes are main trunk lines on the air-map of America.

Legend

DELTA AIR LINES
CONNECTING ROUTES
SCALE BY HOURS
½ HR. | 1 HR. | 1½ HRS.

Delta was justifiably proud of their 1941 route map. Their new Cincinnati-Lexington-Knoxville-Atlanta route was the first new route in seven years.

Delta's new DC-3 was featured in almost all print materials. This 1941 baggage decal sports the DC-3 and the motto, "The Airline of the South."

with an intermediate stop at Knoxville, began on July 15, 1941. Cincinnati became, and remains, a significant Delta city, and Delta was no longer just a southeastern airline. Immediately after World War II, this route would be extended to Chicago and Miami.

For two years, 1942-44, Delta's headquarters was designated an Army Air Corps Modification Base. In order to expedite production, many aircraft types were produced with only basic equipment. The modifications for their specific use, as well as later improvements, were performed at modification bases. Delta modified nearly a thousand airplanes in Atlanta.

Across town in Marietta, the Bell Aircraft plant was producing B-29s. A Delta team commuted to Bell and performed essential, last-minute modifications. The Delta base and personnel were so well regarded that it was the last in the country to be closed. Delta also participated in a number of training programs for the government.

All of America's airlines performed essential transport functions during the war and continued to fly their domestic routes as best they could. Delta's fleet during most of the war was comprised of only five DC-3s. They led the industry in aircraft utilization, which translated into financial success in a difficult time. There were few route awards during the war, but Delta did win a critical Dallas-to-New Orleans route, with significant stops en route.

As the war ended, Delta ordered new Douglas aircraft, issuing stock to provide the funds. The longest route that had ever been awarded to that

PROPOSED AIRWAYS

Having just gained their first new route, this 1941 "Proposed Airways" map seemed overly ambitious. Actually, it was almost prophetic.

point by the Civil Aeronautics Board (CAB) gave Delta Chicago-to-Miami authority on August 23, 1945. Other routes requested were awarded to competitors. Through it all, Delta was still operating a crop dusting service. In fact, until October 29, 1945, the company name was Delta Air Corporation. On that day it became Delta Air Lines, Inc.

In the late 1940s, as Delta and the entire airline industry enjoyed rapid growth, Eastern and Delta became strong competitors. Delta obtained the first DC-4s in the east, and Eastern responded with bigger, faster Lockheed Constellations. Delta, a staunch Douglas customer, took the DC-6 and set a southern transcontinental speed record on the delivery flight.

It became obvious in the early 1950s that jet transports were right around the corner. The Lockheed plant across town was building Boeing, all-jet B-47s, and Boeing had already indicated they were working on jet airliners. The characteristics of these aircraft made long-haul flights, with larger numbers of passengers, a necessity. Delta had few such routes, and was generally regarded as a regional carrier and a trunk airline. The CAB was aiding postwar startup "feeder" airlines. Two that would both compete and "feed" Delta's longer flights were Atlanta-based Southern Airways and Piedmont Airlines.

Yet another innovation of the times was the "interchange" arrangement. Under this plan two airlines would pass an aircraft from one airline's crew to another to allow passengers to remain on the same airplane as it crossed from one airline's route to the other. Delta's first west coast service was as an interchange with American. A similar arrangement with TWA added Detroit to Delta's Midwest destinations.

There had been occasional conversations between C.E. Woolman and the heads of other airlines on many matters, including possible mergers with Memphis-based Chicago & Southern (C&S) and Northeast Airlines.

M. Steiner Archives

62

Serious merger discussions began between Delta and C&S in 1951, and an agreement was reached in Spring of 1952. The various CAB hearings and other financial and governmental actions added a full year to the process. Finally, on May 1, 1953, Delta-C&S became a reality.

After the merger with Chicago & Southern (C&S) an interim corporate name and logo was utilized. It combined the winged "Delta" with the stylized "C&S" as seen on this DC-7.

It would be years until a merger with Northeast occurred.

This was the first merger for each of these carriers, and they sometimes found that they were writing the plan as they went. Technically, the legal name of the airline remained Delta Air Lines, but *all* public references were Delta-C&S. C&S brought Caribbean vacation destinations, including Puerto Rico, Dominican Republic, Haiti, Cuba, Jamaica, Aruba, Curacao, and Venezuela. These were all served out of New Orleans. C&S also brought Lockheed Constellations to the merged fleet. Up until now, Delta had been primarily a Douglas operation, with DC-3s, DC-4s and DC-6s making up the thirty-two aircraft fleet.

Delta's DC-7s boast the new airborne radar. "Deltaliners fly the best weather route!"

delta route maps

The Best Weather Route

An air line map is a wonderful expression of clear and direct thinking. It gets right to the point — by the straight line method — and with all possible speed.

But the straight line is not always the smoothest route when rain or storms lie along the way. Under these conditions Delta flies where the weather is best and all Deltaliners are being equipped with Radar weather-eyes to detect disturbances up to a hundred miles ahead.

As your plane flies above most weather, you may not be aware of any deviation from course, but to insure that your trip is as comfortable as it is quick, Delta pilots will fly the *Best-Weather Route*.

Delta AIR LINES

General Offices: Atlanta Airport, Atlanta, Georgia

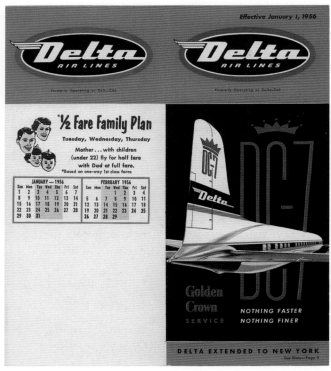

Delta found itself dragged into the jet age. The first available pure jet was a Boeing aircraft, and Delta had no prior relationship with them. Arch-rival competitor Eastern had ordered the Lockheed Electra turbo-prop and would have a speed advantage over Delta on competitive routes. Douglas would be the last to deliver, but Delta was a Douglas customer. On Valentine's Day 1956, Delta ordered the Douglas DC-8 and decided to skip the interim option of turbo-props such as the Electra.

The DC-8 was a large, long-range airliner. The thought of a companion, mid-range jet took Delta to Convair and their CV-880. Convair was anxious to get their fair share of the jet market and was willing to deal. Delta was impressed and ordered ten 880s on June 26, 1956.

September 18, 1959 saw the first DC-8 revenue flight in the world. The delivery flight from San Diego to Miami of the CV-880, the fastest commercial airliner, set a record that stood for almost twenty years.

As traffic grew, the need for more capacity on the money-making long haul routes became critical. Douglas addressed this need with the DC-8 Super Sixty Series jetliner. Known simply as the "stretched" DC-8, capacity was increased significantly.

Delta was the only airline that had operated a separate cargo operation. Even though the jets had significant cargo space, Delta needed cargo container capable freighters. In 1966, Delta bought three L-100s, the civilian version of the military C-130 Hercules from its neighbor in Marietta.

Boeing had lost the military competition for what became the C5-A to Lockheed. Boeing then took their design and directed development of a "wide-body" commercial airliner. The result would be the largest passenger plane ever produced, the Boeing 747. Pan Am placed the first order in April 1966 for twenty-five aircraft.

The race was on. American Airlines had a history of taking their specifications for required airliners to the manufacturers for consideration.

Left: By January 1, 1956, "Delta, formerly Delta-C&S" was the new corporate name. This schedule included the long-sought New York-to-Atlanta route. The motto, "nothing faster, nothing finer" with Golden Crown service was designed to offset competitor Eastern Air Lines Lockheed Electra service on this route.

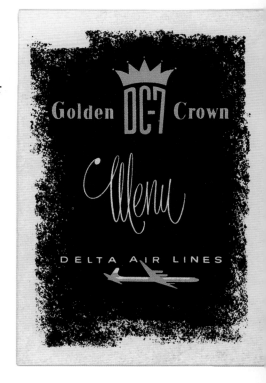

M. Steiner Archive

Right: Delta purchased three L-100s from Lockheed in 1966 to boost its cargo container capacity.

Below: The Douglas DC-8 would become one of the longest serving airliners in Delta's fleet history. It would be "re-engined" with newer power plants to take advantage of the latest technology and "stretched" to carry more passengers. Many would eventually be sold to corporate friend UPS.

This time American approached Douglas for a medium-range wide-body. This specification launched the DC-10 design effort.

Lockheed had also responded to the general needs outlined by American. Their entry, the L-1011 TriStar, would mark Lockheed's first commercial passenger liner since the troubled turbo-prop Electra. To offset the airline's reluctance to consider the TriStar by the airlines, Lockheed had encouraged the active involvement of the airlines in almost every aspect of the design.

The beneficiaries of these three entries were the airlines and the traveling public. Delta was impressed with Lockheed's resulting design and with the available delivery schedule. In April 1968, Delta placed the largest aircraft order in its history for twenty-four TriStars, valued at over $350 million.

The first prototype 1011 flew on November 16, 1970. Less than three months later, the 1011 engine manufacturer, Rolls-Royce, went into receivership, and the entire project was in jeopardy. With delivery of the Lockheed in doubt, Delta scrambled and placed an order for five DC-10s, with the first delivery set for late 1972.

Delta still wanted only one wide-body in their fleet, the Lockheed TriStar. A fleet standardization program had been developed by Delta, and the wide-body dilemma was putting the program to the test. In an unusual move, the airlines with on-order TriStars advanced partial payments to Lockheed and Rolls-Royce. This action, coupled with other governmental assistance, saved the project and production was resumed. With the TriStar back on track, Delta sold the on-order DC-10s to United Air Lines with a leaseback arrangement which allowed them to release the DC-10s as they received each TriStar.

Delta took delivery of the first TriStar in October of 1973 and began service December 15th. Within six months, ten TriStars were in service, and by 1977 over twenty bore Delta's logo. The first Douglas DC-10 arrived in October 1972 and began service on November 22nd.

In addition to being a "crowd pleaser" among Delta's passengers, the TriStar cargo compartment was designed to handle the standard freight containers. This allowed Delta to sell its three Lockheed L-100 (Hercules) freighters and eliminate the maintenance burden of what had been their only turbo-prop aircraft.

Even as the Lockheed TriStar drama unfolded, another landmark occurred with the merger of Northeast Airlines into Delta on August 1, 1972. Northeast had been an elusive catch, with the pursuit going back over twenty years.

Delta's initial trans-Atlantic service was through an interchange agreement with Pan American. At that time, Pan Am had few domestic routes, so their passengers had to change planes and airlines just to get from one Pan Am international flight to another. Under the interchange, a Delta crew would board an inbound Pan Am flight at New Orleans, fly it through Atlanta to Washington, where another Pan Am crew would take the flight to Europe. Many of these flights had both Pan Am and Delta flight numbers, and allowed passengers and their luggage to remain on the same plane. Eventually, Delta would gain their own routes to London, Paris and many other European destinations.

The early seventies had seen few significant route decisions, but the CAB decided to do its first review of the trans-Atlantic routes. Not since the flurry of route assignments right after World War II had there been much change in this market. Delta put its entire effort on one route, Atlanta-to-London. Delta made much of its prior experience with the Pan Am interchange in its 1973 filing. It was October 21, 1977 before Delta would finally win this route. Other international routes would follow.

Comair's first relationship with Delta was as a participant in the Deltamatic computer reservation system (CRS). Essentially the Cincinnati-based regional carrier was no more than a subscriber to the service.

On May 1, 1984, Atlantic Southeast Airlines became a Delta Connection Partner with Atlanta serving as their hub. Delta continued to build its Delta

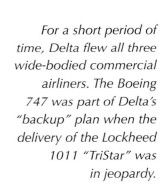

For a short period of time, Delta flew all three wide-bodied commercial airliners. The Boeing 747 was part of Delta's "backup" plan when the delivery of the Lockheed 1011 "TriStar" was in jeopardy.

M. Steiner Archive

66

In 1966 the new "Stretched" Douglas DC-8 became the largest capacity airliner in the world. Seating up to 250 passengers, it was created by inserting two fuselage sections into the standard airframe.

The Boeing 727 was the first tri-jet introduced into commercial service. When Delta purchased Northeast Airlines in 1972, the company began its long Boeing 727 operation.

Connection network with the addition of Comair in September 1984. These Connection partners would code share, meaning that Delta flight numbers would be assigned to the partner's flights. Delta later purchased 20% of ASA on May 23, 1986 and 20% of Comair later in the year.

Expansion also came the old fashioned way, by purchase and merger with another established airline. Among the historical airlines of America, none had a richer history than Western Airlines. Western came into being in 1925 in order to bid on the first round of air mail contracts. It was awarded the Los Angeles-to-Salt Lake City route, which it first flew on May 26, 1926. Western added passenger service the very next month. It grew first into a large regional carrier after WWII, entered the all-jet age ahead of many airlines, and was flying transcontinental routes in the mid-1980s.

Delta saw a nearly perfect fit of routes and purchased Western on September 9, 1986. The airlines were merged on April 1, 1987.

SkyWest Airlines operated as Western (Airlines) Express out of Western Airlines' Salt Lake City hub. With the purchase of Western, SkyWest became a Delta Connection partner.

In November of 1987, Comair joined Delta in establishing a hub at Orlando, Florida. In a somewhat unusual venture, Comair established the only flight school owned and operated by an airline. Comair Aviation Academy was started in 1989 and is located in Sanford, Florida near Orlando. This academy trains flight crews from a number of airlines.

The July 18, 1991, *ATL* summed it up, "Delta goes global." Delta had prepared a $260 million offer to acquire Pan Am's European routes. It seemed an honorable offer for part of the assets of America's historical flag carrier. Pan Am was trying to avoid the agony of a slow death by selling major portions of its operation. The purchase would provide Delta with a Frankfurt, Germany hub and a number of transatlantic routes.

By August, Delta had paid $460 million for the European routes and also the Pan Am Shuttle. The Shuttle was basically a reincarnation of the Eastern Air Shuttle, serving the Boston, New York and Washington corridor. In addition, Delta had offered $140 million to aid the downsized Pan Am to restructure, an effort that ultimately failed.

On March 22, 1999, ASA was bought out by Delta. Comair also was acquired by Delta as a wholly-owned subsidiary in January, 2000. Comair was named the Regional Airline of the Year 2000 by *Air Transport World* magazine.

A strike by their pilots on March 26, 2001 shut down Comair for 89 days. In 2004, Comair gained unwanted attention when a crew scheduling computer failed and caused cancellation of all flights on Christmas Day and the day after.

Yet another Delta Connection carrier joined the system. Chautauqua Airlines began service in the Florida market in November of 2002. A subsidiary of Republic Airways, its sister subsidiary, Shuttle America, also became a Delta Connection partner in the Northeast.

In yet another effort to adapt to the changing world of the airline business, Delta created Song, a low-cost airline brand owned and operated by Delta. Service began on April 15, 2003. In many ways it was reminiscent of Air Atlanta, providing spacious leather seats and free beverages. The new twists included free entertainment centers at every seat with MP3 selections and satellite television. Song competed directly with successful JetBlue in the Northeast to Florida tourist market. It also flew from Florida and the Northeast to the West Coast.

At its peak, Song operated over 200 flights a day. Service was transferred back to Delta on May 1, 2006, and the forty-eight Boeing 757s began their conversion back to Delta livery.

On August 15, 2005, Delta sold its wholly owned subsidiary, ASA, to SkyWest, Inc., another Delta Connection carrier. On September 8th, ASA began operations as a wholly-owned subsidiary of SkyWest, Inc.

On September 14, 2005, Delta Air Lines voluntarily filed for reorganization under Chapter 11 of the Bankruptcy Code. Their public announcement stated their intent to build a "simpler, more efficient, and cost-effective airline." They reaffirmed that their customers were the number one priority, that the full schedule would continue to operate, and that all "SkyMiles" would be honored. Delta acted aggressively to reduce costs. Its subsidiary, Comair, served the Cincinnati and Atlanta hubs, and also served "focus" destinations, including New York's La Guardia, Boston's Logan International, and Washington, D.C.'s Ronald Reagan National Airport.

In October 2005, Freedom Airlines became Delta's newest Delta Connection partner. Freedom was started in 2002 to operate CRJ-900s as America West Express. Freedom, a wholly-owned subsidiary of Mesa Air Group, began operations from Orlando, Florida, serving twenty-one destinations, primarily in the Southeast. New York (John F. Kennedy International Airport) became Freedom's second Delta Connection hub in July of 2006, serving eleven destinations from Richmond to Maine. This hub served the principal northeast corridor airports, including Boston, Hartford, Philadelphia, and all three Washington area airports (Reagan-National, Dulles

Delta put the McDonnell Douglas DC-10 tri-jet into service on November 22, 1972.

Chautauqua Airlines is a Republic Airways company based in Indianapolis. It services Delta routes with Embraer 145 jets. The aircraft are in Delta livery and bear Delta flight numbers.

Freedom Airlines – one of a family of partner airlines that typically serve smaller markets – operates a number of Delta routes in aircraft that appear to be Delta planes. Freedom is a subsidiary of Mesa Air Group, based in Albuquerque.

and Baltimore). This was essentially the same route of the many high-density "shuttle" services of the past by Eastern and PanAm.

In spring 2007, Delta continued to operate their Delta Connection program. The Connection partners included ASA, Comair, SkyWest, Chautauqua Airlines, Freedom Airlines, and Shuttle America. Of the more than 2500 "Connection" flights, ASA and Comair each operated 35%, SkyWest about 17%, and Republic Airways subsidiaries (Chautauqua and Shuttle America) about 13%.

Delta is one of only a few surviving "legacy" airlines. Over the years, it has purchased such historic lines as Chicago & Southern, Northeast, Western, and portions of Pan Am. Only American, Northwest, and United remain of those carriers that started with the Contract Air Mail routes in the 1920s.

AMERICAN AIRWAYS

American Airways became one of the first airlines to serve Atlanta through a series of acquisitions and mergers of the many early air carriers. At that time, airlines still derived most of their revenues from air mail. The second round of Contract Air Mail (CAM) awards in 1927-28 created four routes into Atlanta. Pitcairn began New York-to-Atlanta service on May 1, 1928 (CAM 19). Pitcairn added Atlanta-to-Miami in December of 1928 (CAM 25). This was to replace Florida Airways, who had initially served Miami beginning April 1, 1926 but was not able to continue that service.

St. Tammany-Gulf Coast Airways won CAM 23 between New Orleans and Atlanta and began service on May 1, 1928. On November 19, 1928, Interstate Airlines began service (CAM 30) between Chicago and Atlanta.

Right: Notes to this 1933 system map include, "Comfort facilities are available on most American Airways planes" and "Schedules have been so arranged that meals may be secured at points where facilities are available…"

M. Steiner Archives

In early 1929, the Aviation Corporation (AVCO) was formed. Within a couple of years, over eighty different aviation businesses were acquired by AVCO and became American Airways. Among these merged companies were both Interstate Airlines and St. Tammany-Gulf Coast Airways.

These merged airlines and their routes had produced a southern transcontinental service from Atlanta to Los Angeles. An American Airways advertising folder published on October 15, 1930 boasted, "passengers by day and air mail by day and night…American offers straight transcontinental airline of more than two thousand miles done in two *days* of flying and a good nights sleep in a real bed in between. Our great ships bring the heart of Georgia to the dooryard of California."

The March 1933 *Sky Lines*, a fifty-page booklet containing all airlines' schedules, shows one daily Chicago-to-Atlanta round trip, with four intermediate stops. It took five hours. A Fort Worth-to-Atlanta route took eight hours, with five stops en route and Houston-to-Atlanta, seven and a half hours, also with five stops.

On February 9, 1934, this all came to an end with the cancellation of all air mail contracts. Further, requests for future bids stipulated that, "no airline which had held an Air Mail Contract could bid for a new contract." American Airways sold out to a newly formed corporation, American Airlines, on April 11, 1934. In anticipation of winning back all of the former American Airways air mail contracts, a number of aircraft were ordered by the new American Airlines.

American Airlines did win most of the contracts previously held by American Airways, but not all. It did not retain any of the Atlanta air mail routes. In fact, the *Official Aviation Guide of the Airways*, October 1941 issue, shows no American Airlines service to Atlanta.

A new, smaller carrier, based in

The cover of the 1933 Sky Lines Air Travel Guide *sponsored by American Airways illustrates the new tri-motored airliners that were just coming into general use.*

The Curtiss Condor was the last biplane commercial airliner and was quite luxurious for its time. American boasted, "The ONLY coast-to-coast service operating…CONDOR sleeper planes."

*Right: In 1994, American
Airlines provided service
to Columbus, Georgia and
a number of Atlantic coast
destinations through its
partner, American Eagle.*

Monroe, Louisiana had bid
for the Atlanta-to-Dallas
contract. Perhaps in reaction
to criticism of the earlier
contract awards that had
sparked the Congressional
investigation, the Dallas-to-
Atlanta contract was awarded
to Delta Air Service. Delta
had been bypassed in 1928,
even though they had
previously been operating
a portion of the Dallas-to-
Atlanta route without any
mail contract.

American did not
return to the Atlanta
market until early 1979,
after deregulation. Today
it serves only two Georgia

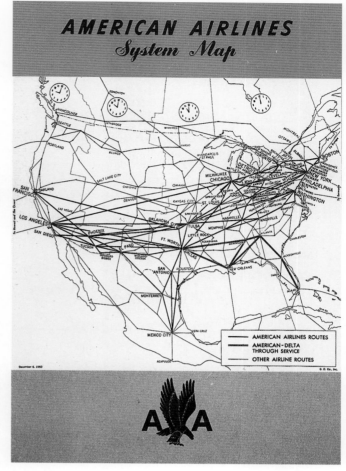

destinations, Atlanta and Savannah. Savannah is served by American's
commuter airline, American Eagle. While Atlanta does have an Admiral's
Club, the business traveler's membership lounge facility, there are no ticket
offices or any other American facilities in Georgia.

By 2007, American non-stop service from Atlanta was available to only
five cities. These included Dallas-Ft. Worth, St. Louis, Chicago, New York
(La Guardia), and Miami.

The once dominant air carrier in Atlanta became a relatively minor player
in this market.

*Below: Reformed into
American Airlines in 1934,
American continued to
court the business traveler
with its Condor fleet.*

M. Steiner Archives

SOUTHERN AIRWAYS

Southern Airways was among the many start-up air carriers after World War II. Like others, they operated the Douglas DC-3 and its military versions, the Army Air Force C-47 and Navy R4D. The airline operation was only the most recent venture for Southern, however.

Southern Airways, based in Augusta, was bought by local pilot Frank Hulse, III. According to his son, Frank Hulse, IV, Hulse bought Southern Airways of Georgia from an Augusta man named Bothwell Lee in the late '20s. Southern operated an FBO and flight school and was active with a Ford Tri-Motor and other aircraft in barnstorming around the South. Some sources indicate that Hulse bought Southern Airways of Georgia in June 1936, which may have been the date of incorporation. Southern moved its headquarters to Birmingham in 1938 and then to Atlanta in 1942.

Frank W. Hulse, III (far left) and Directors of Southern Airways.

Georgia Aviation Hall Of Fame

During World War II, Southern had operated a number of Contract Training Schools for the Army Air Forces. Among these locations were two in Georgia, Atlanta and Bainbridge. While operating these contract schools, Southern had filed with the Civil Aeronautics Board (CAB) for local service carrier routes across eight southern states. Following the end of World War II, the entire aviation industry was attempting to convert enthusiasm, skills, manufacturing capacity, and fleets of surplus aircraft into successful businesses. The former warplane manufacturers rushed to fulfill an expected demand by returning pilots for personal and sports planes. There was an expectation that the airplane, like the automobile, would be at every American home, or at least owned by the family. What was missing was a marketing organization.

While waiting for the CAB route decisions, Southern Airways became the Georgia distributor for Republic Aircraft's "Seabee" amphibious aircraft in January of 1947. This arrangement was short-lived as production of the plane

REPUBLIC AIRLINES.

WHO, WHAT AND WHERE.

REPUBLIC
AIRLINES
We're building your kind of airline.

Usually when companies merge, one of the names or brands survives. The Southern and North Central merger created a new airline brand: Republic Airlines.

was discontinued in October of that same year. Prior to the Seabee, Southern had also marketed Piper aircraft and subsequently became Beechcraft's largest distributor.

Headquartered in Atlanta, Southern's hangars were adjacent to Delta's. Their flight attendant school occupied an old World War II Quonset hut across the street from the hangars, and corporate offices were in a nearby office park.

Southern initiated scheduled airline operations in 1949 with a single Douglas DC-3 and 39 employees. At one time or another, Southern would operate 29 DC-3s as a truly regional carrier, with routes from Louisiana to the Atlantic and Tennessee to North Florida. The 1949 route map shows twenty cities. Routes radiated from Atlanta with two distinct routes out of Columbus, Georgia. This was the first airline service to many of the cities they served.

In 1961, the first Martin 404s were received from Eastern Air Lines. The Martin airliner presented an immediate problem to the maintenance department: it wouldn't fit into the hangar because the tail was too high. Southern's ingenuity won the day. By building a jack arrangement onto the towbar, the nose could be raised enough for the tail to clear the hangar door. Once inside the hangar, the nose wheel would be lowered to the floor and work could proceed.

Eventually, 26 Martins served the south with the last DC-3 being retired on July 31, 1967. That same year, Southern began the move into the pure jet

Southern's start-up route map shows twenty cities.

M. Steiner Archives

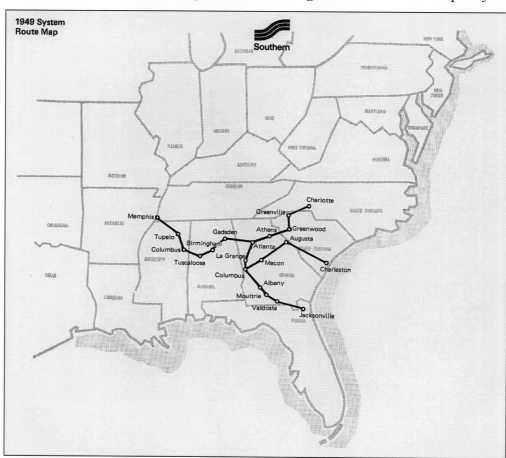

world with early DC-9 Model 10s. These were the shorter, 65-75 passenger models. Later DC-9s would be the 85-95 passenger model 30s. With the arrival of these jets, Southern expanded its routes to include New York and Chicago, as well as Columbia and Charleston, SC.

Southern weathered a number of challenges in the seventies. Fuel shortages, which also produced escalating fuel costs, occurred in 1972. In a regulated industry, government (CAB) approval was required for any fare adjustments to compensate for this additional cost. Gasoline shortages did bring additional passengers, however, who ordinarily would have driven. Southern had paid $2 million ransom to Cuba after a flight was hijacked to Havana. This money eventually was returned in 1974.

Above: Southern celebrated its 15th anniversary with these green and yellow decals that still depicted the original "bird in flight" logo.

Southern celebrated its twenty-fifth anniversary in 1974 while in the throes of building new hangars and service buildings and installing a new reservation system. An image update was in process with new colors (Southern Airways Blue), new logo (the FlightMark), and even airborne "wine tastings" for off-mealtime flights.

Operating twenty-seven jets and its last seven piston aircraft, Southern was now carrying 95% of its passengers on jets. Frank Hulse, III, moved up to Chairman of the Board and CEO. Long-time Executive Vice President, Graydon Hall, became President.

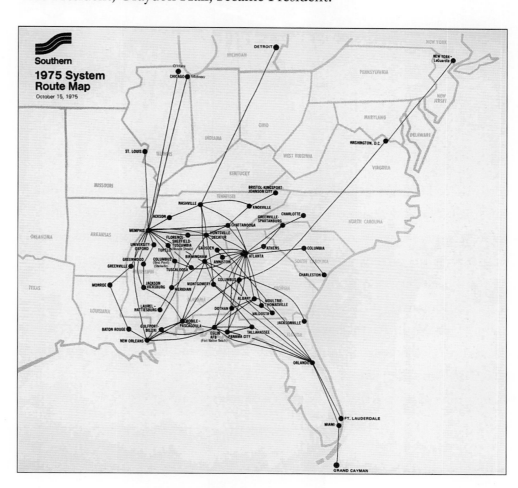

Right: By 1975, Southern served 50 cities in 2 countries.

The end of the 1970s was a time of mergers and consolidation in the airline industry. Deregulation was having its effect. Southern and Minneapolis/St. Paul-based North Central merged on June 30, 1979 and became Republic Airlines. It seemed like a marriage made in heaven. The two airlines' routes had eleven points in common with no duplication of routes. At that time, Southern served 50 cities in 17 states plus the Cayman Islands. Republic Airlines' new transitional logo featured a "Southern Airways Blue" goose flying wing-to-wing with a "North Central Aqua" goose. The "Southern Aristocrat" had flown north.

M. Steiner Archives

WORLD AIRWAYS

In many ways, World Airways was like the other 2,000-plus airlines formed in the late forties and early fifties, each trying to take advantage of a burgeoning economy and wide interest in air travel. Most of these new airlines never got off the ground. Many of those that did fly, did not last very long.

World Airways' operations began in 1948 with three retired Pan Am Boeing 314 Clippers (Flying Boats). Service was from New York to San Juan,

World Airways Captain's wings with logo.

M. Steiner Archives

Puerto Rico. This formerly glamorous fleet was now only one step from the scrap heap. World began moving through a succession of readily available aircraft. The seaplanes were replaced with two leased war surplus Curtiss C-46 Commandos. In convertible form, they could carry cargo or 50 passengers. The Caribbean service continued from New Jersey's Teterboro Airport, World's headquarters at the time.

By 1950, World Airways was a non-operating airline with $250,000 in debt and two leased airplanes. Then came 27-year-old Ed Daly. Daly was not unlike Pan Am's Juan Trippe or Delta's C.E. Woolman: a strong "father" that ran an airline as an extension of his own character and style.

Left: After World War II, World Airways purchased Pan Am's giant Boeing B-314 Flying Boats. World was the last airline to operate these legendary aircraft.

World Airways

He also possessed some of the unconventional traits of Howard Hughes. Daly bought World Airways for $50,000.

In 1951, under Daly's leadership, World Airways bid, won and operated its first U.S. government supplemental cargo airlift contract. This mission supported the U.S. involvement in the Korean

Below: The Curtiss C-46 was designed primarily as a WWII military cargo aircraft. World utilized them for both cargo and passenger purposes during their early years.

World Airways

This World Airways plane was the last flight out of Da Nang, Vietnam, at the end of the war. A grenade was thrown onto the taxiing airliner just before takeoff causing serious wing damage.

World Airways

conflict. Government, and specifically military airlift, contracts have continued to be a major element throughout World's corporate life. A Civil Aeronautics Board (CAB) decision in 1952 forbidding non-scheduled passenger service (civilian charters), made military and industrial charters the only game in town. World was already there.

By 1954, Daly's tight management style had brought profits sufficient enough to buy two Douglas DC-4s. These four-engine transports provided true intercontinental range. But recession and hard times forced return of the leased planes and sale of the DC-4s. World became an airline only on paper. That paper was its operating certificate.

World then bid and won a supply contract for the Distant Early Warning Line (DEWLine). With no airplanes, Daly leased three C-46s *and* crews from another airline, performed the contract and took his profits back to the used aircraft market. Daly found a derelict Royal Air Force Douglas C-54 Skymaster (military version of the DC-4) in a remote, unheated hangar in England. The plane had burned and only its engines were serviceable. In typical Daly style, the plane was repaired to "ferry-able" condition. He used a rented limousine that doubled as his hotel room at night and parts supply vehicle during the day. Ninety-three days later, the plane was successfully ferried to Teterboro Airport.

Almost simultaneously, the Military Air Transport Service (MATS) made four-engine aircraft a requirement for all future contracts. Daly added

World Airways operated a number of different commercial airliners. This post card illustrates World's "stretched" DC-8 with their "Swoosh" logo.

M. Steiner Archives

a second DC-4, was awarded one MATS contract and bid on a 4,000-mile daily Pacific rim contract, winning the second contract as well. The Pacific trip may have been the longest newspaper route in history. The cargo was the Pacific Edition of the military newspaper, *Stars and Stripes*, to Japan, Okinawa, Manila, and Taiwan. Corporate headquarters were moved to Oakland, California in 1956. Additional government contracts began to be received in the area of humanitarian missions. The first of these was to transport Hungarian revolution refugees from Europe to the United States in 1956.

By 1957, World had become America's largest charter airline, operating fifteen aircraft, including eight Douglas DC-6A/B aircraft, as well as four Lockheed Super Constellations and three Lockheed Starliners. The CAB even began allowing some limited public charter flights under a domestic supplemental air carrier arrangement. In 1962, World became the first jet charter operator with the purchase of new Boeing 707-320Cs. Shorter range Boeing 727s joined the fleet in 1966.

It was a famous flight by one of these 727s in 1975 that revealed Daly's and World Airways' soul. Known as the "Flight from Hell," it was an evacuation flight from Da Nang AFB to Saigon as Vietnam was falling to the Communists. That flight gained a spellbound audience for a CBS television special. It was later featured in *American Heritage* magazine.

World built its own maintenance facility in Oakland and began performing outside work as well. The huge facility had been built to accommodate Boeing 747s. The first Boeing 747 joined the fleet in 1973. Again, World was the first charter operator of a new model jet aircraft. World's 747 featured the front-loading doors, which essentially was Boeing's design for the military wide-body transport competition. The Lockheed, Marietta, Georgia-built, C-5A Galaxy had won that contract.

In 1974, World became a major air carrier in the Muslim pilgrimage, Hajj. Its performance was so well regarded that it later took on the management of the airlift for this intense 70-day annual event.

On April 11, 1979, World earned the wrath of the largest U.S. scheduled air carriers when it gained approval for its $99.99 New York-to-Los Angeles scheduled service. Like the "no frills" carriers that would come many years later, no long advance purchase was required and tickets were available at any

The World Airways logo is familiar to many of today's U.S. military personnel who have flown to or from their overseas assignments by World Airways charter.

M. Steiner Archives

Ticketron outlet. Unfortunately, 1979 was not the best of years for World. An American Airlines DC-10 had crashed in Chicago and all DC-10s, World's mainstay, were grounded. Almost immediately, World experienced a strike and lost months of revenue. The 1980s saw World moving more and more into scheduled service.

World Airways aircraft generally are the backdrop for news coverage of American troop movements. Desert Shield, Desert Storm, and Iraqi Freedom have all utilized World under their MATS contracts. Today, World is the largest commercial carrier of U.S. military personnel.

In May of 2001, World moved its corporate headquarters to Peachtree City. By 2007, they operated sixteen McDonnell Douglas MD-11s and Douglas DC-10s in passenger service for both civilian charter and the Air Mobility Command. Increasing air cargo requirements caused the addition of MD-11F freighter aircraft.

World Holdings, Inc. (World Airways' parent) acquired North American in 2006, bringing Boeing 767s and 757s into the combined fleet. These smaller aircraft allow access to a significant market that did not require the larger capacity of the MD-11 and DC-10 aircraft.

The story of World Airways is probably best told by a simple display in the lobby of their executive offices – a colorful quilt that was hung on the wall. Stitched on the border was the message, "With gratitude and affection for World Airways maverick flight April 2, 1975, 'Operation Babylift', a true friend of the children of Vietnam." The quilt was hand-made with pieces of clothing worn by the Vietnamese orphans when they came to the United States. World Airways and its president, Ed Daly, launched this humanitarian effort with a daring, unauthorized flight from Saigon on the night of April 2, 1975, carrying 57 orphans to waiting families in the United States.

World Airways corporate offices and a reminder of the airline's many humanitarian efforts...the "babylift" quilt.

World Airways

ATLANTIC SOUTHEAST AIRLINES (ASA)

It was an unlikely scene, a deHavilland Twin Otter aircraft departing from Atlanta's Hartsfield Airport on June 27, 1979. The Otter, a bush plane more at home in Canada or the Caribbean islands, was probably the only Otter in town and among only a few in the Southeast region. This was Atlantic Southeast's first flight, departing for Columbus, Georgia. Another post-deregulation airline was looking for its niche and hoping for survival. ASA would go on to accomplish far more than just survival.

The industry was unsettled to say the least, and growth was slow. Established carriers, like Southern Airways, were moving up the industry ladder. Larger aircraft, usually jet, moved them into larger markets and left smaller communities available for newer, smaller, regional carriers like ASA. An entire generation of turbo-prop airliners was developed and put into service by these carriers.

ASA utilized both the Embraer Bandeirante "Bandit" and the deHavilland Dash 7 turboprops. In April 1983, ASA acquired Southeastern Airlines, a commuter airline that served such cities as Memphis, Ft. Walton Beach, Athens (GA), and of course, Atlanta.

In 1984, the major carriers embarked on building networks of regional partners. These were essential to feed their hubs and their long haul routes. ASA became one of the first "Delta Connection" partners in May of 1984, feeding Delta's Atlanta hub. Later that year, ASA began operations to feed Delta's Memphis hub.

Many of these feeder routes were essentially free of competition and highly profitable. Delta decided to participate in this profitability by purchasing 20% of the ASA voting stock in May of 1986. ASA took on additional Delta hubs and adjusted

ASA'S NEW DASH 7

The Dash 7. It's ASA's newest aircraft. And it'll fly you non-stop to Atlanta in quiet, air-conditioned comfort. The Dash 7 has wide-body seating for 48 passengers. And many other features.

And like all other ASA flights, the Dash 7 flies conveniently to gate B-1 of Hartsfield Airport. Next time you want to get to Atlanta fast—dash to Atlanta on ASA's new Dash 7.

Spacious wide-body seating, and plenty of legroom and stand-up headroom.

Four turbo-prop engines speed you to Atlanta quickly and quietly.

Overhead and under-seat storage for carry-on luggage.

Lavatory for freshening up before arrival.

Courteous flight attendants offer you a choice of beverages.

ASA 535 Central Ave., Hapeville, Ga. 30354 1-404-761-2234

ASA
Atlantic Southeast Airlines

TIMETABLE
Effective May 15, 1983

NEW DASH 7 SERVICE
ATLANTA — HUNTSVILLE
ATLANTA — AUGUSTA
ATLANTA — ALBANY
ATLANTA — ASHEVILLE

ATLANTA'S LARGEST REGIONAL AIRLINE.

Above: ASA's May 15, 1983 schedule was their first after the merger with Southeastern. It boasts new cities and a larger fleet, including the deHavilland Dash 7.

Left: ASA's 1997 route map shows two hubs and flights to New York, Detroit and Cleveland among the cities served.

M. Steiner Archives

Right: Perhaps the most widely used commuter aircraft was the Brazilian built Embraer Bandeirante. Here, ASA's "Bandit" is readying for flight at the Atlanta Airport.

Atlantic Southeast Airlines

service to dovetail with Delta's needs. Dallas/Ft. Worth was next, followed closely by termination of the Memphis operation.

As its fleet continued to grow and modernize, the airline garnered recognition in the industry. *Air Transport World* named ASA the "Regional Airline of the Year" for 1986. The *Atlanta Journal-Constitution* named ASA the sixth best-performing, publicly-held Georgia company. This success allowed the airline to move into jet service for the first time in late 1995. Within a year, ASA placed the largest single airline order received by Bombardier Aerospace for their Canadair Regional Jet (CRJ).

ASA's management team won prestigious global recognition in 1998 when *Aviation Week & Space Technology* identified ASA as "one of the industry's best managed companies." Growth continued and Delta Air Lines acquired all ASA stock, making ASA a wholly-owned subsidiary. As anniversaries and other special events afforded the opportunity, ASA celebrated with special livery designs. International service took ASA to Canada and Mexico. When ASA entered the jet age, their route map eclipsed that of Delta's, even though Delta had entered the jet age in the early 1960s.

Below: ASA's first aircraft was a Canadian built deHavilland Twin Otter. Here, the Twin Otter sits on a ramp at Atlanta's airport terminal.

Atlantic Southeast Airlines

Rampant growth came to ASA in every measurable form. Passenger boardings, fleet size and number of destinations all would continue to increase. At the same time, the parent corporation, Delta Air Lines, Inc., found itself in increasing financial distress. In order to both generate cash and to protect the assets of ASA, Delta sold ASA to another Delta Connection carrier, SkyWest, Inc., in 2005.

ASA continued to excel and operated as a separate entity and as a Delta Connection partner. From a single lumbering Twin Otter to one of the youngest all-jet airline fleets in the world, ASA moved far beyond survival.

Below: The "ATL" airport newspaper cover for December 15, 1991, showed this impressive line of ASA aircraft. The headline read, "Leaps and Bounds…ASA races to the forefront of commuter airlines."

M. Steiner Archives

AIR ATLANTA

Federal deregulation of scheduled commercial airlines spawned a number of new airlines. Many of these new carriers shared some common attributes. They utilized older jet aircraft that had been retired from service at the larger and more established airlines. These aircraft generally cost less to lease, had readily available parts, but had higher operating and maintenance costs.

Employees of these start-ups received lower salaries than the industry average and frequently had few, if any, benefits. Personnel with considerable

Boarding Pass

Name

Seat No.

Origin   Flight   Date

Origin   Flight   Date

Destination

Seat No.
Non Smoking

Seat No.
Smoking

AIR ATLANTA.

Boarding passes were still in use during Air Atlanta's operation. There were also smoking sections and non-smoking sections.

Right: Air Atlanta "hatched" a new concept in air travel. It courted the "overlooked and underserved" business traveler.

M. Steiner Archives

experience were widely available. Many were retired from major carriers and seeking a few more years in the industry. Opportunities in senior management that had eluded them at larger carriers became available at these new carriers. Roden Brandt, for example, had been Senior Vice President of Airline Planning at Pan Am. With twenty-one years of experience, he served as Air Atlanta's President and CEO. The former Chief of the FAA Regional Flight Standards Division, with thirty six years experience, was hired as Vice President of Operations. Most of Air Atlanta's senior operating management team had that same level of experience.

While Air Atlanta fit much of this model, it also had some significant differences. Creative financing at Air Atlanta included numerous barter deals. Everything from office furniture to advertising was frequently paid for with airline tickets. As much as possible, cash was directed to acquiring terminal facilities and expansion.

Air Atlanta received its operating certificate in July of 1982 and was the first airline formed after the Airline Deregulation Act of 1978. Founded by Michael Hollis and a group of investors, the basic idea was to create a minority-owned airline. Hollis and the directors set up offices in downtown Atlanta to organize the airline. Their intent was to provide the business traveler with upscale service at fares that were equivalent to the major airlines. That strategy avoided the risk of a fare war with the more established and financially stable carriers but challenged them to meet Air Atlanta's higher level of customer service. As operations became more imminent, operational offices were set up in part of the vacant 1961 William B. Hartsfield International Airport. The old Eastern Airlines concourse became home to the staff.

Air Atlanta actually began operations on February 1, 1984, at a time when air traffic controllers were on strike. As a result, there were fewer takeoff and landing "slots" available at major airports. In Atlanta, the only available gates were

at the end of midfield Concourse D, then the most distant concourse from the main terminal. Initial service was to three cities: Atlanta, Memphis and New York (JFK).

Air Atlanta turned each obstacle into an opportunity to excel. The leased Boeing 727 aircraft were refurbished into a low-density, wider, leather seat configuration. Fine china with first-class caliber food and superior cabin service were offered at competitor's coach fares. This customer-focused strategy varied significantly from the typical start-up model of high-density seating with minimal cabin amenities and typical coach class airline food.

In addition, Air Atlanta circumvented their inconvenient gate location by introducing a service named "GateExpress." Ticketed passengers entered an Air Atlanta waiting area immediately inside the North Terminal lobby. Equipped with its own x-ray unit and security, passengers were transported on converted rental car buses directly to the ramp below the gate area. An escalator took passengers to a comfortable waiting lounge offering complimentary beverage service. Carry-on items were taken on board by cabin staff much like the valet service at a five star hotel.

Air Atlanta also established its "Founders Club," a business frequent flyer service. Typical offerings of the Founders Club were noted in the August 30, 1984 newsletter: A free upgrade at the Ritz-Carlton Atlanta or Buckhead hotels, an Avis rental upgrade, free flight "guest" passes, advanced seat

Navigating Atlanta's Hartsfield International Airport involves long walks, a train ride , then more long walks. Air Atlanta provided "limousine" service – almost curbside to departure gate – with converted minibusses.

M. Steiner Archives

Air Atlanta flew to such cities as Philadelphia, New York and Detroit, where Atlantan Vic Hewes encountered more than the occasional snowstorm.

Collection of Vic Hewes

Vic Hewes

Vic Hewes in his BT 13-A Vultee Vindicator at Maxwell Auxiliary Field, Alabama, c.1942.

Collection of Vic Hewes

As an RAF cadet during WWII, Basil Victor "Vic" Hewes was sent to Carlstom Field in Arcadia, Florida for air combat training. He was given command of a communications squadron which was a mixed bag of aircraft: three J-3 Cubs, four Harvards (AT-6s), five Expeditors and six Dakotas (C-47s). Two Spitfires were used for photo-recon. The squadron also had two flying boats for air-sea rescue. Thinking ahead, Hewes knew that he wanted a career in aviation after the war and looked for an experience other than that of fighter pilot. He began flying the Expeditor figuring that the training in transport aircraft would serve him well in the future. The RAF Expeditor was at least twenty mph faster than the Dakotas, their seats were softer and, "they were very much in demand by the VIPs I flew."

After WWII, Hewes relocated to the U.S. and flew for Delta Air Lines. When he reached mandatory retirement age in 1982, he wondered what he could do next. He didn't have to wait long. He was hired that same year as a consultant at the start-up of Air Atlanta, the first African American-owned airline in the country. Air Atlanta commenced service with five Boeing 727s on February 1, 1984 and catered to business travel. Hewes' first task as an airline executive was to establish an office in the "old green terminal" at Hartsfield. He then was made Director of Flight Operations, Safety & Security – a "fantastic experience," says Hewes.

Hewes is well respected in the airline community for his commitment to issues involving security. He has served as Chairman of the Fire & Rescue Committee for the Air Line Pilots Association (ALPA) and as International Vice President of the ALPA. At the annual safety forum in August, 1998, Captain J. Randolph Babbitt, then president of the Airline Pilots Association, presented Hewes – already a 1961 ALPA Air Safety Award recipient – with a special award for 50 years of service to improve aviation safety.

Vic Hewes flew out of Cochran Field in Macon in 1942.

Collection of Vic Hewes

selection, and more. This same newsletter stated, "Expect the Unexpected on Air Atlanta ... prize winning wines, freshly squeezed orange juice, crabmeat and avocado salad, and ..."

In the April/May 1984 schedule (the first year of operation), Air Atlanta used the motto, "Born to Serve Business," and made this assurance: "To the hassled business flyer long overlooked and underserved, we dedicate Air Atlanta, with better business schedules and a lot more comfort."

In March, 1984, Air Atlanta affiliated with Pan American as a "Pan Am Express" carrier. Under this arrangement, Air Atlanta scheduled their New York (and future Miami) flights to connect with Pan Am international service. An Air Atlanta schedule dated December 1, 1986 shows an expanded service map which includes an intermediate stop at Philadelphia on some New York flights and Greenbrier-Lewisburg on others. A new Florida route included Atlanta to Orlando, Tampa and Ft. Myers. Atlanta to Detroit had recently been added and Atlanta to New Orleans service was scheduled to begin on February 1, 1987. Air Atlanta had created the "Liberty Pass II" with unlimited travel for five months. This program was designed to move cash flow forward and gain customer commitment for future travel.

The new program never materialized as Air Atlanta filed for bankruptcy on April 4, 1987. The company ceased operations and laid off all employees. One of the most ambitious and unusual post-deregulation airlines had suddenly become history. According to the Wall Street Journal, the situation had become "a classic struggle between a hard-charging entrepreneur and a professional manager," implying that corporate officers and the board of directors had become directly involved in the operations of the airline causing experienced and capable management to leave.

 # AIRTRAN AIRWAYS

ValuJet, the forerunner to AirTran Airways, may have been the most successful airline ever launched in the United States. It was profitable almost from its very first flight in 1993.

In many ways the ValuJet startup paralleled the earliest days of airline development. Strong, aviation experienced founders combined their individual

Below: ValuJet personnel carried peel-off, happy-go-lucky "Critter" decals to give to passengers.

Above: ValuJet operated only one type of aircraft, the Douglas DC-9-30 shown here on a postcard.

values and talents with their management experience from a number of different airlines. The earliest ValuJet operations also mirrored the first Eastern Air Transport air mail flights sixty five years earlier. ValuJet's first flight from Atlanta to Tampa, with stops in Jacksonville and Orlando, took place on October 26, 1993. This was the same route first flown as an air mail route by Eastern on December 1, 1928.

In most aspects, ValuJet was like other low-cost, "no frills" startups. These low-cost carriers utilized older jet aircraft retired from the major carriers. Usually, only one or two types were used, and generally they were leased, requiring minimal startup cash. Maintenance was outsourced to avoid the costly construction or acquisition of hangars and equipment. Operations were among a limited set of destinations with low frequency of service to each.

There was a difference at ValuJet, however. The airline's sole aircraft, an ex-Delta Air Lines Douglas DC-9, sported the company's logo, a happy-go-lucky dancing airplane, known simply as "Critter." This logo accurately captured the spirit of the new airline's mission. Flying, whether for business or pleasure, should be a relaxed and pleasant experience. ValuJet uniforms were neither military styled nor designer fashioned. Simple, straight-forward, ValuJet knit polo tops and casual slacks outfitted not only the cabin crews, but also the executive office personnel.

Below: This bumper sticker promises "Good Times Great Fares!" reflecting ValuJet's strategy of attracting vacationers on limited budgets.

M. Steiner Archives

One financial analyst identified ValuJet's primary competition as the interstate highway system. ValuJet was actively courting the traveler who ordinarily drives to and from his destination. With fares as much as 60% below the major carriers, ValuJet became an attractive alternative to that long drive.

ValuJet took on one of the nation's strongest airlines, Delta, at its home base in Atlanta. In June 1994, ValuJet made its initial public offering. Within one year their stock had appreciated 500%. During this time period, their fleet of DC-9s had grown from one to 28. Much of this early success can be attributed to the airline's savvy group of founders. Lewis Jordan, born in

Griffin, Georgia, had reached senior management at Southern Airways when it was bought out and became part of Republic Airlines on June 30, 1979. He became the President and Chief Operating Officer at ValuJet, after serving in the same capacity at Continental Airlines under Frank Lorenzo.

Jordan graduated from Georgia Tech as an aeronautical engineer. He was not the traditional student, but participated in Tech's co-op program. Jordan remembers the co-op counselors advising him on what it would take to get a job and keep it. "You're not…here to have fun and go to football games and fraternity parties. You are…in a co-op program that requires a real commitment to something!" That commitment to his co-op employer, Southern Airways, led to a 17-year career with them.

Jordan, remembering not having enough money to go to college, developed a discipline of frugality. ValuJet's executive offices were described as stark, with plain metal desks and space similar to the single-class environment on board their DC-9s. Even the office supplies were meted out only when required. This had also been a Rickenbacker discipline at then profitable Eastern Air Lines.

Another ValuJet executive from those days at Southern was Robert L. Priddy. Priddy had helped start Atlantic Southeast Airlines and became Chairman of ValuJet. Other experienced airline executives included Maurice "Maury" Gallagher, Jr., a founder of WestAir, a commuter airline, and Timothy P. Flynn. Flynn had worked with Gallagher at WestAir and also served in executive capacity at Mesa Airlines and Pacific Express.

On May 11, 1996, management savvy, business success, and operational efficiency were not enough. A ValuJet DC-9 crashed in the Florida Everglades and the airline nearly went down as well. The FAA grounded ValuJet for over three months. In September ValuJet was allowed to restart service on a restricted basis. Customer confidence had eroded, as did load factors and cash flow. Subtle changes started to take place. "Critter" was no longer on the front of the published schedules. The June 12, 1997 schedule did not list three cities previously served. In a variation of hub and spoke operations, ValuJet introduced "FlightLink," an express *bus* service from Macon, Dalton, and Chattanooga to Atlanta. These buses replaced previous inbound feeder flights.

On July 11, 1997, ValuJet announced the purchase of Orlando-based AirWays Corp., owner of AirTran Airways and the planned merger of the two

Above: ValuJet launched a massive media campaign following their lengthy grounding in 1996-97. Folders such as this contained various press releases designed to promote their return to the low fare market.

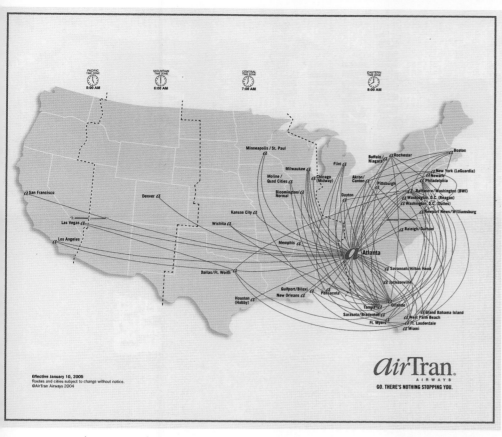

*air*Tran.
AIRWAYS
GO. THERE'S NOTHING STOPPING YOU.

Above: In advertising to the vacation market AirTran took on a more serious tone, "Go, there's nothing stopping you!" appeared on their system route map.

Left: Colorful decals were worn by Valujet's flight attendants.

M. Steiner Archives

carriers. This was accomplished on September 24, 1997. AirTran, though much smaller, was the surviving brand. This "reverse merger" would be the Phoenix bird for this highly capable but challenged airline.

The original AirTran was incorporated in 1994 and began operations with Orlando as a primary destination for flights from various cities in the Northeast. It was mainly a vacation-oriented carrier. In 1996, AirTran became a signatory airline at Orlando International Airport and on November 17, 1997, after the merger, the company selected Orlando as its headquarters site. The majority of the new (post merger) AirTran operations revolved around their hub in Atlanta. Forty three destinations were served from Atlanta including the west coast and the Bahamas.

On January 6, 1999, Joseph B. Leonard was elected Chairman, CEO, and President of AirTran Holdings, Inc. He brought experience from the Eastern failure, a two-year stint at Boeing Aircraft and the Northwest resurrection. Armed with the new, longer range Boeing 737s, Leonard aggressively expanded AirTran's reach with the West Coast, Mexico and Bahamas destinations.

With the acquisition of eighteen Eastern Airlines' gates at Atlanta's Hartsfield Airport, the stage was set for a duel with home town Delta. AirTran pursued the disgruntled Delta business traveler. With 60% lower fares, newer aircraft, and strong on-time performance, AirTran succeeded in luring that business traveler.

In 2007 AirTran continued to outpace the industry and, more importantly, its competition. Even with an announced revised delivery schedule for eight Boeing 737s, AirTran continued to increase its passenger capacity by 20% a year. Officials at AirTran described the delayed deliveries as strategic "fine-tuning." AirTran's financial reports resembled the Delta reports in the 1960s and 1970s. Gross margins routinely exceeded 25%. These consistent profits allowed new aircraft purchases, resulting in one of the youngest fleets in the industry.

With high fuel costs the obstacle for most carriers, AirTran's new high-efficiency aircraft further reduced the impact of fuel costs while also minimizing their maintenance costs. The airline operated 87 Boeing 717-200s. This was Boeing's new designation for the McDonnell Douglas MD-95, arising from the merger between Boeing and McDonnell Douglas. Even before the merger with ValuJet, AirTran was the launch customer for the MD-95. AirTran ordered 50 MD-95s with options on another 50 in October 1995.

The MD-95/717-200 was discontinued as a result of the Boeing merger with McDonnell Douglas. In fact, the Long Beach, California plant where the 717 was built was being closed after more than sixty years of aircraft production. AirTran had already ordered "New Generation" Boeing 737-700s to acquire greater range capability. Some of the undelivered, on-order 717s were to be replaced by additional 737s.

AirTran continued to press their competitive advantage with enhancements to their amenities. AirTran broke the single-class mold of low-fare carriers by offering a business class for a nominal fare increase. All seats on all flights featured XM satellite radio, a first in the industry. With over 100 channels of digital, commercial-free service, the old on-board audio service was replaced. Other services that belie the low cost airline image included online reservations, check-in and advanced seat selection. An award-winning frequent flyer program was also offered.

Industry accolades continued to be awarded to AirTran. Among these were the *Aviation Week & Space Technology* Laureates Award for Commercial Air Transport in 2004, awarded to Chairman and CEO, Joe Leonard. In 2006, *Entrepreneur Magazine* awarded AirTran Airways their Best Airline Value award. They had previously awarded five annual Best Low-Fare Airline awards to AirTran.

By 2007, AirTran had become the tenth largest airline in the United States. They operate with 7,800 "crew members" (employees) and over 120 aircraft, serving 50 destinations with over 700 flights each day.

Above: AirTran ticket jackets promoted the fact that they were the "Launch Customer for the Boeing 717." This new aircraft was flown only by AirTran.

Below: AirTran is moving toward a Boeing 737 fleet.

M. Steiner Archives

UNITED PARCEL SERVICE (UPS)

Mention UPS to most people and they might visualize a global fleet of brown delivery trucks. To people at Boeing and Airbus, however, UPS is regarded as the ninth largest airline in the world with 336 aircraft in operation or on order, more on options, and 384 under various charter arrangements.

Corporate headquarters for UPS was moved to Atlanta from Greenwich, Connecticut in 1991. UPS Airlines, the company's own designation, operates out of Worldport in Louisville, Kentucky. Their fleet includes Boeing 727, 747, 757 and 767s. Douglas aircraft, now part of Boeing, include DC-8 and MD-11 types. Airbus 300-600s, with A380-800Fs on order round out this essentially all-cargo airline.

UPS Airlines is a relatively new business, having only been formed in 1988, but the parent company operated air express service as early as 1929.

In 1907, the parent corporation American Messenger Company was established in Seattle, Washington by nineteen-year-old Jim Casey. American Messenger was a local message and package courier. By 1913, the company had changed its name to Merchants Parcel Delivery to reflect its primary business of delivering to retailers. With a fleet of four automobiles and five motorcycles, it was time for a company color scheme. Casey preferred yellow, but his partners reminded him that Pullman cars on trains were painted a drab brown so they wouldn't readily show dirt and require frequent washing. Brown it was, and brown it still is today.

Top Image: Like the U.S. mail, packages on United Air Express were bagged. Each bag was stenciled with the destination. Service was only in the West.

UPS Airlines

Bottom: An early UPS truck delivers parcels to a Maddux Airlines Ford Tri-Motor. All air parcels traveled on regularly scheduled airlines.

UPS Airlines

Growth continued with purchase of an Oakland, California delivery company in 1919. A company name conflict caused Casey to adopt United Parcel Service in 1922. A Los Angeles delivery company was acquired in 1924.

In the years following the first air mail contracts in 1926 and growth of their airline operators, businesses sought to involve air travel in some form. UPS followed the pattern of the postal service and utilized space on passenger flights to deliver parcels. This service, known as United Air Express and only available on the West Coast, began on February 15, 1929. The stock market crash of 1929 would eventually put an end to this venture, although United Air Express did manage to operate successfully for over two years before the Great Depression finally took its toll.

United Parcel Service–Air was reinstituted more than twenty years later on January 22, 1953. This wholly-owned subsidiary of UPS of America began operations with only eastbound and northbound service from California to points including Seattle and New York. Within three months, the return service was established. To increase transcontinental volume, a lower rate, offering four- to five-day delivery rather than the standard two days, was later established.

This transcontinental airborne service continued with few changes for eleven years. On November 6, 1967, UPS-Air converted all service to two-day delivery under a brand name of "Blue Label." Since UPS owned no aircraft of its own, all parcels were transported by contract carriers. Blue Label service was expanded in a very slow and deliberate fashion. One reason for this was federal legal restrictions placed on ground transportation of air packages. UPS was not licensed as a Common Carrier and could not legally transport airborne freight. Since UPS handled both pickup and delivery of its Blue Label parcels with its familiar brown fleet of trucks, expansion was piecemeal into some states and commercial areas of larger cities. On July 1, 1980, all Common Carrier restrictions were lifted, and by mid-August, UPS Blue Label went national.

UPS had earlier established an operations center in Louisville, Kentucky. Louisville was the western-most point in the Eastern Time Zone, allowing later pickup in the east. Louisville also was the closest point to the West Coast of any city in the Eastern Time Zone. Now, with full national service, this center was expanded. A fleet of twenty Boeing 727-100s was purchased. All flight operations and maintenance was outsourced since UPS was not an FAA-certified air carrier. Having their own air fleet did eliminate the time lost in transferring parcels to and from the other UPS contract air carriers.

UPS retraced the steps of their United Air Express past when they introduced "Next Day Air" on the West Coast. During 1982, they rapidly expanded across the country. This expansion allowed lower than industry average rates, but it also required more capacity and aircraft. Much larger Douglas DC-8s were purchased from Flying Tiger Airlines, and additional 727s were acquired by year's end.

UPS founder, Jim Casey, retired from the Board of Directors in 1983 at the age of 95. He died a month later.

A fleet of Orion Airlines Boeing 727 air freighters on the ramp. Orion served as the sub-contractor with the airline operating certificate. Orion was UPS Airlines.

UPS Airlines

UPS Airlines purchased the aircraft of Flying Tigers cargo airline.

M. Steiner Archives

Destinations continued to be added, and by August of 1984, three Boeing 747s, six stretched DC-8s, and four more 727s were added. Within months, more 747s and DC-8s were added. Within three years, UPS had grown from no company-owned aircraft to a fleet of sixty-two air freighters. The year 1985 brought ten more aircraft and the ability to deliver to every address in the continental U.S., Hawaii and Puerto Rico.

Senders' packaging options were greatly expanded. Many of these changes were in direct response to its primary competitor, Federal Express. Next Day

Air Letters and Air Packs (bubble-pack pouches) were added, with UPS providing all the shipping supplies for these services. The resulting increase in volume required that additional aircraft be ordered. The Louisville operations center added U.S. Customs Clearance to its capabilities.

UPS Airlines was certified by the FAA in 1988. Operation of the first UPS-owned aircraft by a UPS crew followed immediately. This began a period of rapid growth.

Hub-and-spoke operations reached their highest level of development with UPS. All cargo and express carriers operated in a similar fashion, but UPS refined it to near perfection. Beginning in 1989, a network of regional hubs was constructed including Philadelphia, PA; Dallas, TX; Ontario, CA; Rockford, IL; Columbia, SC; and Hartford, CT.

In Georgia, UPS opened an air cargo sort facility at the Southwest Georgia Regional Airport in Albany. Operations began in August 2006. The airport constructed a $1.7 million site including a 5,270-square-foot building. To complete the project, the community blended budgets from Special-Purpose, Local-Option Sales Tax (SPLOST), FAA, Georgia Department of Transportation, and the airport. Nearly ninety employees operated the facility and UPS became the largest tenant at the airport. Albany's cargo facility became the second largest in Georgia, right behind Atlanta.

The 1990s saw UPS Airlines turn its attention to a global capability. Until then, UPS had served Asia through contract carriers. The first UPS-owned and operated aircraft serving Asia began operations utilizing their regional hub in Anchorage, Alaska in January 1990. Direct U.S. to Japan service followed in 1991. Service offered to Europe had been limited to two flights a week in 1991. By 1994, UPS was offering next day (before 8 AM) service between many major U.S. and European cities.

In 1998, UPS announced plans for a 1.1 billion dollar mega hub in Louisville to support expected worldwide growth. This center, named "Worldport," was designed to handle over 300,000 parcels per hour when completed. The MD-11 was designated the company standard, long-range, wide body aircraft. A firm order was placed in November of 2000 for thirteen aircraft, with options for twenty-two additional. The first MD-11s were scheduled to join the fleet in 2002, coinciding with the Worldport opening.

Top: UPS Airlines Boeing 767 in new company livery.

Bottom: An artist's impression of the new "Super Jumbo" A380 in UPS markings. UPS became the only customer for the freighter version of this new aircraft with ten on order.

UPS Airlines

On March 25, 2003, UPS made its first change to the airline's logo. Utilizing a new paint technology, a three-dimensional form of the familiar "Shield" logo was unveiled on a new Boeing 767-300ER.

Many of the new technology aircraft operated with a two-man crew versus three on most of the older models. In 2003, UPS was confronted with the possibility of having to furlough 100 pilots. This was avoided by voluntary early retirements.

China became the major newest route and volume expansion for UPS. Agreements with the Chinese government have increased the allowable frequency of flights. By 2005, UPS was operating 21 flights each week to China, including non-stop service directly from the U.S. The sharp increase in Asian business was supported by an intra-Asia hub at the historic Clark AFB site in the Philippines.

With the first flight of "Super Jumbo," the double-decked Airbus A380, and UPS's order for ten of these aircraft, the very latest of heavy lift technology would soon be joining the fleet. A single A380 can carry the equivalent of eight times the load of the original Boeing 727s. Announcements of delays in the Airbus delivery schedule were being addressed by UPS, which increased orders for MD-11s and expected deliveries of Boeing 747-400s.

In 2006, UPS Airlines announced planned expansion of their Worldport. At a cost of 1 billion dollars, the capacity would be increased to nearly 500,000 packages per hour.

UPS Airlines may very well be the fastest growing airline in the world, even if it also may still be the least known.

Right: UPS Airlines'
"Worldport" sorting
complex in Louisville,
Georgia will double
in size.

UPS Airlines

UPS Louisville Expansion

AGRICULTURAL AVIATION IN GEORGIA

If the tiny boll weevil can be credited with creating Delta Air Lines, it can also be said that it was in large measure responsible for launching the agricultural aviation industry in Georgia.

In 1921, following successful aerial applications of lead arsenate to eliminate sphinx moth larvae in Ohio, Delta's founder, C.E. Woolman, and Dr. Bert Coad began in earnest to experiment with the more powerful calcium arsenate on the devastating boll weevil presence in Georgia. Their efforts – and their successes – convinced the U.S. Government to endorse the use of aerial application in the Southern states, where it was said that "Cotton is King." In 1922, modified Curtiss JN-6 "Super Jenny" aircraft were used to dust cotton fields near Tallulah, Louisiana to control boll weevils. In 1923, Huff-Daland Dusters, Inc. – the forerunner of Delta Air Lines and the first

Delta Air Transport Heritage Museum

commercial agricultural flying company in existence – performed the first commercial dusting of crops with their own specially-built aircraft.

The first agricultural aircraft were called "dusters" because they worked with dry chemicals, mostly insecticides. Dust had been applied by hand since 1918 and farmers were reluctant to change to spray. Early aircraft were lightweight and weak-framed, having been modified for use as crop-dusters, and flying such aircraft often proved hazardous to the pilots. Modern aerial applicators dispense mostly liquid products to control pests and diseases and to provide nutrients to the plants and soil.

It wasn't until after World War II that aerial pest control was widely accepted by the farming community. The availability of sturdy, war-surplus aircraft launched an era of rapid growth and experimentation in the crop-dusting industry. Three of the most often-used aircraft for crop dusting were the Boeing PT-17 Stearman, the Navy's N2S and the Piper J-3 Cub. The abundance of inexpensive, open-cockpit Stearmans gave many veterans an opportunity to get into the business. Other pilots got their start in the agricultural-aviation industry (ag-aviation) in war-surplus Cubs. The L-4 military version of the Piper J-3 was nicknamed "Grasshopper" for its ability to get in and out of tight spots, and it was easy to maintain. The aircraft was in plentiful supply. By 1947, 14,125 Piper Cubs had been built.

By the 1950s, the ag-aviation industry began to develop airplanes made especially for aerial application. Later, larger airplanes like the Ayres Turbo-Thrush (manufactured in Georgia) and Grumman Ag-Cat carried as much as 800 gallons of chemicals, were powered by turboprop engines and cost a million dollars or more. Advanced GPS navigational technology helped pilots maintain pinpoint accuracy.

Agricultural aviation became a $1.9 billion industry in the United States. In 2006, in the state of Georgia, $100 million of that total was represented by twenty large-scale aerial application operators.

More than 2,200 professional ag pilots with thousands of hours of experience operated in the United States. Training continued throughout a pilot's career. They must meet federal and state requirements both for flying skills and for the safe handling of chemicals. Ag pilots are committed to the control of chemical drift through research, technology and innovation. They take responsibility for making sound decisions in the field, for the benefit of the crop being treated, and for the protection of everything surrounding the field. Aerial applicators must hold an FAA Part 137 certificate to operate an aerial application business. Pilots must have a commercial pilot's license as well as a letter of competency to work as an ag pilot.

Facing Page: A Huff-Daland duster working in 1924. This original Huff-Daland had a 400 HP Liberty WWI engine.

Facing Page: Jackie Cochran and Col. Chuck Yeager share a light moment after a flight at Edwards Air Force Base in 1962. Yeager helped Cochran transition to jet-powered aircraft; the two pilots enjoyed a lifelong friendship.

Below:
Jacqueline "Jackie" Cochran had a message for people everywhere: "Flex your mental muscles and get cracking under your own power. Derive emotional satisfaction from a good try and then another and another and still another if the first ones fail."

Georgia Aviation Hall Of Fame

Women in Georgia Aviation

From the early days, men weren't alone in learning to fly. Inspired by the likes of Amelia Earhart, Mabel Cody and Mathilde Moisant, several women in Georgia took to the skies, leaving their own marks upon the industry. The contributions to aviation made by six of these pioneers have been recognized by the Georgia Aviation Hall of Fame.

JACQUELINE COCHRAN

Perhaps one of the most recognized names in women's aviation is Jacqueline "Jackie" Cochran. Much has been written about this dynamic competitor. The word "can't" simply was not in her vocabulary. Born into poverty, she was eight years old when she moved with her foster family to Columbus, Georgia.

Cochran earned her pilot's license in 1932. By 1935 she had entered her first Bendix Air Race (an air race coast-to-coast across America) and owned a multimillion dollar cosmetics manufacturing company. Three years later, she won the Bendix and was honored with the William E. Mitchell Memorial Award for having made the greatest contribution to aviation in 1938. It's no wonder that Amelia Earhart was one of her best friends.

In 1939, as World War II neared, Eleanor Roosevelt suggested that Cochran approach General Hap Arnold with plans for using women pilots. Arnold rejected the idea. Undaunted, Cochran continued to compete, winning air races, establishing altitude and speed records. Arnold eventually came around to her way of thinking and, at his request, Cochran organized a group of twenty-five women pilots to fly for Great Britain. In her new capacity, Cochran became the first woman to pilot a bomber across the North Atlantic (June, 1941).

A severe shortage of male pilots prompted Arnold to once again turn to Cochran. At his behest she returned to the United States and began training women pilots, eventually establishing the Women Airforce Service Pilots (WASP) program at 120 airbases across the U.S. For her efforts during the war Cochran received the Distinguished Service Medal.

After the war, Cochran returned to air racing and established new transcontinental and international records. In 1953, in an F-86 Sabre, Cochran became the first aviatrix to break the sound barrier, just ahead of France's Jacqueline Ariol. For this achievement Cochran received the Collier Trophy of 1953. By 1959 the two women's informal competition was being conducted at speeds above Mach 2. Ariol set her last record in June, 1963, when she flew a Dassault Mirage III R at 1,274 mph. Cochran topped this in 1964, emerging as the overall winner. She still holds more international speed, distance and altitude records than any other pilot, male or female.

Cochran died in 1980. She was inducted into the Georgia Aviation Hall of Fame in 1992.

HAZEL JANE RAINES

Hazel Jane Raines was born in Waynesboro, Georgia in 1916 and grew up in Macon. Shortly after graduating from Wesleyan in 1936, Raines accepted a dare to take flying lessons at Herbert Smart Airport. Although born with asthma and a heart condition, Raines was determined not to let her medical condition or any discrimination against female aviators prevent her from becoming an accomplished pilot. She was one of the first woman in Georgia to earn her pilot's license and began her career as a stunt flyer performing in air shows.

Jackie Cochran with General Hap Arnold. By the spring of 1942, he had come around to her way of thinking and appointed Cochran Director of Women's Flying Training.

Georgia Aviation Hall Of Fame

During WWII, Jackie Cochran recruited Raines for both the ATA and the WASP programs. Raines returned to England in 1954 as WAF Advisor for the Third Air Force.

Georgia Aviation Hall Of Fame

Raines' early reputation as one of the South's premier stunt flyers caught the attention of fellow aviation pioneer Jackie Cochran.

Georgia Aviation Hall Of Fame

One of the few female pilots chosen to be an instructor for the Civilian Pilot Training Program, Raines taught at Cochran Field and at a Ft. Lauderdale aviation school until 1942. It was then she was chosen by Jackie Cochran to fly for the British Air Transport Auxiliary (ATA) as a ferry pilot – one of only twenty-five women to be selected for the often dangerous task. The women flew unarmed and without radio contact to prevent detection in the German-patrolled skies, delivering planes to bomber stations and damaged aircraft to repair facilities. Raines logged more flight hours than any other pilot in the ATA and learned to fly nearly every type of aircraft. She survived her only plane crash when the engine on her Spitfire failed. The two men on the ground who raced to the crash site were stunned to find a woman, very much alive, in the wreckage.

Raines returned to the U.S. in 1943 and moved to Texas to join the new WASP program. There she worked as a test pilot, another risky job, flying recently repaired planes and pulling targets for aviation cadets participating in live ammunition practice. The WASP faced hostility and resistance at home from groups and individuals who were adamantly opposed to women actively serving in the military. When the organization disbanded in 1944, Raines went south to teach the theory of flight to Brazilian student pilots, lecturing five hours daily in Portuguese. The WASP were finally recognized for the service to their country in 1977, long after Raines' death.

When the Korean War began in 1950, Raines was the first female reserve pilot called into active service. After the war, she acted as advisor to the British Third Air Force and recruited pilots for the Women in the Air Force (WAF) and the Women's Army Corp. She became staff advisor for the WAF in 1954 and assisted young women with their careers as pilots. That same year, at the age of 40, Raines died of a heart attack in London. In 1989 she was inducted into the Georgia Aviation Hall of Fame as Georgia's First Lady of Flight for her contributions to aviation in peace and war.

Evelyn Greenblatt (signature)

EVELYN GREENBLATT HOWREN

Evelyn Greenblatt Howren was born in Atlanta, Georgia in 1918. After graduating from Vanderbilt University she returned to Atlanta determined to pursue a career in aviation. She began flight instruction at Candler Field in 1939 and received her private pilot rating on November 3, 1941. One month later Howren joined the newly formed Civil Air Patrol (CAP) where she became a member of the first all-women's squadron of the CAP.

In the spring of 1942, Howren became one of eight female air traffic controller trainees – the first class ever. Only three were pilots. In November of that same year she was chosen to join the newly formed WASP program and completed training at Ellington Field in Houston on April 24, 1943 – one of 23 women to graduate that month. She remained a WASP throughout World War II, ferrying planes and test flying various types of aircraft.

Howren returned to civilian life at the end of the war, became a flight instructor and established Flightways, Inc., one of only a handful of flight operations managed by a woman. Flightways was sold to Lockheed in 1968.

Evelyn Greenblatt Howren was inducted into the Georgia Aviation Hall of Fame in 1994. She died four years later.

MARION STEGEMAN HODGSON

Marion Stegeman grew up in Athens, Georgia, the daughter of the University of Georgia's legendary coach H.J. Stegeman. She earned her pilot's license while attending UGA, where she graduated in 1941 – just ahead of Pearl Harbor. She answered the U.S. government's call for licensed women pilots and reported to Sweetwater, Texas for WASP training in March, 1943. After six months of intensive training, she received her silver wings and was ordered to Love Field in Dallas, Texas.

Hodgson served with the 5th Ferrying Group, picking up aircraft at factories and delivering them to air bases around the country. She was the first woman to be inducted into the Order of Daedalians, an organization of military pilots. Hodgson has received numerous honors and awards, including the Citizens Patriot Award from the Department of Defense. She was inducted into the Texas Aviation Hall of Fame in 2004 and the Georgia Aviation Hall of Fame in 2005.

JUNE MAULE

June D. Maule is CEO and sole owner of Maule Air, Inc., the world-renowned manufacturer of Maule STOL airplanes. She was the wife and business partner of the late B.D. Maule, aircraft designer and manufacturer. Maule operated the administrative side of Maule aircraft and aircraft parts manufacturing facilities for 55 years. She was inducted into the Georgia Aviation Hall of Fame in 1999.

CHARLOTTE FOGG FRYE

In 1898 Charlotte Barbara Fogg moved to Atlanta from Wichita Kansas. In 1916, she married Dr. Augustus Frye, a pilot, and lived in Griffin until her death in 1983. She learned to fly at Candler Field in 1931. Beeler Blevins and Wesley Raymond were her instructors. Georgia claimed only 6 women pilots at the time. Frye flew in air shows and took leading roles in promoting aviation in Georgia. She called the 1930s the "best years and happiest years – when we were flying." Frye was the only woman sworn in during the celebration of the twentieth anniversary of air mail service in May 1938. She flew the mail from Griffin to Atlanta and became one of the first female airmail pilots. Mrs. Frye became a charter member and vice president of the Georgia chapter of the Ninety-Nines and served as governor of the Southeastern Section in 1941. She was also a member of the Atlanta Aero Club, Carolina Aero Club and the Georgia chapter of the National Aeronautical Association.

Charlotte Fogg Frye was inducted into the Georgia Aviation Hall of Fame in 1991 as one of Georgia's pioneer women pilots and one who actively promoted aviation in her state during the 1930s.

Above: Charlotte Frye and husband Augustus, both pilots, raised a family of fliers. All three of their children became involved in aviation.

Georgia Aviation Hall Of Fame

MYRTLE "K" THOMPSON CAGLE

As early as 1961, Randolph Lovelace, director of the New Mexico clinic where the Mercury 7 astronauts had undergone their physical exams, along with Jackie Cochran, wanted to prove that women were equally qualified to be astronauts. Twenty highly qualified female pilots underwent identical tests given the all-male Mercury astronauts. Thirteen passed, proving they too had the "right stuff." These women were known as the FLATs (First Lady Astronaut Trainees) and one of them has ties to Georgia.

While serving as a flight instructor in Macon, Myrtle "K" Thompson Cagle received an invitation to join the 1961 Lovelace Clinic tests. A pilot since age 12, she had logged an impressive 4,300 hours of flying time – more than some of the Mercury 7 men. She already held a Commercial Pilot's license with Single and Multi Engine Land ratings, and an Instrument Rating. She earned certifications as Flight Instructor, Flight Instrument

Instructor and Ground Instructor. She earned an Airframe and Power Plant (A&P) license, and was also a licensed nurse.

Cagle accepted the invitation to participate in the Lovelace Clinic tests and passed with flying colors. Ultimately, NASA refused to place any of the finalists in the official NASA training program. "Captain K" returned to Georgia and resumed her role as flight instructor and pilot with the Civil Air Patrol (CAP). She was inducted into the Georgia Aviation Hall of Fame in 2003.

A pilot by age 12, Cagle was keen on joining an aeronautics class in her high school. Her mother convinced the principal to allow her daughter to participate. She did so well that when the instructor was drafted, she stepped in and finished the year as teacher.

Georgia Aviation Hall Of Fame

World War II Boosts Construction of Air Bases and Airports in Georgia

Unlike Europe, where commercial aviation developed quickly after World War I, the United States still generally regarded flying as "stunts" and not serious transportation. That attitude did little to support the building of dedicated "landing fields," and aviators were relegated to taking off and landing their aircraft at fairgrounds, ball fields, pastures and the like.

Georgia was no exception to this attitude. While they were enamored with flight and the touring barnstormers, Georgia communities were not quick to build airports. In 1920, a small book entitled *Municipal Landing Fields and Airports* was written to "present to the public… the entire problem involved in the creation and administration of flying routes, landing fields, and airports." The book listed only eight municipal fields in Georgia: Albany, Fort Valley, McRae, Macon, Marshallville, Montezuma, Savannah and Waycross. Military fields added four more to the list including Americus, Augusta, Brunswick and Columbus. Noticeably missing was Atlanta.

Facing Page: Atlanta Airport, c. 1940s.

Delta Air Transport Heritage Museum

By 1937, just prior to the massive buildup of aviation training bases in anticipation of World War II, only seventeen municipal fields existed in Georgia. Atlanta finally had one; Augusta and Brunswick's military fields had become municipal fields; and Dalton, Douglas, Gainesville, Griffin, Lavonia, Moultrie, Social Circle, Thomaston, Thomasville and Valdosta had joined the ranks. Rome and Stockbridge were listed as commercial airports, but no definition of commercial or municipal was provided.

Up to this point, airports were still considered landing (or flying) fields where the focus was on the operation of the aircraft, not passengers. Hangars and shops were provided, but little provision was made for the incidental passenger. Those few passenger air terminals that were built emulated train stations with large common waiting rooms, ticket-purchasing facilities and doors that led to the landing field and waiting aircraft.

In 1941 Washington D.C.'s National Airport became the first modern American air terminal and served as a model for air terminals of the future. But advances in airport design were put on hold when World War II began. The war had significant impact on almost every aspect of aviation across America, but especially in Georgia. A large number of military training fields and auxiliary fields became operational in 1942. Many of these would become commercial or general aviation airports after the war, while others would remain military bases. In some cases, communities converted these fields into industrial parks, community colleges and other non-aviation use.

SAVANNAH
Hunter Army Air Field
Chatham Army Air Field

Savannah has the earliest and perhaps most comprehensive aviation history in Georgia. Charles Cevor's balloon works were located in Savannah, and most of his flights originated there from approximately 1835 through the Civil War.

On November 25 and 28, 1911, Savannah was the second of five Georgia cities to host demonstrations of air mail flights performed by the Curtiss Exhibition Team. The Savannah flights, with Beckwith Havens piloting a standard Curtiss Model D pusher, took place on the first and last days of the Athletic Park Aviation Meet and were part of an aggressive marketing plan by the Curtiss Aeroplane Company.

Like other cities, Savannah had its local airplane experimenters. Matthew Batson and his Aero Yacht Company built what appeared to be a small cabin on floats with tandem wings and three engines. All three engines drove a single shaft with a propeller at each end, one at the front of the craft and the other at the rear. The Aero Yacht never flew. A smaller version, the Dragonfly, made only one uncorroborated claim to flight. The assets, including the Aero Yacht and the Dragonfly, were sold when the company went bankrupt in 1915.

Savannah had no direct aviation role in World War I, although some of its men did gain fame by their service, most notably Frank O'Driscoll Hunter.

There were the occasional barnstorming visitors to Savannah. Although the 1920 *Municipal Landing Fields and Airports* lists Savannah, the only detail provided is that the field is "under the control of the city government or Chamber of Commerce." It is known that a portion of Daffin Park was designated as a landing site in 1919, and the Savannah Golf Club also had landings on occasion.

Savannah began the process of acquiring an airport site on January 31, 1928. Perhaps this was due to the national surge of interest in commercial aviation which followed the Lindbergh national goodwill tour late in 1927. The Belmont tract, southwest of the city was favored, approved and eventually purchased. Plans were to create a grass landing field 4,500 by 3,500 feet that would allow operations in any direction. No runways were designated.

M. Steiner Archives

In September, 1929 Eastern Air Express (not related to Eastern Air Transport), announced twice-weekly service from New York to Miami via the coastal route and Savannah. Eastern intended to increase its frequency to daily service by December. Service was infrequent and eventually stopped altogether. The *Official Aviation Guide* of February, 1930 does not even list this airline or their service.

Even with this false start, the need for an airfield continued. In June, 1930 the landing field was officially named the Savannah Airport.

April 1, 1931 saw the coastal air mail and associated passenger service officially begin with Eastern Air Transport. This route bypassed Atlanta by leaving Eastern's main route at Richmond and going through Charleston and Savannah, rejoining the main route at Jacksonville. In October an agreement was signed with Eastern for daily service and an airport beacon was installed, allowing night operations. An additional route from Savannah through Augusta to Atlanta was added on December 1, 1931. For this first flight, the mayor's daughter, Ida Hoynes, "christened" a propeller blade of Eastern's Curtiss Condor with a bottle of Savannah River water.

The airport was officially dedicated the Savannah Airport on August 13, 1932. No sooner had the ribbon been cut than controversy arose. Many wanted the airport to be named after Savannah's World War I ace, Frank O'Driscoll Hunter. A compromise was reached on November 30, 1932. The airfield would be named Hunter Air Field, and the airport would remain Savannah Airport.

Airfields in the Savannah area would change missions, ownership and identification more than in any other area of the state. The Department of Commerce Descriptions of Airports and Landing Fields in the United States, January, 1937 lists it simply as the "Savannah Airport, municipal" with an L-shaped pattern of two runways, a beacon and an office building.

During Savannah Aviation Week in May, 1940, the airport was renamed Hunter Municipal Airfield. Then Lt. Col. Frank O'Driscoll Hunter stopped in Savannah during the event on his way to his assignment as U.S. Air Attaché to France.

On August 30, 1940 the Army Air Corps decided to build an air base at Hunter. They renamed it Savannah Air Base on February 19, 1941. The base served as both a training base and a staging base for airmen bound to the European Theater of Operations. Many were B-17 crews on their way to England. It was at Savannah Air Base that the VIII Bomber Command (later the 8th Air Force) was activated on January 28, 1942. Brig. Gen. Ira Eaker,

Above: After WWI ended, Frank O'Driscoll Hunter remained in the army, attaining the rank of Major General. He commanded the 8th Air Force Fighter Command in England during World War II, and retired from the USAAC in 1946.

Left: Hunter Municipal Airfield opened during Savannah Aviation Week in May, 1940. Lt. Colonel Hunter surprised the crowd, visiting the field on the first day of Aviation Week while en route to France.

Georgia Aviation Hall Of Fame

commander of this group, would move his headquarters staff to England within a month.

Although the Army Air Force allowed the commercial airlines to continue operations from Savannah Air Base, the city decided to build another municipal airport on a site northwest of downtown. Much of the construction was accomplished as a Works Progress Administration project, and the WPA District Director was former Savannah mayor Hoynes. The airport included three runways, a terminal and hangars.

In 1942 the Army Air Corps found it necessary to take over this new airport even though construction was not yet complete. Named Chatham Field, it became a training base for Consolidated B-24 Liberator bomber crews and fighter pilots. The civilian airport was not moved from Savannah Air Base. After the war, the Savannah Air Base served as a separation center for returning troops. In June, 1946 the airport was returned to the city for civilian use. Many of the former military buildings became industrial facilities, some became a college campus, and others were used as apartments and an orphanage.

In 1948 the Georgia Air National Guard took over Chatham Army Air Field and changed the name to Travis Field. The name was a tribute to the Travis brothers from Savannah, Brig. Gen. Robert F. Travis and Col. William L. Travis, both highly decorated World War II Army Air Force officers. Travis Air Force Base in California is also named after Robert Travis.

In January, 1949 the newly activated 2nd Bombardment Wing, Medium, transferred into Chatham Air Force Base (the name had changed to Air Force Base when the Air Force became a separate service in 1947). The base was found inadequate for the unit's needs, and the Air Force considered moving out of Savannah. In a move to retain the Air Force operations, Savannah offered to swap Hunter back to the Air Force and move the civilian airport to the Chatham site, now Travis Field. The Air Force accepted, moved their operations to Hunter and changed the name from Savannah Air Base to Hunter Air Force Base.

Later in 1949 the city took title to Travis Field, and commercial airline operations were moved there in 1950. The city set about making improvements to the airport, including a new terminal building in 1960. Gulfstream Aerospace Corporation built its manufacturing facility at Travis. Delta Air Lines, which served this airport since operating the very first commercial flight in 1950, began jet service in 1965.

The 2nd Bombardment Wing and 308th Bomb Wing, operating B-29s and transitioning to B-50s, were located to Hunter AFB. The 308th Wing Commander was Col. Paul Tibbets, the pilot of the *Enola Gay*. This wing

(continued on page 114)

Brig. General Robert L. Scott: God Was His Co-Pilot

They referred to it as "flying the hump." In the early stages of America's involvement in World War II, volunteer pilots had the dangerous mission of flying supplies from bases in India into the embattled lands of Burma and China. In lumbering C-46s and C-47s, the American pilots launched from field elevations of six hundred feet and began their formidable climbs over the Himalayas. The twin-engine cargo planes were loaded with everything from carbon paper to ammunition – jammed to the gunwales, unprotected, and flying in some of the most treacherous weather in the world. With the closure of the Burma Road by Japanese forces, the hump pilots were the only source of supply for British forces and a small group of Americans known as the Flying Tigers. Without them, Japanese domination in that portion of Asia would be complete.

Having been something less than a stellar student, the Georgia boy named Robert Lee Scott bullied and manipulated his way into West Point. His academic career was tumultuous, but in his true fashion, he worked the system. After numerous close calls, Scott graduated in 1932 and received his commission in the U.S. Army Air Corps.

Over the next several years he built his hours and worked his way up through the ranks, gaining extensive experience flying fighters. In 1939 he was assigned to the West Coast Training Center with the title of Assistant District Supervisor. Shortly after, he was given command of the Air Corps Training Detachment, better known as Cal-Aero. By the time the United States entered the war, Scott was a Colonel. And he was also thirty-four years old.

Colonel Robert Scott had never given up his dream to fly fighters in action. He tried every trick in the book to get out of the Training Center, all without success. At his age, not only was he too old to command a fighter squadron, he was too old to fly fighters in combat at all. Only through his persistence was he able to convince one general to bend the rules. But it would not be in the cockpit of a fighter.

After the attack on Pearl Harbor, American leadership became intrigued with the idea of a counter attack against mainland Japan. One of the resulting plans was to send a flight of B-17s, launched from India, on a bombing run over Tokyo. Scott was offered the job to fly one of the Flying Fortresses. When asked if he had ever flown a four-engine ship, he lied that he had flown one for eleven hundred hours. In fact, he had never flown a B-17 for even one minute. Scott got the job and wheedled his way through a B-17 checkout.

Illustration: Sue Mabry

Scott ferried his bird from South America across the Atlantic to Africa. From there, he and his crew turned north, then east, working their way across the continent toward India. Once at their destination of Karachi, they discovered that the mission had been cancelled due to increasing Japanese expansion in the theatre. Two weeks later he was told to report to a remote base on the India-Burma border. His new job would be flying supplies over the 15,000 foot ridges of the Himalayas to the front. His primary customer would be a man named Claire Chennault, commander of the American Volunteer Group (AVG) – the Flying Tigers.

Chennault was officially commissioned in the Chinese Army. He was the commander of the AVG personnel. They were on the Chinese payroll, essentially as mercenaries. Payments to the Americans were funneled through a company known as CAMCO – the Central Aircraft Manufacturing Corporation.

Scott quickly befriended Chennault and made a proposal. Would the AVG consider loaning him a P-40 for use in escorting the transport aircraft back and forth over Burma? To Scott's great surprise, Chennault agreed. A P-40E Kittyhawk would be his to fly. Two days later it arrived and Scott wasted no time in having the trademark shark's mouth painted on the front cowling. This classic nose art, used on all the AVG fighters, would become the one of the most recognizable images of the entire war.

Robert Scott wasted no time in putting his new toy to use. If he wasn't flying escort, he had the warplane out on solo sweeps, looking for targets of opportunity. During the first full month, he logged 215 hours of flight time. His first kill was a Mitsubishi medium bomber, known as a "Betty" to the Allies. He caught it being serviced on the ground and reduced it to a flaming hulk with two passes. Barges, trains, and troop columns continued to fall under the guns of his plane, "Old Exterminator," all month long.

In June of 1942 the announcement that the AVG would be absorbed into the U.S. Army reached the men. Unfortunately, it was described to them in a very unappealing way. They could join the Air Corps and keep their commissions, or they could expect representatives from their draft boards to meet them at the docks when they returned to San Francisco. Feeling angry and betrayed, only five pilots and thirty ground crewmen stayed on. Claire Chennault resigned from the Chinese Army to accept a Brigadier General's commission in the U.S. Army. He would remain as the chief of the new 14th Air Force. The AVG would become the 23rd Fighter Group and Scott received orders to take over as its commander.

The scrappy Georgian hadn't worked all those years to accede to a desk. He scored his first two aerial victories at the end of July. He had been CO of the group for less than a month. Two months later, he was an ace with five confirmed kills. By the time he was rotated home in January, 1943, he was a celebrated double ace.

Back in the United States, Colonel Scott hit the trail promoting war bonds and making speeches. After a speech in Buffalo, New York, a man named Charles Scribner introduced himself. The publishing mogul had been electrified by the story Scott told and suggested that he consider writing a book. Jack Warner of Warner Brothers Studios came to the same conclusion a few months later and purchased movie rights before the book was even written. The title of the book and film became a permanent credo for aviators: *God Is My Co-Pilot*.

After the war, Scott remained in the Air Force and took command of the first jet fighter school, located at Williams Field, Arizona. In 1950 he was reassigned to Germany as CO of the 36th Fighter/Bomber Wing. He later graduated from the National War College and was promoted to Brigadier General. Finally, in 1957, after thirty-six years in uniform, Brigadier General Robert L. Scott retired from service and returned home to Georgia.

(continued from page 111)

would receive its first B-47 Stratojet bombers on November 25, 1953, as part of the Strategic Air Command (SAC). Hunter also was home to SAC's transports, such as the Douglas C-124 Globemaster and a variety of air-refueling tankers.

In 1964 the Department of Defense announced that Hunter AFB would be closed over the next three years. Closure had not yet taken place when the Secretary of Defense decided to transfer Hunter to the Army as a helicopter training base. This came about when the war in Vietnam created a greater need than the Army Aviation School at Fort Rucker, Alabama could satisfy. On April 1, 1967, the base was renamed Hunter Army Air Field. It is the largest Army airfield in the continental United States.

Another cycle of deactivation and reactivation occurred between 1973 and 1975 when Hunter became a hub in the Rapid Deployment Forces capability. In 1980, the 24th Infantry Division was assigned to the Rapid Deployment Force at Hunter. During 1990 this division was totally deployed from Hunter to Kuwait in only six days validating the rapid deployment concept. In 1998 the Truscott Air Terminal was dedicated. The terminal serves passenger and cargo arrivals and departures from Hunter. The base also serves as Coast Guard Air Station Savannah, the largest Coast Guard helicopter unit. Hunter is the home of the Georgia Air National Guard 117th Tactical Control Squadron. With an 11,375 foot runway, Hunter is also an alternate landing site for the NASA Shuttles. Hunter is actively involved in all military operations today.

In 1983 Travis Field became Savannah International Airport (IAP). Savannah IAP moved into its new terminal building in May, 1994 with room for 19 gates. With increased traffic destined for the South Carolina coastal resort areas, the airport was renamed Savannah/Hilton Head International Airport in 2003. The 165th Airlift Wing, Air National Guard, became tenants in 2005 with C-130H aircraft. Gulfstream Aerospace Corporation continues to make its world headquarters at Savannah/Hilton Head International Airport.

ALBANY
Turner Air Field

Turner Air Field near Albany, Georgia was named after 2nd Lieutenant Sullins Preston Turner of Atlanta, who died in an airplane accident at Langley Field, Virginia. The selection of his name was popular across the aviation community in Georgia. "Tops," as he was known to his friends, was an Emory graduate and his father was a Latin professor there. Turner had expressed an

Facing Page: Darr Aero Tech and the Lakeland School of Aeronautics were founded in 1940 by Mr. Harold S. Darr. Darr Tech, located across town from Turner Air Field, became one of the largest Army air training detachments in the country.

M. Steiner Archives

interest in developing an aviation center at Albany even before he graduated, but he did not live to see it.

Turner Air Field was one of a number of training bases that would be built in Georgia as the threat of World War II grew. During the summer of 1940, the Albany Chamber of Commerce was approached by a representative of the United States Army, Major Peacock, whose mission was to locate a site near Albany that would be suitable for an airfield. The Chamber set out to locate a site that offered access to the railroad, then the primary means of heavy shipping. Utilities, terrain and sparse population were other considerations.

The Chamber and the army selected a site about four miles east of the city and the Flint River. The Chamber of Commerce's Industrial Committee raised funds to purchase the land from the R. L. Jones family. The site was presented to the City of Albany, who in turn leased it to the United States Government for $1.00 a year. Similar transactions provided four auxiliary fields nearby as well.

Other military facilities were established in Albany including enrollment and separate housing for black and white soldiers and Woman's Army Corps (WAC). The Georgia Northern Railroad was contracted to construct a spur from their main line onto the base site. Albany Water Gas and Light extended utilities to the site and numerous local contractors performed other tasks. All of these activities and facilities led to the quick construction and completion of Turner Field. Construction began on March 25, 1941 and Turner opened on June 25, 1941 as an Advanced Training Base for pilots. Also included was a navigator school. Colonel John B. Patrick, who had been assigned as the Project Officer for the development of Turner on April 23rd, became the first base commander in July, 1941. Patrick had previous Georgia assignments at both Ft. Oglethorpe and at the Atlanta Municipal Airport (Candler Field). Lt. Colonel John R. Skeldon piloted the first plane into Turner on July

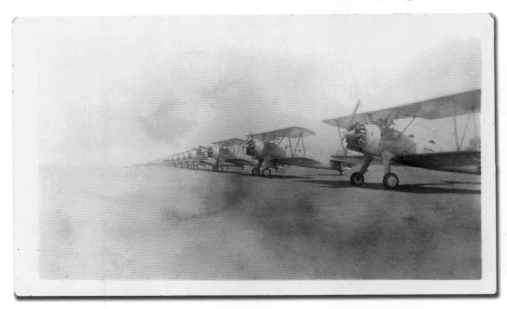

17, 1941, and the first class graduated on October 31, 1941, just five weeks before Pearl Harbor.

Turner also served as an orientation base for British Air Cadets who trained in Georgia and adjacent southern states. This training program came to be known as the "Arnold Scheme," so named because the concept was developed by U.S.

Army Air Force Lieutenant General Henry H. "Hap" Arnold. It was part of the "Hands Across the Sea" policy that also included the more widely known "Lend Lease" program. The first RAF Advanced Flying School class graduated at Turner. These were the first of over seven thousand RAF cadets that would ultimately train in the southeast.

In September of 1942, the navigator school moved to Monroe, Louisiana, allowing the pilot program at Turner to be expanded.

Turner Air Field was closed on August 15, 1946. The dust had barely settled when, in 1947, the newly established United States Air Force reopened the facility as Turner Air Force Base. The initial unit assigned was the 9th Air Force, 31st Fighter Wing. This was the first unit flying the Republic R84G reconnaissance aircraft. One of its pilots, Lt. Frances Gary Powers, would go on to some fame years later when his Lockheed U-2 reconnaissance aircraft was brought down over the Soviet Union. Turner was Powers' first base assignment upon graduation with class 52-H.

The reconnaissance role was expanded in 1957 when the Strategic Air Command (SAC) took over the base and moved in Martin RB57D aircraft. Further expansion, including a 12,000 foot runway, came in 1958 when Boeing B-52 Stratofortresses were moved to Turner. Notable with SAC bases were Air Defense sites around the base armed with nuclear tipped, Nike Hercules missiles. The Air Force ended its stay at Turner in 1967.

Phoenix-like, the base rolled into its next tour as Navy Air Station (NAS) Albany.

Again, reconnaissance was the mission, this time by United States Navy pilots. When not at sea on carrier cruises, two units called Albany, Georgia home base. RVAH-12 Speartips, and RVAH-3 Sea Dragons, both equipped with North American RA-3 Vigilantes, flew out of Albany. NAS Albany closed the gates on military use of Turner in the mid 1970s.

There was some civilian use of the facility, including a training base for nearby Thrush Aircraft agricultural pilot training, but all flight activities ended in the late 1970s. Miller Brewing built a substantial plant on the site in 1978 and continues to be the primary occupant of the old base site.

"High Flight Over Darr" Oil Painting By James W. (Red) Hall, Member of RAF in Albany Committee

The Royal Air Force
in Albany
1941 - 1943

A Remembrance In Word, Music and Fellowship

FIFTIETH ANNIVERSARY REUNION
OCTOBER 19 & 20, 1991 ALBANY, GEORGIA USA

Above: On June 8, 1941, the first United Kingdom (British Royal Air Force) cadets arrived. After the last American class was completed on July 14, 1941, Darr Aero Tech trained British Cadets exclusively. This was prior to Pearl Harbor and America's entry into the war. Seven British cadets are buried in Albany's Crown Hill Cemetery.

M. Steiner Archives

HINESVILLE-FT. STEWART
Liberty Army Air Field
Wright Army Air Field

With over 280,000 acres sprawled across the pine and palmetto thickets of eastern Georgia, Fort Stewart near Hinesville, Georgia is the largest military installation east of the Mississippi. Today, it is primarily known as the headquarters of the 3rd Infantry Division, U. S. Army. Liberty Army Air Field, located on the base, has a unique place in aviation history. While the airfield may appear incidental to the mission and the resident military units, in fact it is central to their purpose, both now and most especially in years past.

Liberty County, west and southwest of Savannah, derived its name from having been a hotbed of patriotism during the American Revolution. General Daniel Stewart, a Liberty County native, served with Francis "Swamp Fox" Marion during that war. This new base would be named after General Stewart and the airfield after its home county.

The World War II resident unit, Company B, 101st Anti-Aircraft Artillery (AAA) Battalion, also had a link to this history. Before becoming the AAA unit, they were initially the Liberty Dragoons and later the Liberty Independent Troop (cavalry), which served in World War I as Company B, 106th Field Signal Battalion.

Like many other Georgia bases, Camp Stewart was funded in June, 1940. Unlike the others, however, the federal government purchased the land

Three WASP receive pre-flight briefing from the anti-aircraft range officer at Liberty Field. Target towing was just one of the high risk assignments for WASP.

Fort Stewart Museum

directly, beginning in July. It would become the site of an anti-aircraft artillery (AAA) training center. The high priority of this mission grew out of observing the German occupation of Europe by use of aerial warfare. Air assault was the primary method utilized by Germany, including bombardment, strafing and paratrooper drops. Anti-aircraft capability was essential to survival against such an adversary.

Above: The Liberty Field WASP unit in formation for inspection. Liberty had one of the largest WASP contingents of any airfield in Georgia.

Fort Stewart Museum

An anti-aircraft unit included searchlights, audio tracking equipment and weapons. Initially, all production of the necessary hardware was being shipped to the war zone. Wooden mockups were provided to the earliest training classes. In November, the base was officially designated Camp Stewart. Since very little of the facility had been constructed, and all of the large area required for live-fire exercises had not been purchased, live-fire practice took place at beach-front sites overlooking the Atlantic Ocean. As the base expanded, this activity was moved back onto the reservation. As training progressed, target practice also included tracking and firing at targets towed over the base by aircraft. The towing aircraft and targets were being launched from Liberty Army Air Field.

Following the attack at Pearl Harbor, a detachment of Women's Air Service Pilots (WASP) was assigned to Camp Stewart to pilot the target towing aircraft for live-fire exercises. This was done in order to make all male pilots available for combat. Actually, flying target tow was almost like being in combat. On more than one occasion, the towing aircraft would be struck by practice anti-aircraft fire.

Below: This in-flight photo reveals why target towing was such high risk. Student anti-aircraft gunners practiced "leading the target" occasionally hitting the tow aircraft.

Fort Stewart Museum

If this mission seemed unusual, the aircraft utilized were even more so. A variety of aircraft types were used for target towing. These included the AT-6 Texan, A-24 Douglas Dauntless (the Air Force renamed it the Banshee), A-25 Curtiss Helldiver and the B-34 Lockheed Ventura. With the exception of the AT-6, these were unusual aircraft in the Army

Air Force inventory, but all had been deemed not suitable for active combat. Both the A-24 and A-25 were Air Force versions of U.S. Navy/Marine dive bombers. The Army Air Force, in reaction to the great success of the German Stuka dive bomber, had ordered these aircraft (the only dive bombers then in American production) only to later decide not to put them into combat.

A typical, target tow flight would have a WASP pilot and an army private (male) in the rear-facing cockpit, reeling out the target and then retrieving it after the live-firing session. This team would criss-cross the firing range a number of times during a typical practice session. These aircraft types were generally used from 1943 on. As early as 1940 the Army Air Corps had drawn up specifications for a radio-controlled target towing drone. Later in the war, these tow aircraft were developed and put into use, providing a more effective,

Right: Liberty Field during WWII. On the ramp in this photo are Lockheed Venturas and various dive bombers, all used for target towing.

Fort Stewart Museum

and certainly safer, means for target practice. The all-wood tow planes included Culver Cadets, first the PQ-8, a modification of Culver's piloted civilian aircraft. In 1944, a larger and faster version with retractable landing gear, the PQ-14, was put into service. These aircraft could be pilot flown as well.

Late in 1943 two Prisoner of War camps were established, one for German and the other for Italian prisoners primarily from the African campaign. Most prisoners were put to work supporting base operations, construction and farming. In Spring of 1944 Camp Stewart became a staging area for the European invasion forces. Seemingly overnight, 55,000 men were housed there. By this time, with air superiority established, the need for AAA was incidental, and the AAA training center was closed. By January, 1945, after the invasion forces had left, Camp Stewart was little more than a POW camp. It would function as a separation center as troops returned after victory in Europe.

The quiet was broken with the Korean Conflict. Camp Stewart was reactivated on August 9, 1950, and the 3rd Army's AAA began training, utilizing Liberty Field. Again, air superiority and the introduction of newer technology and air defense systems lessened the need for AAA capability. This time the Department of Defense began to recognize the need for more permanent facilities, and Camp Stewart was designated permanent and renamed Fort Stewart on March 21, 1956.

The Cuban Missile crisis brought a short flurry of activity, including a visit by President John F. Kennedy. By then, the helicopter had become more than just a medical evacuation or VIP vehicle. Liberty Field and Fort Stewart became the home of the U.S. Army Aviation School, moved from Fort Rucker, Alabama.

In 1967 the U.S. Air Force decided to close Hunter Air Force Base in Savannah, and the Army Aviation incorporated Hunter as an Army Air Field. Much of the helicopter capability in Vietnam came out of this expanded program. By 1973 the cycle started again with Fort Stewart and Liberty Field becoming inactive, except for the summer National Guard encampments. The kudzu had scarcely begun to engulf the base

Above: A target tow aircraft taxiing out for a mission. The target was deployed after the aircraft reached the assigned target range.

Fort Stewart Museum

when the Army Rangers arrived to make this home base. The old World War II wooden (temporary) structures were finally replaced with permanent structures. Late 1974 saw the 24th Infantry Division Rapid Deployment Forces settle in.

From 1984 on, the airfield was known as Wright Army Air Field. It was used as a readiness exercise site by Lockheed C-130 equipped Tactical Airlift Groups. A unit would be airlifted in with all support facilities such as kitchen, medical and field tents, and perform field exercises. Today, Wright is heavily used as a helicopter field. The 24th was redesignated the 3rd Infantry Division on April 25, 1996. It continues to call Fort Stewart and Wright Army Air Field home.

The lack of use by fixed-wing aircraft allowed the runways, lights and other improvements to degenerate. At the same time, the local community did not have an adequate airport. The Department of Defense and local government agencies have now developed a joint-use arrangement in order to provide a local airport for Hinesville, Liberty County and adjacent area. This arrangement is the result of many years of effort. First suggested by Ft. Stewart in 1996, the idea lay dormant until 1999, when a joint study was launched. This study resulted in an agreement on October 24, 2002 that includes reworking the two runways, extending one, providing lighting and general improvement of the entire physical plant. A ground-breaking for a new passenger terminal took place on April 4, 2005, and the MidCoast Regional Airport became a reality.

WARNER ROBINS
Southeast Air Depot
Robins Army Air Field
Wellston Air Depot
Warner Robins Air Depot

There may be more confusion about the correct name and spelling of this base and facility than any other in Georgia. It all started with Congress authorizing construction of army air logistics bases just before World War II. This program was different from the build-up of training bases that brought about so many other army airfields in Georgia. Macon and Bibb County, anxious to win this base, issued bonds and purchased over 3,000 acres near Wellston, Georgia, a small community south of Macon, and then offered to donate it to the federal government.

The Macon Chamber of Commerce and the City of Macon had already achieved some success with the growing defense needs of the country. Three previous "free land" offers had resulted in a naval ordnance plant (Reynolds Metals), an infantry replacement training center (Camp Wheeler), and an Army Air Corps training center (Cochran Field).

The Georgia military community has often benefited from a strong presence in Congress. In this case, Congressman Carl Vinson was

Below: In 1945 Macon hosted the world premier of God Is My Co-Pilot, *a film based on a book of the same name written by native son Robert L. Scott. In 1988 the Museum of Aviation at Robins AFB held a second "World Premier" as a fund-raising event.*

M. Steiner Archives

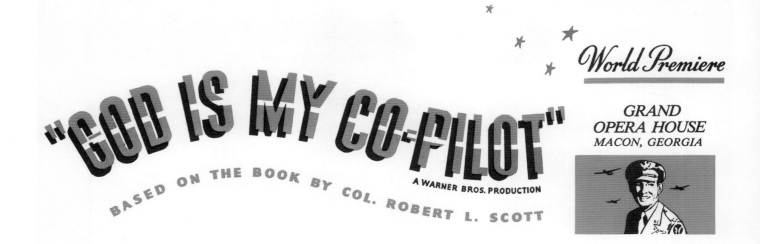

instrumental in recommending the Wellston site. With this gift of land and strong Congressional support, the decision to locate the depot at Wellston was announced in June, 1941. An official ground-breaking ceremony took place September 1, 1941 and the Southeast Air Depot was named in November.

There had been other contenders for the depot, including a site at Ellenwood, southeast of Atlanta. An Air Corps survey team visited the Atlanta site, then Wellston, followed by Albany, Dublin, Milledgeville and Vienna. The primary difference was that the Wellston site was level, required little grading, and had a number of artesian wells on the property. The Atlanta site would have had to pipe in water, required extensive earth movement, and would have had to be purchased. Each of the other sites had similar drawbacks.

The Georgia Air Depot, as it was generally known, would be built in phases. Some buildings were put into use as early as April, 1942, even though the first phase was not completed until the following August 31st. The base was officially named Robins Field on January 23, 1942, and the depot, Wellston Air Depot, on March 14th. On September 1, 1942 the town of Wellston became Warner Robins, and on October 14th, the depot became the Warner Robins Air Depot.

Both are named for Brigadier General Augustine Warner Robins. Gen. Robins had been Chief, Materiel Division, Army Air Corps from 1935 through 1939. He had died in an airplane crash while Commandant at Randolph Field, Texas in 1940. One source states that this base and depot were renamed seven times during World War II.

While under construction, base operations took place at Macon's Herbert Smart Airport, with administrative and supply functions operated from offices and warehouses in Macon. The remainder of the base was essentially completed the following spring (1943).

Initially, the air depot maintained and repaired the aircraft of the many Army Air Training bases in the area. This included managing civilian sub-contractors, as well. In August, 1943 the depot was made responsible for maintenance and repair of all the major aircraft types in the Army Air Force inventory. These included C-47 transports; B-17, B-24 and B-29 bombers; and P-38, P-47, and P-51 fighters.

Even though the geographic area of responsibility was constantly being changed, as were the types of aircraft, the depot was responsible for some 6,500 aircraft, at any point in time. Even more important was the training of the field aircraft mechanics, known as air depot groups, and the many civilian employees.

In 1955 Robins Air Force Base was headquarters for the Warner Robins Air Materiel Area (WRAMA). The flagship aircraft at that time was the B-57, a U.S. version of the British-developed Canberra bomber.

M. Steiner Archives

In 1946 the depot was renamed the Warner Robins Air Materiel Area (WRAMA). After the establishment of a separate Air Force in 1947, the base was renamed Robins Air Force Base. Like most other military installations, the depot downsized significantly after the war. There was a flurry of activity in 1948, as the Berlin Airlift went into operation. Much of the Douglas C-54 Skymaster (DC-4) fleet went through Warner Robins en route to participate in the Berlin Airlift. The last C-54 transports arrived at Robins AFB in 1949, on their way to Germany.

In October, 1949 the Headquarters 14th Air Force was moved to Robins AFB from Orlando, Florida. This gave the base a second major activity, an operational air force. Runways were extended, and heavier concrete aprons built.

The 14th also brought significant history to the base. It was the direct descendent of Gen. Chennault's American Volunteer Group (AVG), also known as the Flying Tigers. Brig. Gen. Robert L. Scott, who would later be one of the founders of the Museum of Aviation at Robins AFB, had been named commanding officer of the 23rd Fighter Group in July, 1942. The 23rd was the re-formed Flying Tigers, which later would become part of the 14th Air Force. Scott was a native of Macon.

The Korean Conflict brought more significant growth, including a number of large permanent buildings, and expansion of staffing. A variety of special units were activated at Robins AFB. These included recruiting groups, aircraft control and warning, air refueling, and logistics support. The aircraft inventory supporting the logistics function included C-124, C-97, C-119, C-47, and C-54 cargo transports. Heavy maintenance functions were provided for B-47, F-86, F-84F, F-94C, B-29, and B-50s. Numbers of cocooned B-29s were unwrapped and refurbished at the depot. Robins assumed prime management and maintenance responsibility for B-57 aircraft and TM-61 Matador guided missiles.

Following the Berlin Airlift and the Korean Conflict, the United States Air Force set about building up its European aircraft fleet. The fastest and least expensive delivery method for operational aircraft moving to Europe, was to ferry them across the North Atlantic. While this had been done during World War II, the jets and their crews had not operated in this manner since the end of that war.

In 1955 the ramp at Robins was occupied by North American F-86 Sabres and Martin B-57s. Boeing B-47s and numerous transports were also frequently seen.

M. Steiner Archives

In March, 1953 Operation High Flight was initiated. These flights originated at Robins AFB after the aircraft had been placed in top maintenance condition. Aircraft received "shake-down" flights and were winterized. Military Air Transport Service (MATS) ferry pilots were involved with their long range, over-water experience. Over 1,000 aircraft were delivered, including Republic F-84 Thunderjet/Thunderstreak, North American F-86 Sabre, and T-33 Shooting Stars. In October, 1954 the first RB-57A Night Intruder reconnaissance aircraft was ferried across. Bases in Germany, France, Spain, Turkey, and others were equipped through this operation.

Additional prime maintenance responsibilities were added in the late 1950s, including the Mace missile system and additional transports. These also included the Douglas C-117 Super DC-3, Douglas C-118 Liftmaster (DC-6), and Fairchild C-123 Provider.

The Strategic Air Command (SAC) took up residency at Robins with the activation of the 4137th Strategic Wing (SW) on March 24, 1959. This was the first SAC unit at the base. It would be 1961 before the wing received its B-52s. This would be the first of a series of bomber units to be based at Robins.

The Continental Air Command (CONAC) Headquarters was moved to Robins AFB in April, 1961. CONAC administered and trained Air Reserve Forces. It would oversee significant reserve involvement in the Cold War activities. The Air Force Reserve would replace CONAC at Robins in August, 1968.

The Vietnam era (late 1960s and into the '70s) saw Robins performing maintenance on the vital, transport fleet that provided the men and material to Southeast Asia. In fact, a large contingent of Robins maintenance personnel were actually located to Da Nang and other air bases in order to quickly return aircraft to service. These included the Fairchild C-123 Provider, Douglas C-124 Globemaster II, and Lockheed C-130 Hercules and C-141 Starlifter. Mission-critical Airborne Warning and Control System (AWACS) aircraft and their onboard systems were assigned to Robins in 1974.

Gunship versions of in-service transports were created during the Vietnam War. All gunship modifications were performed at WRAMA, and the

resulting models were supported by the depot. These included the Douglas AC-47 "Puff, the Magic Dragon," the Fairchild AC-119 Shadow/Stinger, and eventually the Lockheed AC-130 Spectre/Spooky II.

As well as the C-130 and C-141 transports, the F-15 Eagle fighter fleet maintenance was assigned to WRAMA in March, 1969. This was even before the manufacturing contract had been awarded. WRAMA joined the team that would evaluate the manufacturer's proposals. The Eagle Country facility and function came online on May 30, 1975, when a prototype was brought in for validation of the maintenance procedures, tooling, and the facility.

In addition to its maintenance functions, Robins also served as a supply base for a number of military actions, utilizing fleets of C-130 and C-141 aircraft. This included re-supply for Israel during the October, 1973 Yom Kippur War. Twelve C-130E transports were ferried to Israel and transferred to the Israeli Air Force. It was during this activity that the need for a stretched and aerial refueled C-141 became apparent. WRAMA performed these modifications to the existing aircraft, creating C-141Bs.

The US action in Grenada, in 1983, also was supplied from Robins AFB. In the late 1980s there was another change of name. During Desert Shield (1990-91), supplies and personnel were provided by transports operating from the Warner Robins Air Logistics Center.

The Spirit of Georgia was officially named during a ceremony at Robins AFB on December 11, 1995. It is one of only 21 B-2 bombers in the Air Force inventory. Most B-2s are named for states. Georgia was delivered to its home base at Whiteman AFB near Kansas City, Missouri, on November 14, 1995, scarcely a month before the public event in Georgia.

The Georgia Air National Guard's 116th Fighter Wing, based at Dobbins Air Reserve Base, had been flying the F-15 Eagle for ten years. In April, 1996 the unit became the 116th Bomb Wing and equipped with B-1B bombers. Due primarily to an air space issue, the 116th was relocated to Robins AFB. The wing occupied the vacated Strategic Air Command (SAC) alert facility.

The Air Force Reserve Command (AFRC) would take up residency at Robins on February 17, 1997. All Air Force Reserve and Air National Guard units report to this command.

The B-1 Bomber program was reorganized by the Department of Defense in the summer of 2001, and the 116th gave up their bombers. The wing was joined with the active duty, 93rd Air Control Wing (ACW), and became the first "blended" wing (active and National

Facing Page: The Mace missile system was another unmanned member of the tactical air force arsenal that was maintained at WRAMA.

Below: The ancestor of today's cruise missile was the TM-61 Matador. WRAMA had prime responsibility for this unmanned all-weather weapon system.

M. Steiner Archives

Guard in a single unit), operating the E-8C Joint STARS (Surveillance Target Attack Radar System) battlefield surveillance aircraft. The merged unit became the 116th ACW on October 1, 2002. This unit received their 17th and final E-8C on April 1, 2005, and continues to operate worldwide.

By 2007 Robins also hosted a number of unique and unusual units. The Air Force Reserve Band is based at Robins, and consists of different performing units who have issued many recordings over the years. With its 12,000 foot runway, Robins became one of the few bases capable of handling the NASA Space Shuttle, when mounted on its Boeing 747 transporter.

The second largest U.S. Air Force Museum is located adjacent to the base. Officially known as the "Museum of Aviation at Robins AFB," it was established in 1981, and continues to add aircraft and buildings to display the Air Force history. The Georgia Aviation Hall of Fame is housed within the museum complex.

Robins AFB and the Warner Robins Air Logistics Center have survived the three (1993, 1995 and 2005) Base Realignment and Closure (BRAC) Commission studies.

Some shuffling of units has occurred, including the recommended transfer of a portion of Naval Air Station (NAS) Atlanta's operations to Robins.

On January 11, 2007 the B-1B "Midnight Train in Georgia" took up permanent residence at the Museum of Aviation at Robins AFB. It was a homecoming for an aircraft that had served with the Georgia Air Guard.

Robins AFB and the Warner Robins Air Logistics Center is the largest single site industrial complex in Georgia, employing over 27,000 people and contributing more than $4 billion (including "ripple effect") to the state's economy. Personnel, both military and civilian, reside in more than 25 central Georgia counties. The Museum of Aviation and the Georgia Aviation Hall of Fame also attract over 500,000 visitors each year and generate substantial revenue to the area.

MOULTRIE

Spence Army Air Field

Spence Air Base

Spence Field

In 1930 the City of Moultrie purchased land northwest of downtown for a municipal airport. Named Clark Field, it was officially dedicated on October 9, 1934. In attendance was Georgia's U.S. Senator, Walter F. George, and other notables. When the Army Air Corps visited Moultrie in early 1941, looking for a training field site, the city assumed they would simply take control of Clark Field. However, the Air Corps deemed the site "inadequate" and instead selected a 1,600-acre site southeast of the city that was planted in tobacco and cotton. The city purchased the land and leased it to the Army Air Corps for $1 a year. The base was named after Lt. Thomas Spence, a World War I flight instructor who had died in a crash when his aircraft broke up over France. By the time of the Pearl Harbor attack, a skeleton crew of 27 officers and 39 enlisted men was already in place at Spence.

Spence Army Air Field was an Advanced Flight Training base. Most graduates became fighter pilots after training in North American T-6 Texans. In February, 1945 the Army Air Force was already anticipating the end of World War II and was quickly reducing the number of active training bases. Two classes of Basic Flight Training were established at Spence to accommodate cadets reassigned there when their original training bases were shut down.

Most Army Air Force training bases were ringed by auxiliary fields, both for practice and also for emergencies. These auxiliary fields might be just a few miles away or as much as 40 to 50 miles away. One Spence auxiliary field served a special purpose. In addition to Advanced Flight School, Spence was to provide Curtiss P-40 Warhawk transition training. This operation was established at the auxiliary field at Tifton Army Air Field, twenty-six miles away, and was intentionally isolated from the Moultrie operations.

When Spence closed in November, 1945, it had produced over 6,000 pilots. While there at Spence, many of those cadets had married or become engaged to local girls, and many returned to South Georgia after the war.

Following the start of the Korean Conflict, the U.S. Air Force re-opened a number of bases. Many Contract Flight Schools were established in order to quickly respond to the increased need for pilots. Hawthorne School of Aeronautics was selected in March, 1951 to open and operate Spence Air Base. When Hawthorne renovated the base early in 1951 they found clues about the many "tenants" – some legal and some not – during the base's five year closure. "No one had to tell us that elephants had lived in Hangar Three," was the report from one early Hawthorne employee. In fact, a circus had wintered at the base one year. More traditional uses included small businesses, a veterans' vocational school, and various agricultural functions. There even was a pimiento pepper processing plant. The old barracks had become a residence for transients.

Hawthorne was still in the process of getting the old base up and running when both aircraft and cadets began to arrive. Class 52-C would utilize the venerable North American T-6 Texan trainer. May 17, 1951 was officially the opening day.

Since it was a Contract Flying School, there was a U.S. Air Force contingent assigned to Spence, to monitor all training. Lt. Col. Stephen H.

M. Steiner Archives

Crosby, 3302nd Pilot Training Group Commander, arrived in May with a small staff. By October, the base was fully staffed and operational, the first class had graduated and 52-G student cadets were on site for training. This second class included cadets from Denmark, Belgium and the Netherlands. The inclusion of cadets from other Allied nations would continue throughout the Hawthorne years (1951-61).

By the base's first Hawthorne anniversary, five classes with a total of over 500 cadets had already graduated. The base held an Armed Forces Day Open House to celebrate their anniversary. The success of the training operation led to additional Air Force improvements to the base.

Community relations was a tradition at Spence. In "Operation Hospitality," a program which actually got its start during World War II, Moultrie families opened their homes to the cadets. Families of foreign cadets still occasionally visit the base site and the families that hosted these young men so many years ago.

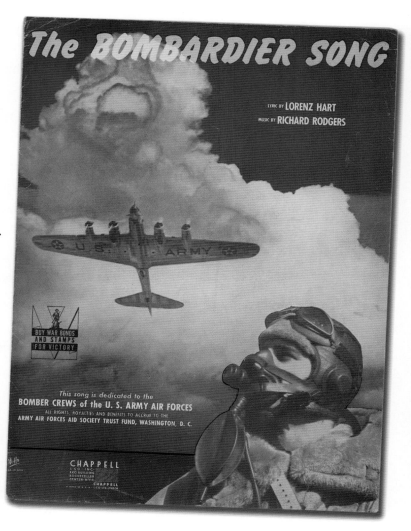

M. Steiner Archives

Late in 1953 the North American T-28A Trojan began to replace the aging T-6 fleet. Also that year, President Dwight D. Eisenhower arrived at Spence in the President's plane, a Lockheed Constellation, *Columbine*. This would become a regular occurrence whenever the President visited friends in nearby Thomasville. One host was his Secretary of the Treasury, George Humphries. Six such visits to Spence took place.

By the end of 1955 Spence had 500,000 flight training hours. An Army training program was added with the Cessna L-19 Bird Dog aircraft. The first jet trainer, the Cessna T-37 Tweetie Bird arrived in May of 1957 as part of Project Palm. Other aircraft that were used during the Hawthorne years included the Piper PA-18 Super Cub and the Beechcraft T-34 Mentor.

Various notables often arrived at Spence. One was the creator of the comic strip "Smilin' Jack," Zack Mosley, who visited in June, 1957 to do research for his comic strip. Spence would be featured in the strip starting that fall for about six months.

The first all jet (T-37) class, 61-F, arrived in March, 1960. In April, 1960 the Air Force announced termination of the Contract Flight School program. Training continued until the end of 1960 with classes 62-A and 62-B graduating. By the end of March 1961, Spence was once again inactive. The Hawthorne years had produced another 6,000 pilots.

This time the former military base took on a more planned and active use after closure. In 1968 it became home to Maule Air, Inc. All three World War II hangars still stand and are used for industrial and commercial ventures. The original control tower and water tank are also still standing. Spence has become a popular large outdoor venue for such events as Sunbelt Ag Expo, the largest agricultural trade show in North America. Most of the old ramp area has had exposition halls built on it, and other special events are also hosted there.

In an unusual move, the Air Force again put Spence to use as a training site from September, 2003 to October 30, 2006. This was the first such lease arrangement by the Air Force in over forty years. It became an auxiliary field to Moody AFB, Valdosta, for touch and go exercises. Improvements to Spence for that use included a new fire station and equipment. The facility officially opened on July 16, 2004 with Georgia's senior U.S. Senator, Saxby Chambliss, and then Air Force Chief of Staff, Gen. John P. Jumper, participating. General Jumper had started his Air Force career at Moody AFB in June 1966. The aircraft involved were the new Raytheon/Hawker Beechcraft T-6A "Texan II" turboprop trainers. Moody (Spence) was the first Air Force Base to put this new trainer into service.

Many of the graduates of Spence became famous. One Spence graduate walked on the moon. Charles Moss Duke attended and graduated the U.S. Naval Academy and was commissioned in 1957. He enlisted in the Air Force, received primary flight training at Spence and advanced training in North American F-86 Sabre jets at Moody AFB.

In April 1966 Duke was one of nineteen astronauts selected for the Apollo program. Serving as Capcom during the first lunar landing, it was Duke's southern drawl that responded to Neil Armstrong's *The Eagle has Landed* with, "Roger, *Tranquility*…you've got a bunch of guys about to turn blue…we're breathing again!"

Apollo 16 landed in April 1972 with Duke as lunar lander pilot. He was the tenth man to walk on the moon.

WWII Era Airports and Air Bases

CITY	NAME
Albany	Turner Air Field
Americus	Souther Field
Athens	Epps Field (operated by the US Navy, not designated NAS)
Atlanta	Candler Field Navy Air Station Atlanta
Augusta	Bush Field Daniel Field
Bainbridge	Bainbridge Army Air Field/Bainbridge Air Base
Brunswick	Glynco Navy Air Station
Columbus	Lawson Field (Fort Benning)
Douglas	Douglas Army Air Base
Hinesville	Liberty Army Air Field Wright Army Air Field
Macon	Cochran Army Air Field
Marietta	Cobb County Army Air Field/Rickenbacker Field/ Marietta Army Air Field
Moultrie	Spence Army Air Field/Spence Air Base/Spence Field
Rome	Navy Auxiliary Air Base (not designated NAS)
Savannah	Hunter Army Air Field Chatham Army Air Field Travis Field
Thomasville	Thomasville Army Air Field
Tifton	Tifton Army Air Field
Valdosta	Moody Army Air Field
Warner Robins	Southeast Air Depot/Robins Army Air Field/Wellston Air Depot
Waycross	Waycross Army Air Base

ATLANTA

Candler Field

Atlanta Municipal Airport

Hartsfield Atlanta International Airport

Hartsfield-Jackson Atlanta International Airport

The Atlanta Airport had a lengthy and difficult birth. After flight activity at Candler Field had increased enough to warrant one, the city struggled a long time over the question of even having an airport. Before it was an airfield, Candler Field was a race track.

Developed by the Asa Griggs Candler interests, Candler Race Track was intended to rival the Indianapolis Speedway that had recently opened. The newest rage in racing was the automobile, and race tracks seemed like certain financial success. The earliest flying at the track was for special events related to auto racing. Lincoln Beachey raced his Curtiss pusher biplane against a Stearns automobile and an Elyea-Austell motorcycle at the Candler race track in 1910. The automobile won.

One of many Curtiss aircraft "air mail" demonstrations took place on November 16 through 18, 1911. The air mail "route" began at Candler Race Track and ended about three miles away at Stewart Avenue, only partway to downtown Atlanta. At that point, the mail was dropped to a waiting postal truck. The whole delivery process – from airplane to truck to post office and finally a postman on motorcycle – only took a few hours from takeoff to delivery.

This restored 1918 postal mail plane visited the Atlanta Air Mail facility in 1968.

M. Steiner Archives

Auto racing in Atlanta did not generate enough fan support, and the Candler investment failed. The race track, and the infield that had served as a landing field for those early events, gradually fell into disuse. The old "airport" and infield became grazing grounds for cattle.

In 1918, Lindsey Hopkins, then chairman of the Aeronautical Committee of the Atlanta Chamber of Commerce, pleaded with the business community to establish an airport. World War I generated great interest in the use of airplanes, and after the Armistice that ended the war, a fleet of seventeen Army planes visited Candler Field. Still there was no action to establish an airport, but three pilots did set up shop at the old Candler Race Track. Beeler Blevins and Doug Davis are quite well known.

James H. Elliott holds a tire from his Curtiss JN-4 Jenny. He professed to have sold both Beeler Blevins and Doug Davis their first Jennies.

M. Steiner Archives

The third, a somewhat shadowy figure, was James Elliott. His reputation was a propensity to make grand – but uncorroborated – claims about his barnstorming days at Candler. He claimed he had the first airplane at the track, was the pilot for the first parachute jump in Atlanta and leased the field from Asa Candler so he could clear a portion of the infield and house his Curtiss JN-4 Jenny inside an army canvas airplane hangar.

In spite of this kind of use by local pilots and the occasional visiting aircraft, there is no listing of an Atlanta airport in a 1920 published list of airports and landing fields. The early '20s were the formative years for aviation in Atlanta and elsewhere. William B. Hartsfield, elected City of Atlanta Alderman in 1923, struck a deal with Candler in 1925 to lease the old race track. Part of the deal was that Atlanta would pay all real estate taxes. After the lease was signed in 1925, Hartsfield convinced Fulton County to remove the property from the tax rolls. Atlanta then had no tax bill to pay.

Hartsfield's reward was to be named chairman of the Aldermanic Aviation Committee. He also became the *de facto* manager of the airport. The Air Commerce Act of 1926 brought air mail service and the race for airway beacons. Hartsfield invited the Assistant Secretary of Commerce for Aeronautics to Atlanta for a site review and within weeks, Atlanta was awarded the beacon route.

Charles Lindbergh stopped in Atlanta on his goodwill tour in October of 1927. Additional Air Mail routes were awarded in 1928. Atlanta exercised its purchase option on the airport in 1929, and passenger service arrived in 1930.

Air races, special events, and the ongoing activities of Doug Davis and Beeler Blevins made Candler Field a real working airport.

The Ford Motor Company sponsored an annual "Reliability Air Tour" from 1925 through 1931. The purpose of these tours was to promote aviation (and perhaps to sell a few Ford Tri-Motor airplanes). The only year that the fleet of participating aircraft came to Atlanta, or any part of Georgia, was 1929. That fleet stopped at Augusta's Daniel Field on the way to an overnight stop in Jacksonville, Florida. The next morning, October 12, the fleet turned north to Miller Field in Macon, and then on to Atlanta.

Atlanta may have been the most memorable stop, but certainly not for the right reasons. It was raining, and the advance plane had broken down in Macon. The advance crew did not telephone Atlanta with the updated schedule, so forty airplanes arrived at Candler Field with very few spectators yet in place. Adding to the confusion was a lack of hotel space. It seems it was the weekend of a Georgia vs. Yale football game in Athens, and most of the Yale fans ("Eli's") were staying in Atlanta hotels.

In 1929 the Chicago Daily News published, "Homeward Flies the Mail," a narrative of a trip which occurred in October of that year from Montevideo, Uruguay to Chicago, Illinois. After describing the various Florida stops, the story noted that "the planes averaged 118 miles an hour…to Macon. …the first revolving beacon was sighted and a moment later Miller Field." And then, "The glow from Atlanta was ahead, then Candler Field, far outside the city…and we were down."

THE "MYSTERY SHIP" OF 1929. In 1929, prior to the National Air Races at Cleveland Airport, Thompson Products, Inc. was approached to donate a cup as first place award for a 50-mile free-for-all speed contest. An outstanding entry for this event was the red and black Travelair Mystery Ship of Douglas Davis, Atlanta, Ga. Davis' plane was powered by the Wright Whirlwind engine that Lindbergh made famous. Hopelessly outdistancing all other contestants, Davis won at an average speed which was remarkable for its day—194.90 m. p. h. His performance sounded the doom of the biplane for super-speed design. It also marked the first occasion a civilian plane had ever beaten military ships in speed competition. It was this 50-mile event of 1929 that suggested the permanent establishment of an annual international, free-for-all race to serve as a practical test of aeronautical progress — the now world-famous Thompson Trophy Race.

The Thompson Products Company sponsored the Thompson Trophy Race at the annual National Air Races and produced a series of color prints honoring the winners. In 1929, Doug Davis won the first Thompson Trophy Race piloting his Travel Air Mystery Ship.

M. Steiner Archives

Also in 1929, Atlanta pioneer pilot Doug Davis won the National Air Races, flying the Travel Air *Mystery Ship*.

The year 1932 was a pivotal year in the history of the Atlanta Airport. The first real terminal building was completed. Designated the Administrative Building, it combined everything then considered necessary for a modern airport. A large common waiting area, reminiscent of a railroad station, occupied much of the first floor. An open air observation area was above that, enabling people waiting for arrivals, and other air-minded individuals, a close-up view of the "giant" airliners of the day. One function not included in the Administration Building was a control tower. A low volume of flights and a lack of radio equipment on most aircraft made control towers unnecessary. It would be March, 1939 before a tower was added to the building.

The building was funded in large part by American Airways, who had insisted on having a proper terminal. That funding was accomplished by the advance payment to the City of Atlanta of ten years' rent. The air mail contracts were cancelled in 1934, and American failed to regain the Atlanta route.

A small Army unit was established at Candler in February, 1934 to oversee the Emergency Air Mail Service being flown by Army pilots and planes. At the conclusion of this "emergency," Delta Air Corporation, with a new air mail contract in hand, resumed service on July 4, 1934 from Ft. Worth to Atlanta. Later that year, Atlanta was stunned when Doug Davis was killed while leading the National Air Races in Cleveland.

In October, 1940, when so many Georgia cities were courting the Army Air Corps, the Army simply declared Candler Air Field an Army Air Field. Army improvements to the field would nearly double its size.

As the United States moved towards war, Delta Air Corporation was still headquartered in Monroe, Louisiana. In 1941 a new Delta General Office and

IVAN ALLEN
Chairman, Board of Directors
Ivan Allen Co.

THE ATLANTA SPIRIT
Altitude + Attitude

by

IVAN ALLEN

Author of *Atlanta from the Ashes, Rotary in Atlanta,*
County Consolidation, Fulton County Centennial.

Published by
Ivan Allen Company
Printers, Lithographers, Office Outfitters
Atlanta, Georgia

Above: Ivan Allen, Jr., then president of the Atlanta Chamber of Commerce, wrote and published this booklet in the 1950s to promote Atlanta and her future as an airline hub.

Left: The new Atlanta Airport was hampered by limited road access. The raw red dirt seen behind the terminal building is Interstate 85 in the early stages of construction.

M. Steiner Archives

134

137—Candler Field, Atlanta's Municipal Airport showing New Control Tower

© PHOTO BY EDGAR ORR

9A-H83

Atlanta's 1932 Administration Building was the hub of activity. The new (1939) control tower resembled a forest ranger tower.

Hangar Building was constructed in Atlanta, at a cost of $150,000, and Delta moved its corporate headquarters to Atlanta. The Delta 1941 Annual Report declared the building, "the most complete building of its type." Today this building – "Mahogany Row" – still serves Delta's senior management.

After the war, the volume of air traffic grew rapidly. New airlines were born, many with fairly modern, military surplus aircraft. The newest design concept for modern airports utilized concourses with gates dedicated to specific airlines. The model for this design was the only commercial airport owned by the United States government, Washington National, just outside

Right, Top: Utilizing plywood open-air concourses, the post WWII growth was quickly accommodated.

Right, bottom: Delta's distinctive round terminals at the end of their two concourses accommodated Delta's "Big Jets."

M. Steiner Archives

135

of Washington, D.C. It was opened in 1940, with the expectation that other cities would quickly follow.

World War II delayed all commercial airport construction. In 1948, Atlanta moved into the new age of aviation by constructing wooden, open-air concourses that used army surplus materials. The main terminal moved into a surplus military hangar, and the old Administration Building became the Air Mail Post Office. This complex was termed the Atlanta "temporary" Airport.

In the 1950s, *The Atlanta Spirit, Altitude + Attitude*, a small booklet by Ivan Allen, stated that "Atlanta has borne, and still bears, a variety of nicknames. Of all these names, I think the Gate City is most fitting. Atlanta has not one but three gates. ... And the third is that of Air Transportation." He goes on to say, "fifteen years ago…70 million people could be reached in twenty-four hours by rail, today half of the entire population of the world can be reached from Atlanta's municipal airport within twenty-four hours." Allen's booklet, and aggressive campaigning by the business community, forced the city to consider a new airport.

Although the initial planning began in 1950, ground was not broken until 1957. The "new" airport opened on May 3, 1961. It was a sprawling series of enclosed concourses requiring long walks to almost any of the 72 gates. Most (almost all) airport amenities were located in the central terminal, with only

Below: A view of the Delta Terminal, c. 1961.

The Atlanta History Center

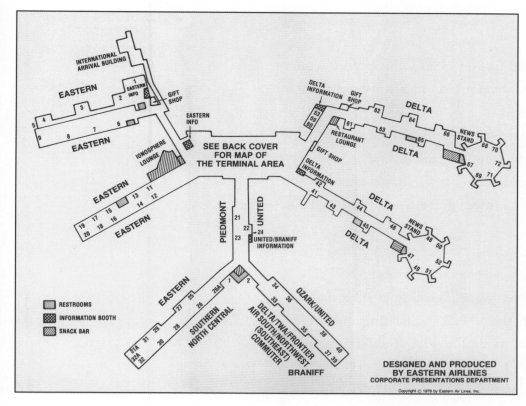

DESIGNED AND PRODUCED
BY EASTERN AIRLINES
CORPORATE PRESENTATIONS DEPARTMENT

Copyright © 1979 by Eastern Air Lines, Inc.

Above: The number of airlines seen on this 1979 map reflects the era of air travel expansion. Many of these carriers either merged or were bought out. Some simply disappeared.

M. Steiner Archives

one snack area on each individual concourse. Intersecting runways were used to adjust for wind direction.

Eastern, with 17 gates, shut down in 1991. National had 2 gates and merged with Pan American Airways in 1980. Southern, with 4 gates, merged with North Central in 1979 to become Republic. Piedmont, with 2 gates, merged with US Airways in 1989. TWA had only 1 gate and merged with American Airlines in 2001. Northwest had only 1 gate and is currently operating under Chapter 11 bankruptcy. Braniff, with 2 gates, quit in 1982, United, with 6 gates, emerged from Chapter 11 in 2006. Delta, with 27 gates, filed for Chapter 11 bankruptcy in 2005. The airport was designed for six million passengers a year, but 9.5 million people passed through the terminal in its first year.

As this "new" airport exceeded design capacity, some airlines began the practice of utilizing shuttle buses to carry checked in passengers to aircraft out on the tarmac. In effect, they created additional "gates" without any construction. In 1964, planning for yet another "new" terminal was begun. Again, the latest design was utilized. This would be a midfield terminal flanked by long parallel runways.

In February, 1971 Mayor William B. Hartsfield died. He had seen nearly a half century of airport and commercial aviation development in Atlanta. The airport was renamed William B. Hartsfield Atlanta Airport. When the airport's first international service was established by Eastern on July 1st, the airport added "International" to its name.

Early in 1977 the new airport began construction. On Sept. 21, 1980 this new "midfield" airport opened with three parallel runways, and a planned annual capacity of 55 million passengers. Four parallel terminal buildings were connected by an automated rail system providing access to the four concourses and 138 gates. The opening was preceded by special sections of the Atlanta Journal-Constitution with a special bannerhead, "Hartsfield Airport…Aviation's New Giant." Opening events included a visit by President Jimmy Carter. Even at the opening of the midfield terminal, it was noted that it already would be at 90% of design capacity. A fourth runway was added in 1984, and the need for either another runway or a second airport became obvious. After considerable study and intensive planning, construction of the fifth runway was started in April, 2001.

In 2003 former Atlanta Mayor, Maynard H. Jackson, died suddenly. He had been a strong supporter of the airport and its growth, and he was mayor when the massive midfield terminal opened. In his honor, the airport was renamed Hartsfield-Jackson Atlanta International Airport on October 20, 2003.

The May 17, 2006 Atlanta Journal-Constitution front page bragged, "cleared for landing" as the airport's fifth runway was ready at last. The ceremonial opening featured bands, champagne, free airliner rides, and speeches. A Delta Air Lines 767 made the official first landing and taxied through the traditional firehose arch of water. The $1.28 billion runway went into regular service on May 27th.

Plans for the future include another nearly $6 billion in improvements. This will include another terminal, almost creating two adjacent airports.

Below: A rainy evening at the Atlanta Airport, c. 1965.

The Atlanta History Center

Henry Tift Myers

Henry Tift "Hank" Myers was born in 1907, the same year that Ben T. Epps made his historical flight in Athens, Georgia. Myers was named after Capt. Henry Harding Tift who founded Tifton, Georgia in 1872. He learned to fly while a student at the University of Georgia and paid for his lessons by boxing at night for $50 a fight. In 1932 he graduated at the top of his Army Air Corps training class. In 1933 he became a co-pilot with American Airlines.

After the attack on Pearl Harbor, at age 35, Myers was ordered back into the Army Air Corps and served as an aide and pilot for Lt. Gen. Harold S. George, commanding general of the Air Transport Command. Gen. George recommended Myers for the job of piloting *The Sacred Cow*, a Douglas C-54 reconfigured as a presidential aircraft for Franklin D. Roosevelt. Myers attained the distinction of being the first presidential pilot and flew President Roosevelt to the historic conference of Roosevelt, Stalin and Churchill at Yalta. During his storied career, Myers flew many international dignitaries and heads-of-state including Eleanor Roosevelt, Winston Churchill and Madame Chiang Kai-shek.

Myers piloted both predecessors to *Air Force One*, *The Sacred Cow* and *The Independence*. He established a number of world records for speed and distance and was the first to fly non-stop across the Atlantic after Lindbergh. He flew the first non-stop London-to-Washington, D.C., the first non-stop Hawaii-to-Alaska and the first non-stop Ceylon-to-Australia. He was also the first to fly around the world at the equator.

Henry Tift Myers was inducted into the Georgia Aviation Hall of Fame in 2007, exactly 100 years after Georgia's first powered flight.

Peacetime Boom

Emerging General Aviation Supports Georgia's Growth

As the United States geared up for World War II, there was a great need for trained pilots and good flying weather. Along with California and the Southwest, Georgia was an ideal location for primary, basic, advanced and navigation training. The Savannah District of the U.S. Army Corps of Engineers was mandated to design and specify everything from large-scale military airfields, to depots and small specialized training airfields. They oversaw the construction of paved and multiple runways, and airfields of every size were spread throughout Georgia; the majority being located in the relatively flat terrain of the southern portion of the state.

Primary aviation schools were constructed in Americus, Albany and Douglas. Basic schools were built in Macon and Augusta and advanced schools in Moultrie, Valdosta and Albany. Robins Field and dozens of auxiliary airfields designed to relieve traffic at other fields were also created.

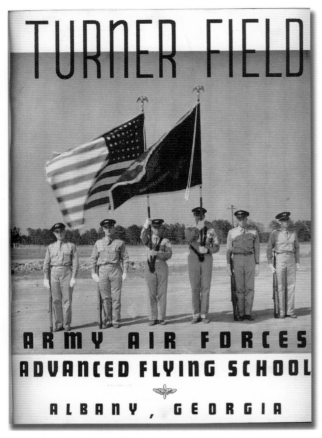

Turner Army Air Field,
a WWII Advanced
Flying School.

M. Steiner Archives

Although Army Aviation's presence in Georgia goes back to the early 1900s, the most extensive development of airports in Georgia occurred during the Second World War. At the height of the war the Army Air Force had twenty-two installations in the state. At the end of the conflict, most of these airfields, depots and bases reverted or were deeded back to the local communities, and this became the basis for Georgia's current airport system.

During World War II, as they were exposed to air travel in newsreels and in movies, Americans became aware that flying was within their reach as another mode of transportation. Glamorous Hollywood movie stars, promoting the sale of war bonds, were seen flying from coast-to-coast.

This collage was made possible by Tuck Jackson, an Aviation Machinist Mate 2nd Class stationed at NAS Atlanta for the duration of the war.

Collection of T. M. "Tuck" Jackson

As the war wound down, Army Air Forces personnel from all walks of life returned home. Some had been officer pilots, bombardiers and navigators. Others had served as gunners, engineers, radio men and mechanics. All of these people had become accustomed to flying while serving in the Army Air Forces. By the time WWII came to a close, the American public was ready to give aviation a go.

THE GROWING POPULARITY OF COMMERCIAL AIR SERVICE

The years following the war were a boom time for the country. Most Americans were working, and they had money in their pockets and leisure time to travel. They now had a more global view, and exotic destinations like Cuba, Hawaii, Bermuda, New York City, and Puerto Rico were now accessible. In Georgia, Delta Air Lines ("The Airline of the South") and Eastern Air Lines (formerly Pitcairn) flew to these locations, and people started packing their luggage.

In the 1950s, Delta opened flights from New Orleans to the Caribbean and Venezuela. In the years following, with the introduction of their first jets, the DC-8s, Delta used the slogan: "Fly Delta's Big Jets to Florida!" and Bob "Super DC-8" Hope was the company's spokesperson. Delta became the launch operator of the Convair CV-880 and the DC-9. By 1970, Delta was an all-jet aircraft airline.

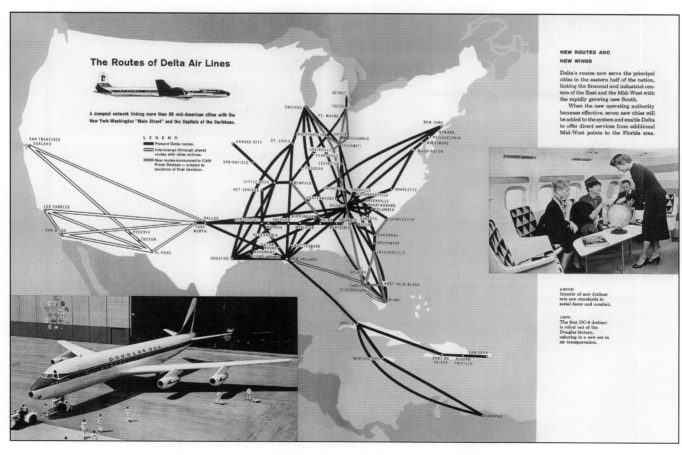

Effective Dec. 14, 1967 thru Jan. 31, 1968

DELTA
AIR LINES

FLY BIG
TO FLORIDA
FLY
DELTA

Bob Hope

DELTA
AIR
LINES

See Bob Hope soon in "The Private Navy of Sgt. O'Farrell"

INFLUENCING GEORGIA'S AVIATION

After World War II, four major advances occurred in general and commercial aviation that significantly affected the aviation industry in the state: military bases were transferred to municipal ownership; commercial aviation enjoyed a growth spurt; business aviation increased in appeal; and Carl Sanders was elected governor (1963-1967). A fifth major factor in the growth of aviation in Georgia came more than a generation later – the visionary airport program of Governor Zell Miller (1991-1999).

As military bases were transferred to municipal governance, city commissioners and chambers of commerce had the task of deciding the fate of the surplus air bases, equipment and buildings; as well as a pool of trained military personnel, military aircraft and aircraft manufacturing operations.

Many of the aviators returning home from the war wanted to remain in aviation, choosing to locate near a former base or existing airport. Some of them turned to crop dusting to continue flying; others offered flying lessons and sold fuel to keep the airports alive and viable. Guy Hill, Sr. was one Georgian who made the transition.

Left: The consummate spokesperson, comedian and actor, Bob Hope.

Delta Air Transport
Heritage Museum

Thomasville – utilized as an air base during WWII – was one of a number of bases transferred to municipal governance after WWII.

Collection of M. L. Shettle

GUY HILL, SR.

Guy Hill, Sr. had an illustrious aviation career. He was a decorated Navy pilot, airplane mechanic, fixed base of operations (FBO) owner and politician. After his years in the Navy, Hill knew that he wanted to remain in aviation – any way he could. After some time in Texas, he came home to Georgia to operate

A youthful Guy Hill, Sr.

Hill Aircraft

a small airport in Fairburn where he worked on airplanes, performed stunts and took passengers on short flights called "hops." In 1951, doing business as Hill Aircraft Services at Fulton County Airport, Hill built up his customer base and eventually leased office space.

Fulton County Airport (later renamed Fulton County Brown Field) began operation in 1950, and the FBO had a couple of owners before Hill bought the operation in 1955 from Gene Barwick. At the time, Barwick Industries was the largest manufacturer of tufted carpet, and Barwick had bought the FBO so he would have a place to house his DC-3. The operation proved to be more trouble than he had counted on, so he decided to sell.

During the 1950s, the FBO business at Fulton County Airport proved to be steady work for Hill, but it really got a boost a few years later when a flight training operation at Hartsfield closed down and sent all of their 100 students his way. By the end of the decade, Hill was firmly entrenched at Fulton County Airport and the business was growing steadily.

In the 1960s, business aviation was emerging as an industry unto itself, and most of Atlanta's major corporations downtown looked to Hill as their closest

Aerial view, Fulton County Airport, 1964.

The Atlanta History Center

provider of general aviation services. Eventually, Hill Aviation was faced with the challenge of losing those same corporate customers when they negotiated with the County to build their own facilities. Coca-Cola was the first to do so, and others followed suit. In later years, Hill faced stiff competition from the "chains," large aviation companies that established fixed based operators all over the country. Hill Aviation survived all those challenges. Today, the company is known as Hill Aircraft and Leasing Corporation and is led by the founder's son, Guy Hill, Jr.

Guy Hill, Sr. died in February 2004 and was inducted into the Georgia Aviation Hall of Fame in April of that same year.

DEKALB PEACHTREE AIRPORT: MILITARY TO GENERAL

Hill Aviation, circa 1950.

Hill Aircraft

War's end also brought change to DeKalb Peachtree Airport in Chamblee just eight miles northeast of downtown Atlanta. Originally a farmland field, the

(continued on page 150)

E. Patrick Epps
02/23/1934

When Ben T. Epps, Georgia's aviation pioneer, was killed in a plane crash in October, 1937, he left behind a wife, nine children and an auto service garage business. Youngest of the five boys, Pat was three when the accident occurred, and he was left with no memory of his famous father. With the outbreak of World War II, eight-year-old Pat watched brothers Ben and Harry enlist in the Army Air Corps and become pilots. Ben Epps, Jr. gained some notoriety by flying C-46s "over the hump" from India to China, and in 1994 was inducted into the Georgia Aviation Hall of Fame. His sisters Evelyn and Virginia worked at the Naval Air Station Atlanta as ground instructors and instrument simulation trainers with a new device called a "Link Trainer." Pat, however, had no strong urge toward aviation.

What Pat did inherit from his dad was a strong interest in building and designing. In high school, he excelled at math and science and set his sights on an engineering degree from Georgia Tech. During his senior year of high school, his brother Douglas finally convinced him to learn to fly, and after six hours of instruction, at the age of 18, Pat Epps soloed. He managed another two hours before closing his log book in the fall of 1952 and heading to Atlanta for his freshman year. Because he had four brothers who served as pilots in the military, Pat joined the Air Force R.O.T.C. program at Tech and received his commission as 2nd Lt. in the spring of 1956. Even though he had a slight astigmatism, he still qualified as a navigator. Prior to beginning his military obligation, he married his high school sweetheart, Ann Hailey, and moved to Seattle as part of the flight test team on the Boeing 707 project.

While at Boeing, Pat met a captain, a navigator, who was there to pick up a B-52. Pat told him that he was headed to San Antonio, Texas for navigator training in the fall, and the captain told him bluntly to do whatever he could to change his designation to pilot. Pat ate carrots from Seattle to San Antonio to improve his vision and his chances. Later, he was allowed to retake his physical, and after some convincing, he began pilot training.

He completed his primary training in Beech's T-34 Mentor and his advanced and multi-engine training in North American T-28s and B-25s. By his own admission, Pat wasn't so great at the military part, but he was a very good pilot and graduated with distinction. For the next two years he flew as co-pilot in one of Boeing's four-engine C-97 Stratofreighters. When it came time for reassignment, Pat requested any base in the south, or, perhaps Wright-Patterson in Ohio. Instead, he received orders to Roswell, New Mexico, where he spent the next three years flying over one thousand hours in twin-engine Fairchild C-123 Providers.

His military career over in 1963, Pat, his wife and two children went to Huntsville, Alabama to work for his brother, George, as an engineer at an aerospace company. In the fall of 1963, Pat answered an ad in a flying magazine about becoming a Mooney dealer. With the purchase of a brand new Mark 20, Pat and George were declared Mooney dealers for all of northern Alabama. Unfortunately, there already was a dealer for northern Alabama, and there wasn't room for two. Wanting to return to Georgia anyway, they eventually bought a Mooney distributorship at Hartsfield-Atlanta Airport. Two years later they needed more space, so Pat met with Ned Woodruff at DeKalb Peachtree Airport, and instead of leasing space, Ned offered to sell his business. In May of 1965, Epps Aviation Services began operation with 19 employees.

Epps Aviation celebrated forty years in business in the spring of 2005 and the aviation heritage of the Epps family continued with Pat's two daughters, Marian and Elaine, and his son, Patrick, Jr. involved with the business. By 2007, Epps Aviation had grown to more than 200 employees. In a small, cluttered room at the back of one of the massive hangars are many of the reminders of the link to the beginning of aviation in Georgia including a sign that reads "Epps Garage, Athens, Ga."

A longtime air show performer in his familiar red, white and blue aerobatic Beechcraft Bonanza, Pat Epps gave an enormous amount of his time and resources to numerous aviation causes and organizations. Among those was his support of the Royal Air Force's program during the 1980s for training handicapped individuals to fly in a specially designed aircraft used by Epps Flight School for that purpose. He was an honoree of the 1988 Gathering of Eagles, an annual event celebrating aviation heritage and honoring distinguished aviation pioneers. In June 1994, he piloted a DC-3 over Normandy as veteran WWII paratroopers jumped to commemorate the 50th anniversary of the D-Day landings. Throughout his career he provided ongoing support to technical schools and organizations involved in aviation education, and he became a board member of the Georgia Aviation Hall of Fame at its inception.

(continued from page 147)

site was the only area in northern Atlanta that had the large, flat, open space necessary to create an airport. The Army utilized the field as Camp Gordon, a World War I training base. After the war, realtor T.R. Sawtell purchased the property, intending to sell parcels of farmland. However, the newly formed Atlanta Aero Club prevailed upon Sawtell to hold 300 acres of the farmland to build an airport. It wasn't until 1940 that DeKalb County finally purchased the land. The first plane landed on dirt runways on February 12, 1941.

From 1940-1945, the property was leased from the County by the U.S. Navy, initially as a Naval Reserve aviation base then quickly expanding into a full-fledged Naval Air Station. By the 1950s, advances in jet engine technology led the Navy to eventually move the Air Station to Dobbins Air Force Base, where it could share the use of its longer runways. In 1959 control of the DeKalb County Airport, as it was known at the time, was returned incrementally to the county which quickly opened the facility to civilians as DeKalb Peachtree Airport – fondly known as "PDK."

Under the supervision of H.F. Manget, Jr., the first airport manager and William E. Jayne, the chief air traffic controller, flight operations increased rapidly. In 1963, FAA personnel and equipment arrived, taking control of air traffic. Improvements on the facility continued and in 1968, a new 5,000 foot all-weather runway was completed, providing a parallel runway system. Sites were leased to private corporations.

Approximately $2.5 million was spent on leaseholder improvements. By 1975, more than 400 aircraft were based at PDK and 48 corporations had headquarters or representatives on the field.

By 1980, PDK had upped the ante, producing a total annual economic impact of $74 million to the DeKalb and Atlanta areas again revealing its worth as a self-sufficient enterprise fund of the county.

Classified as a general aviation reliever airport for the Atlanta metropolitan area, PDK generates impressive economic numbers. In 1991, for example, a total of 563 aircraft based at PDK paid a total of $2.3 million dollars to the county in personal property taxes on their aircraft. Additional income for the county comes from the purchase of fuel for each aircraft. These "fuel flowage fees" exceeded over three-quarter million dollars in 1990-1991.

DeKalb County collected over $2.5 million in rents from tenants on the airport for the same period. Add to that the number of people employed at

Naval Air Station Atlanta, from the air, circa 1946.

Collection of M. L. Shettle

This is the Naval Air Station/Chamblee patch of the 1940s.

M. Steiner Archives

the airport (1,200 in 1991) who likely live in, spend their paychecks in and pay taxes to the county.

Over the past 30 years, PDK has averaged approximately 230,000 takeoffs and landings per year. In 1999 alone, a total of 239, 230 flights were recorded at the airport. In 2006, the state listed 608 aircraft based at PDK. Fuel flowage fees generated $1,223,418 from FBOs and $19,800 from the corporate sector. $2,150,000 (about $179,000 a month) in rent was collected from tenants. Also in 2006, PDK was ranked as the second busiest airport in Georgia in number of flight operations per year.

By 2007, the airport was ranked the third largest property taxpayer in DeKalb County with more than 800 people employed in aviation-related jobs there. The airport also generates $50 million in travel and operating cost savings and 3,600 jobs created by non-airport businesses which have indicated they would leave the county if the airport were to close.

All told, PDK is responsible for an estimated 7,300 jobs in DeKalb County, generating $130 million in personal income for county residents. In terms of economic output for the county (total dollar value of all goods and services produced), the airport is directly and indirectly responsible for $819 million of the gross product in the county.

Carl Sanders, B-17 pilot.

Governor Carl Sanders

CARL SANDERS

Carl Sanders, Governor of the State of Georgia from 1963 to 1967, and native son of Augusta, was one of the many returning WWII aviators, having served as a pilot of a B-17 "Flying Fortress" out of England. Sanders came home brimming with enthusiasm for aviation, convinced that it could boost the economic future of the state. He also discerned that a love of flying had emerged among the general populace.

The newly elected Sanders had a vision to build and improve airports all across the state. His ultimate motivation was to put an airport in every county in Georgia. He came close to achieving his dream. In 1968, a study found that nearly 70 percent of the state population lived within 25 miles of one of the twelve major carrier airports.

Sanders also hoped to attract new businesses and industries to Georgia by offering them easy access to every region of the state and by encouraging the expansion of local communities and their airports. To accomplish this, he used his secret weapon, John Bennett.

Bennett was consumed with every aspect of flying, and as head of the Aviation Division of the Georgia Department of Industry and Trade, he was the perfect person to generate excitement in small communities and to convince their leaders of the value of an airport. In a 1966 interview, Bennett jokingly shared his complicated method of choosing sites in rural Georgia to build new airports: he threw darts at a large state map hanging on a wall in his office. Soon, every community Bennett visited was sending a representative to Governor Sanders to hear that the FAA's share in building the airport was not nearly as important as the effort of the Chamber of Commerce and County Commissioners.

Tapping into the Federal Aviation Administration's (FAA) matching funding program for airport development, and looking to attract federal funds, Sanders asked communities to contribute $25,000 which the state would then match. Sanders' program provided the seed money – $25,000 in state funds – to attract $50,000 from the FAA in order to get these communities interested.

Sanders was the first Georgia Governor to dedicate a new airport. At the 1963 dedication in Washington, Georgia, Sanders declared that "every dollar

Governor Sanders at the dedication of the Louisville airport in July of 1966.

City of Louisville

we invest in airports will be returned a hundredfold." He believed that airports would enable the growth of industry and used this promise to convince counties and localities to build airports.

In 1963, four new airports were completed in Georgia. In 1964, seven more completed airports were added. And in 1965, sixteen airports were either newly constructed or improved. The Louisville Airport was the most quickly constructed in the state, being completed in only two months. State, city and federal funds totaling $150,000 went in to building the airport with a 3,500 foot runway.

A total of forty-two airports were built during Carl Sanders' four-year term. Fifteen of those airports were built in the span of two years and airports were still being built or were on the drawing board after he left office – a tremendous impact.

The towns that benefited the most from the governor's airport program were those rural places that had been nearly isolated by the interstate highway system. Airports put these small towns in the middle of Georgia's industrial boom as business after business followed most every airport.

To ensure the building of an airport, Governor Sanders often dipped into the Governor's Emergency Fund to pay

Governor Sanders flew to most airport dedications, piloting the aircraft himself.

Governor Carl Sanders

shares of matching funds owed by small localities that could not otherwise collect funds through taxes and other levies. Blairsville, Georgia is a good example.

In 1964, Blairsville had a population of 434 – the area was poor, the kind of place tourists passed through but certainly wouldn't stop to have a bite to eat or rest before setting off on the next leg of their journey south to Florida or north, toward home. Sanders believed an airport would vitalize the mountain town and construction began in earnest – in part, from monies produced out of the Emergency Fund. In the end, the Blairsville Airport in Union County cost the people of Blairsville $6,000 to build. The total cost of the field was $175,000. Three weeks after completion, as if to once again emphasize the idea that airports attract industry, a shoe factory moved into Blairsville and employed nearly every person of working age in the town and surrounding area. In 1966, the airport was being used daily by poultry company officials, doctors and private pilots looking for a place to land before heading into the rugged mountains.

Economic development was Carl Sanders' touchstone. The number of airports in Georgia rose by 46 percent from 1962-1968 due to his fervent belief in aviation. As governor, Sanders developed more airports than any other Georgia official, giving the state the modern airport system it enjoys today. Carl Sanders was inducted into the Georgia Aviation Hall of Fame in 1997.

THE ECONOMICS OF AVIATION

Carl Sanders took office and pledged to bring $1 billion in industry to the state during his administration, and he did just that – primarily through air transportation. Invariably, when a new airport was built, a new industry appeared adjacent to the field.

In his quest for industries, Governor Sanders said that the first question asked by the business community was usually, "Where is the nearest airport?" In a 1963 interview, Governor Sanders explained why business executives emphasize the importance of air service in selecting a site for a plant: "To get executives where they must go, to place parts and technicians where they are needed, and to make emergency deliveries, more and more companies are operating their own aerial fleets."

In 1963, nearly one-half million private aircraft were being used, mostly by businessmen. Aviation service for executives and their companies remains tremendously big business.

Carl Sanders happened to be in town the day Eastern Air Lines landed the first commercial jet airliner at Bush Field in Augusta.

Governor Carl Sanders

AUGUSTA

Official Quarterly Publication of Augusta Chamber of Commerce   50c   WINTER 1967

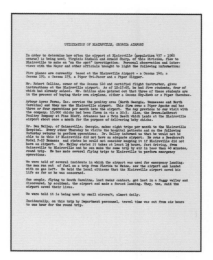

Georgia DOT personnel flew from Atlanta to Blairsville for an "on the spot" investigation. The last line casually mentions that "travel time was cut from six hours to one."

Other airports were "custom-built" to accommodate industry: JACKSON COUNTY AIRPORT

Jackson County Airport (JCO), near Jefferson, Georgia, was originally developed in 1954 as a private airport for Jefferson Mills, Inc. By 1966, the mill was purported to be the world's most modern textile mill. The original airport consisted of a 3,100-foot, north/south runway and a 2,700-foot east/west runway. The first corporate aircraft owned by Jefferson Mills was a Twin Beech D18. This was replaced by a Beech Twin Bonanza. Eventually, the mill purchased a Beech King-Air.

In 1965, the airport was converted to a public facility. Since that time, four different fixed base operators have provided services at JCO. The airport was officially dedicated on May 5, 1968 with two former governors, one former congressman and several other distinguished citizens participating in the ceremony. It is interesting to note that, while a 1961 improvement on the Atlanta Municipal Airport cost $22 million, an improvement program for Jackson County Airport during the same period cost approximately $247,000.

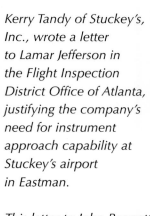

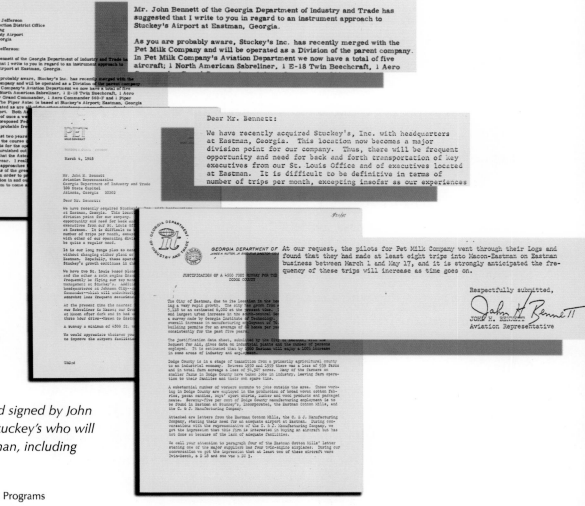

Kerry Tandy of Stuckey's, Inc., wrote a letter to Lamar Jefferson in the Flight Inspection District Office of Atlanta, justifying the company's need for instrument approach capability at Stuckey's airport in Eastman.

This letter to John Bennett from Stuckey's explains that Macon is the closest airport with a runway capable of accommodating company aircraft.

This memo addressed to the Georgia Department of Industry and Trade and signed by John Bennett, lists companies other than Stuckey's who will benefit from a longer runway in Eastman, including Winn-Dixie and Pepsi-Cola.

Georgia Department of Transportation Aviation Programs

WASHINGTON-WILKES AIRPORT

In the early '60s, the Pet Milk Company in Washington, Georgia was threatening to leave Wilkes County because the airport was sorely in need of improvement. Company executives wanted to visit the facility more often, but the 2,500-foot strip could not accommodate the company jet, a Sabreliner. The company's owner made it clear that if improvements were made to the airport, not only would Pet Milk stay in Georgia, he would expand the plant and increase employment. County commissioners assured Pet Milk that an adequate airport would be provided and set the process of funding and building in motion.

Governor Sanders in the cockpit of the state-owned Twin Beechcraft H18.

Governor Carl Sanders

In the end, a $151,000 air terminal was constructed as promised, and the Washington-Wilkes airport was dedicated in April, 1963. It was a joint city-county project, built in cooperation with the FAA. One half of the amount was furnished by the FAA, and one fourth each by the City of Washington and Wilkes County. The Pet Milk Company responded by expanding its milk collecting and processing facilities, hiring 150 new employees.

CARROLL COUNTY AIRPORT

Carrollton's 2,500-foot runway was lengthened to 3,100 feet because industry began moving in larger planes. Airport administrators approved an extension to 4,500 feet when a giant wire manufacturing plant, Southwire, located there and started a partnership with a company that owned a JetStar. The world's first executive jet, the JetStar was produced in Marietta, Georgia.

Statistics prepared in 1965 by the FAA's Regional Planning Office in Atlanta reveal that, as of December 17, the average number of publicly-owned airports across the country was 38 percent while in Georgia, that number was 49 percent. Nationwide, the average number of airports open to the public was 68 percent compared with 75 percent of the public in Georgia enjoying access to the state's airports. And, the nationwide average of paved runways was 28 percent while in Georgia, that number was 40 percent. The figures were based on a total of 159 airports.

On April 12, 1966, in his dedication speech at the Roosevelt Memorial Airport, a new, $150,000 facility three miles north of Warm Springs, Sanders reminded attendants that President Franklin Delano Roosevelt never shied away from bold innovation and imaginative approaches to a solution. He said that Roosevelt "fully realized that industrial and technological changes required equally great social and economic changes."

Sanders closed his dedication by emphasizing that, "What was true during the 1930s is even more true today. The nation, the state, or the community which wants to keep abreast of our changing times, and which wants to take advantage of the many economic and social benefits offered by modernization and growth, must never be satisfied simply with the way things are and have been."

The Federal Program and ACCG

In October of 1963, the U.S. government announced that – under a $76 million allocation from the Federal Aviation Agency – federal construction funds would be made available for improvements or additions to civil airports in Georgia. Local governments had to match the funds on a 50-50 basis. The emphasis was to be on development of the smaller, general-purpose airports. Because more counties were becoming the operating agencies for the airports, they were deeply involved in the FAA aviation and airport program. Governor Sanders made state grants available, advising county commissioners to "get your airport construction plans in order, tell us what you want to do and we'll try to help you do it."

The Association County Commissioners of Georgia (ACCG) encouraged its membership to embrace the development of a modern airport as a source of economic development. ACCG ensured that its membership was aware of these opportunities by featuring articles in its Georgia County Government magazine on successful airport ventures made by various counties, as well as providing information on how a county could qualify for financial assistance in the federal aid airport program.

The FAA made grants to communities of up to 50 percent of the cost of land and approved airport construction on projects programmed. All airport facilities were eligible except buildings. To qualify for federal aid, each community had to be included in the National Airport Plan, which was revised annually by the FAA. The State Aviation Division offered assistance to Georgia communities in preparing a request for federal aid, planning and site selection.

Through Sanders' leadership, guidance from the Department of Industry and Trade and support from ACCG, dozens of counties built airports which not only helped them gain new industries but also encouraged existing companies to stay and expand.

Aircraft Built In Georgia

Georgia's aircraft manufacturing industry covers the entire range of fixed-wing aircraft. Georgia-based manufacturers produce aircraft that are considered the smallest and largest, slowest and fastest, least and most expensive, and most basic to most luxurious in the world. In addition, numerous other companies across the state provide manufacturing support to the aerospace industry in Georgia and elsewhere.

With historical roots that date back to 1930, **Gulfstream Aerospace Corporation** today produces the Gulfstream G550 – the flagship in the company's family of business-jet airplanes and the acknowledged leader in executive/corporate aircraft.

Located in Savannah since 1967, Gulfstream has produced over 1,500 of the most technologically-advanced business aircraft for corporate, government, private and military customers around the world. Of the 275 Fortune 500 companies that operate business-jet aircraft, more than 100 of them operate Gulfstream jets.

On the plant floor at Gulfstream Aerospace Corporation.

© Gulfstream Aerospace Corporation

The latest version of the largest air transport, the C-5M Super Galaxy, took to the skies on June 20, 2006 at the **Lockheed-Martin** plant in Marietta, Georgia. Lockheed reopened the U.S. Army's vacated "Bell Bomber" plant in 1951. This same plant continues to produce the venerable C-130 Hercules, and more recently, the most advanced war plane in the world, the F-22 Raptor.

Based in Moultrie since 1968, **Maule Air, Inc.** produces a wide variety of short takeoff or landing (STOL) configurations including traditional tail draggers, tricycle gear, float and amphibious float versions. Power plants range from 180 HP to the Allison turbine of 400 HP. Maule is the oldest of the few small aircraft manufacturers in Georgia and ranks as the third largest single-engine aircraft manufacturer in the U.S.

Thrush Aircraft, Inc. in Albany produce agricultural distribution aircraft, better known as crop dusters. The Thrush history in Georgia dates back to 1970 when Rockwell Standard moved production of their Ag Commander S-2 to Albany. Today, the Thrush is generally recognized as the most reliable of the three major producers of this agricultural distribution aircraft.

Aircraft Manufacturing & Development Co. (AMD) was established in Eastman in 1997 to produce the Zodiac XL. The inexpensive Zodiac and its big brother, the Alarus, are all-metal, low-wing, two-seat entry level aircraft.

Leroy "Roy" Grumman was a quiet, unassuming and brilliant engineer. He flew as Naval Aviator No. 1216 in the early days of military aviation, earned a degree in aeronautical engineering from MIT and founded an aircraft repair shop, The Grumman Aircraft Engineering Company, with four former associates from Loening Aeronautical Engineering Corporation.

© Gulfstream Aerospace Corporation

 # GULFSTREAM AEROSPACE CORPORATION

Like many early aviation companies, Gulfstream Aerospace Corporation came from humble beginnings. In January of 1930 Leroy "Roy" Grumman and a few other aviation pioneers, all formerly with Loening Aeronautical Engineering Corporation, rented a small garage in Baldwin, New York and founded the Grumman Aircraft Engineering Company. It was not the best time to start a business. The Great Depression was taking its toll and many companies were fighting just to stay alive. Initially, Grumman survived by repairing Loening aircraft and by building aluminum pontoons and truck bodies. Then, on April 2, 1931, Grumman won its first contract to build a new airplane for the U.S. Navy.

A well-educated aeronautical engineer and test pilot, Roy Grumman was more interested in building the best aircraft than he was in building a big business. Nevertheless, the XFF-1 was a great start for both. Nicknamed "FiFi," Grumman's two-seater XFF-1 became the Navy's first fighter to use retractable landing gear. It was durable and dependable, and pilots loved the way it handled. Orders for the XFF-1 provided the company enough revenues to add employees and expand into a factory location in New York at Valley

Stream, Long Island. A year later, the company relocated to Farmingdale, Long Island. Through the decade of the 1930s Grumman continued to develop aircraft for the Navy, including the F2F and F3F, and in 1936, the company moved again to a permanent home at Bethpage, Long Island.

Grumman Aircraft moved to Bethpage in 1936. In 1945, Grumman set a number of U.S. production records including the most planes of a single type in one month. In March 1945, 605 Hellcats were built.

© Gulfstream Aerospace Corporation

Roy Grumman knew airplanes and he was also a visionary. He recognized that aviation had a future outside the military and that his company could be part of it. In 1936 the company decided to enter the commercial aviation market and introduced the Grumman Model G-21 Goose, an amphibian aircraft ideally suited for reaching remote areas. The Goose was originally conceived by a group of wealthy businessmen who were also avid outdoorsmen. Only ten were built for commercial use, however, before the military recognized its potential, and orders for hundreds of the versatile aircraft poured in from the Army, Navy and Coast Guard. Grumman followed with development of the Widgeon, a smaller version of the Goose, which also found a ready military market in the U.S. and abroad.

In 1938, the same year that Grumman went public, the company began production of the F4F fighter, better known as the Wildcat. During World War II, Grumman became the primary source of the U.S. Navy's air fleet, which included the Wildcat, Hellcat, and Avenger. In the Battle of the Coral Sea in 1942, Navy aviator Butch O'Hare (for whom O'Hare International Airport is named), piloting a Grumman Wildcat, single-handedly shot down five Japanese bombers and damaged a sixth, earning him the Congressional Medal of Honor.

As the war came to an end, the U.S. government encouraged its industrial providers to seek other markets. To prove the point, on August 15, 1945, the day after the Japanese surrendered, the federal government canceled 85 percent of its orders with Grumman. However, Grumman was able to continue some of its Navy business when it developed its first jet-powered combat plane, the F9F Panther, which became operational in 1949 and was the Navy's primary jet fighter in the Korean conflict. Later, during the 1950s, Grumman continued to produce Navy surveillance aircraft. The S2F Tracker in 1950 was followed by the EA6B Prowler and the E2 Tracker.

After WWII, as America's economy surged forward and factories were being built all over the country, so grew the demand for business aviation. Roy Grumman renewed his interest in developing business aircraft, and among his early creations was the luxurious amphibian aircraft, the G-73 Mallard. Powered by two 600-horsepower Wasp engines, the Mallard could seat up to 12 passengers and featured a plush, business-class interior cabin. Regarded as one of the most admired amphibians ever designed and built, only 59 were

© Gulfstream Aerospace Corporation

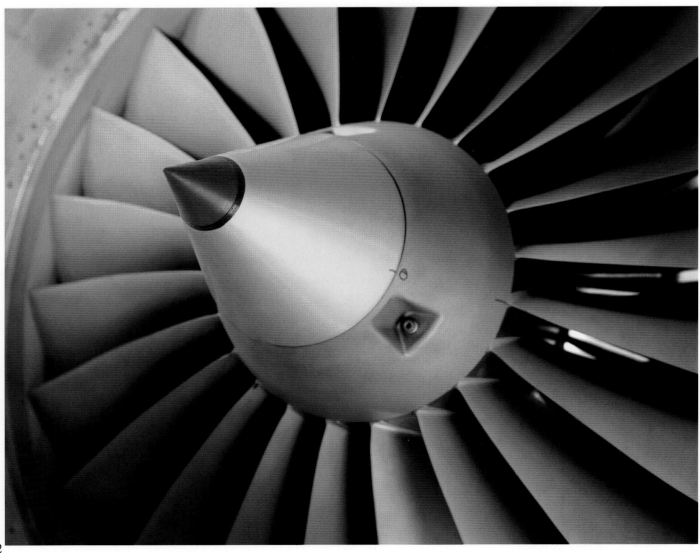

Grumman sold 200 Gulfstreams, later the GI, during its 11-year production life. Some of the early customers to take delivery were Owens-Corning Fiberglass Corporation, Texaco, Dow Chemical, Upjohn Company, United States Steel, Martin Marietta, Brown & Root, the Columbia Broadcast Company (CBS), and Walt Disney. The FAA bought two.

© Gulfstream Aerospace Corporation

manufactured between 1946 and 1951. Surplus military aircraft and a growing number of civilian airports severely reduced the market for amphibian aircraft.

One of Grumman's first non-military aircraft successes was the AgCat, a single seat, piston-powered biplane which, as its name implies, was directed at the agricultural distribution business (crop dusting). The AgCat first flew on May 22, 1957. Grumman licensed all production to Schweizer, who eventually purchased the manufacturing rights in 1981.

By the mid-'50s, Roy Grumman was pressing his engineers to develop a modern, marketable business aircraft. The time was right. The development team at Grumman sought advice from prospective customers to determine what they would like to experience in a corporate aircraft – a research technique that Gulfstream practices to this day. One customer suggestion, the trademark large elliptical windows, has been a mainstay of every Gulfstream aircraft produced since that time.

The result of Grumman's intense research and development was the "Gulfstream," which got its name from Roy Grumman himself. Many of the company's executives vacationed in Florida, where the Gulf Stream current flows northward off the coast. Later to be known as the Gulfstream I, or GI, the design was introduced in 1957. It was a twin turboprop-powered (Rolls-Royce Dart) transport that resembled a small passenger liner. It could seat 12 passengers comfortably and accommodate as many as 24. The first prototype flew on August 14, 1958, and on May 21, 1959 the aircraft received its FAA certification. Sinclair Oil was the first customer to take delivery of the Gulfstream I.

Although the Gulfstream I design was targeted toward the business executive, it proved attractive to both the Coast Guard and the Navy. The Coast Guard purchased a military variant designated VC-4A, a VIP transport, and the Navy ordered the TC-4C, equipped for instrument and navigator/bombardier training for the A-6 Intruder. This variant, known as the Academe, first flew on June 14, 1967 and deliveries began in late 1967 through mid-1968.

By the mid-1960s, there had been more than 200 deliveries of the Gulfstream I. The airplane was a great success and the fulfillment of Roy Grumman's dream to build aircraft that would serve the emerging business aviation market. Not only was the airplane itself attractive to corporate America, so was the company's somewhat controversial policy of providing aircraft support directly to customers. Grumman became the first aircraft manufacturer to provide direct, full-scale support including training and maintenance programs. Unorthodox at the time, it has since become an industry standard.

The company also adopted a policy of continual product improvement, and recognizing the shift from turboprops to jets, Grumman set about developing a jet-powered aircraft. The result was the Gulfstream II, powered by twin jets, aft-mounted on the fuselage. It was announced in May 1965. No prototype was ever built; the first production model served that purpose. The first flight was on October 2, 1966, with FAA certification in October 1967 and first customer deliveries in December 1967.

The Gulfstream II was the first large-cabin business jet to employ an autopilot during its first flight. Like its predecessor, it was a success, and again the military was interested with orders coming from both the Air Force and the Coast Guard with the designation VC-11A. These were primarily VIP transports. NASA purchased a special variant, the C-11A STA (Shuttle Training Aircraft), which provided landing training for the space shuttle crews. The STA was modified to simulate an orbiter's cockpit motion, visual cues and handling characteristics. Two STAs were based in Houston.

On the corporate side, Campbell Soup, Proctor & Gamble, Ford, Texaco and host of other companies received deliveries of the GII. Northrop Corporation, a leader in the aerospace industry, bought one and was the first to receive a certificate to charter the aircraft. Another notable purchaser of the GII was the Rockefeller family. One by one, the GII set a number of performance records, not the least of which was becoming the first corporate aircraft to fly nonstop from the U.S. to Europe.

The GII set a number of performance records and became the first corporate aircraft to fly nonstop from the U.S. to Europe. The GII's comfort, range and prestige made it a favorite of royalty around the world.

For practical and economic reasons, production of the GII was transferred to Grumman's new Savannah, Georgia plant in 1967. Savannah offered a climate better suited for year-round flying and flight training, there was a ready and able workforce in the region, the plant was adjacent to an airport, and the city of Savannah offered economic incentives. The move also served to separate the company's military and corporate manufacturing operations.

During the early 1970s, when inflation and spiraling costs were crippling the nation's economy, Grumman was facing its own challenges including losses on its F-14 contract with the Navy. Following that was a difficult merger of its Gulfstream program with American Aviation, creating a subsidiary called Grumman American Aviation. By 1976, however, the company was recovered, thanks in large part to its production of a light aircraft line that included the Lynx, T-cat, and twin-engine Cougar. The four-seat versions of the T-cat, the Cheetah and Tiger, were produced through 1979, the end of the company's production of piston-powered aircraft.

In 1978 Grumman American was acquired by American Jet Industries,

headed by Allen E. Paulson. Like Roy Grumman, Paulson was an aviation innovator first and a businessman second, and like Grumman he proved to be good at both. After the acquisition, Paulson became CEO and president of the company and changed the name to Gulfstream American. Among his first priorities was development of the Gulfstream III.

The Gulfstream III first flew out of Savannah on December 2, 1979. It featured a wider

wingspan, new drag reducing winglets, a new nose profile, greater range, and a modest stretch to the fuselage. Production of the GII ended in late 1979, and the first customers began to receive the GIII in late 1980. The first 10 airplanes sold for $7.4 million each.

The military version, designated VC-20D, was acquired for long-range, low passenger load, distinguished visitor airlift. These were equipped with commercial and military communications capability. In June of 1983 the C-20 was selected to replace another Georgia product, the Lockheed C-140 JetStar. Three were immediately delivered to Andrews AFB for use by the 89th Airlift Wing, which also operates the *Air Force One* aircraft. Eventually, eight more would be delivered including Air Force, Army, and Navy models.

In the early '80s, Gulfstream continued to grow in spite of a recession. The *Savannah News* reported in March 1982 that the company employed about 2,500 people in Georgia. In 1982, Paulson changed the name of the company to Gulfstream Aerospace Corporation to better reflect the company's global market (60% outside the U.S.) and Gulfstream's "future technological goals." In 1983 he took the company public and offered each employee 50 shares of stock.

In 1982 the Gulfstream IV project was publicly announced. After considerable design and development the GIV was introduced in September

The GIII made its first flight out of Savannah on December 2, 1979. Test pilots noted that in many respects the GIII handled more gently than its predecessor. Certification by the FAA was received in September of 1980.

© Gulfstream Aerospace Corporation

of 1985, ahead of schedule. Powered by two Rolls-Royce (Tay) engines, the aircraft was labeled by Gulfstream's preeminent engineer, Charles Coppi, as "evolutionary in design and revolutionary in concept." The GIV became the epitome of the large-cabin business jet, and after receiving its Type Certification from the FAA in April 1987, the aircraft set astonishing world speed and distance records that surpassed all estimates, including those of Gulfstream's own engineers. By December of 2002, 500 Gulfstream IV, and enhanced IV-SP, aircraft had been built.

In 1985 the Chrysler Corporation purchased Gulfstream and kept the Paulson management team. The 1987 Wright Brothers Memorial Trophy was awarded to Paulson for his contributions to aviation as a pilot, designer, entrepreneur, industry leader, and employer during a career that spanned forty years. In 1990, after Chrysler's near-brush with bankruptcy, Paulson partnered with Ted Forstmann, a founding partner in Forstmann, Little & Company, to buy back Gulfstream. Paulson was named chairman and CEO. Two years later, after his shares were bought out by Forstmann, Paulson stepped down and remained on the board as a director and chairman emeritus. That same year, 1992, Allen Paulson was inducted into the Georgia Aviation Hall of Fame.

In fall of 1992, the official launch of the next generation Gulfstream, the Gulfstream V, was featured in the Gulfstream chalet at the Farnborough (England) Airshow. Although based on the Gulfstream IV, the upgraded design objectives dictated a longer fuselage, a totally new wing design produced by Vought Aircraft Industries, and the first use of the new BMW Rolls-Royce BR-710 turbofans.

The first Gulfstream V flight took place on November 28, 1995, with the first customer delivery in June of 1997. As if to emphasize its preeminence in the intercontinental market, the GV had already set nearly 40 records within a few months of its first delivery. These records included city-pair flight times,

time-to-climb and altitude. To cap off their efforts, the Gulfstream V Industry Team was awarded the 1997 Collier Trophy by the National Aeronautic Association (NAA).

Just as Grumman had diluted its reliance on the defense market by developing the Gulfstream in the 1950s, General Dynamics did so by purchasing Gulfstream Aerospace from Forstmann Little in July of 1999. At the time of this acquisition, the GV was the company's premier product, capable of carrying a crew of two (four for longer flights), eight passengers (although seating for 19 can be accommodated), two lavatories, a computer workstation, and dining/conference areas. In late 1999, just after the National Business Aviation Association (NBAA) conference, the GV recorded its 60th world record. Remarkably, the longest nonstop flight from Asia to the United States – a 6,471 nautical mile trip completed in 13 hours and 21 minutes – was actually a business trip and not intended to be a milestone record-setting flight.

In October of 2000, Gulfstream introduced the GV-SP, "the world's most technologically-advanced business jet." This aircraft would feature an advanced cockpit with a state-of-the-art vision-enhancing system and even greater performance than the GV. Two years later, this model would be redesignated the G550, the flagship of an entirely new family of business jets.

The first Gulfstream V flight took place on November 28, 1995, with the first customer delivery in June 1997. Within a few months, the GV had set nearly forty records including city-pair flight times, time-to-climb and altitude. The Gulfstream V Industry Team was awarded the 1997 Collier Trophy by the National Aeronautic Association.

For the second time, a Gulfstream team – the G550 Team – was awarded the Collier Trophy.

At the September 2002 NBAA Annual Meeting and Convention, Gulfstream announced their entire family of products including new designations, consisting of the Gulfstream G100, Gulfstream G150, Gulfstream G200, Gulfstream G300, Gulfstream G400, Gulfstream G500 and the Gulfstream G550. In October of 2003 the G550 set a time and distance record with a direct flight from Seoul, South Korea to Orlando Executive Airport in Florida. The flight of 7,301 nautical miles lasted 14 hours and 30 minutes with an average air speed of 572 mph. At the 2003 NBAA convention the Gulfstream G450 was added to the fleet and in February 2004 the company introduced the Gulfstream G350 at Asian Aerospace in Singapore.

Gulfstream today is one of Georgia's major manufacturers and Savannah's leading employer and corporate citizen. The Gulfstream brand is recognized around the world and its markets are global, but the company focuses much of its resources on the Georgia community including partnerships with and support for education, aviation heritage and other community-oriented programs and initiatives. Targeted support for education includes Georgia Tech's Savannah campus, Savannah Technical College and the Savannah

College of Art and Design (SCAD). Many of Gulfstream's executives serve on boards and the company contributes to the arts and the Mighty 8th Air Force Heritage Museum, which is located just a few miles from the manufacturing plant.

Bryan Moss, who was named president of Gulfstream in 2003, is a Georgia Tech graduate with a stellar career in business aviation. He worked for Lockheed-Georgia Company until he joined Canadair in 1979. In 1992, he was appointed president of the Business Aircraft Division of Bombardier Aerospace Group. In 1995, Moss accepted an offer to become vice chairman of Gulfstream and chief executive of Gulfstream's new subsidiary, Gulfstream Aircraft. Eight years later on April 11, 2003, after some corporate restructuring and a reinvigorated marketing effort, Bryan Moss was named president of Gulfstream Aerospace. In November of that same year, he was also named executive vice president of Aerospace Group, General Dynamics.

On April 9, 2007, Moss handed the presidency over to Joseph Lombardo, former Gulfstream chief operations officer. Moss continues with the company as president emeritus, focusing his efforts on international sales.

 # MAULE AIR, INC.

Maule Air, Incorporated, based in Moultrie, Georgia, is a family-owned aircraft manufacturing company that produces single-engine, 4-place STOL aircraft. The company was founded in 1942 by Belford David "B.D." Maule and his wife, June. Of the few small aircraft manufacturers in Georgia, Maule is the oldest and to date has produced more than 2,300 airplanes. The company ranks as the third largest, single-engine aircraft manufacturer in the U.S. and produces fifty or more airplanes a year.

The STOL abilities of the Maule series of airplanes have proven useful to bush pilots in Alaska, on dense jungle airstrips in Brazil and as float planes on Canadian lakes. When Maule introduced its M-4 "Rocket" in 1962, its advertisements depicted an M-4 which appeared to be standing on its tail wheel, aimed steeply into the sky. This was no creative artwork, but rather an accurate representation of a takeoff by the high-performance STOL aircraft.

Originally located in Jackson, Michigan, Maule's M-4 was an impressive performer. Factory specifications included a 210 HP, 1,190-pound aircraft with a useful load of over 900 pounds, cruise speed of 165 mph, stall of 40 mph, and a takeoff run of only 300 feet.

Originally certified in 1961 as a basic, high-wing tail dragger, this structural design has remained virtually unchanged for nearly half a century. In later years, very few modifications

A 2007 Maule Air, Inc. logo.

M. Steiner Archives

America's
Performers of the Sky
M-4 ASTRO-ROCKET   M-4 ROCKET
M-4 STRATA-ROCKET

the aircraft designed and built to
give you what you want in an airplane.

Speed—Economy—Short Field Capability

MAULE aircraft corporation MOULTRIE, GEORGIA 31768

M-4 ROCKET **MAULE** M-4 STRATA-ROCKET
AND NOW THE
M-4 ASTRO-ROCKET

The name Maule has been well-known and respected in the aviation industry for decades. Now, the same engineering skill and manufacturing capabilities that have provided quality components to aircraft manufacturers throughout the world bring you three of the highest performance airplanes in their class. Construction is extremely rugged with strength limits for above normal tolerances. The welded steel tubing fuselage is a veritable fortress of strength. M-4 Strata-Rocket, M-4 Rocket and M-4 Astro-Rocket offer the ultimate in their power and price range in performance and economy. Whether your cargo is people or things, you'll get it there fast, easily and economically in a Maule.

The Rocket, Strata-Rocket and Astro-Rocket are three of the few aircraft that combine true STOL characteristics with low cost and high-speed economical cruise. The aircraft accomplishes its short field performance with flaps of an unusually high-lift capability and without elaborate spoilers, slots or other items normally associated with STOL design. A choice of exterior and interior color schemes is available to meet the individual tastes and needs of the buyer.

BY **MAULE** AIRCRAFT CORPORATION
SPENCE AIRFORCE BASE • MOULTRIE, GEORGIA 31768

were necessary to create an Allison turbine powered, tricycle gear version of the original airframe.

B.D. Maule was one of the last of America's old style inventors, cut from the same cloth as Alexander Bell or Thomas Edison. He was born in Ohio and grew up in Pennsylvania, where he worked in his aunt's tearoom and ice cream shop. Because he did not like churning ice cream by hand, he developed a motorized unit to do the job. Ice used in the churns was hand-cut from frozen creeks in the winter, a process that B.D. also motorized.

He joined the army in 1929 and served in the 19th Airship Company at Langley Field, Virginia. While he was in the service, he earned his mechanics license. His work on the Army's dirigibles may have sparked the designing and building of his first airplane, the M-1. Like many of the early airplane designers, B.D. made use of a lightweight motorcycle engine in his single-seat airplane. He left the Army after two years, shipped his plane home to Pennsylvania, read a book on "how to fly", and then made two flights in his M-1. He married June Aderhold in 1934, and they lived near both the Piper Aircraft and Lycoming Engine plants. Their first home was a "housecar" built on a truck chassis, much like today's RV, except heat and cooking relied on a pot belly stove. "Mr. Maule", as June refers to him, got a "good job" at Lycoming engine works, and the Maules bought land out in the country to design and build their first real house.

In 1939 while working for Lycoming, B.D. developed a mechanical starter for light aircraft, and although Lycoming was interested in it, no deal was ever struck. The following year the Maule family moved to Jackson, Michigan and established the Mechanical Products Company to manufacture the starter, known as the "Hummer." The inertial starter was eventually sold to Piper Aircraft. Other aviation inventions followed, including a full-swiveling, steerable tailwheel and much later a non-destructive fabric tester to satisfy the FAA-required annual fabric checks. As the U.S. drew closer to involvement in World War II, demand for starters diminished and the need for tailwheels and subcontractor parts increased. In 1942 B.D. formed the B.D. Maule Company to produce subcontractor parts and tailwheels. Although improved over the years, Maule's tailwheel is still in production today.

For years, B.D. had envisioned a four-place, go-anywhere airplane for pilots who love flying. The design was drawn on butcher paper, and then B.D. set about building it. After his prototype flew in 1957 and he won the award for aircraft design at the Experimental Aircraft Association (EAA) Oshkosh, B.D. began the FAA certification testing. Type certification came in 1961, and the first production plane was delivered in the spring of 1962. The first Maule M-4 "Bee Dee" had a modest 145 HP. With a thick, high-lift wing and cambered wingtips, it was the ultimate STOL aircraft.

Above: The Maule Aircraft Corporation was originally located at Belford Maule Field in Jackson, Michigan. Here the production of the M-4 would provide a basic private aircraft with outstanding STOL performance.

The Maule Family

The fast-cruising M-4 was produced in the small company factory in Napoleon, Michigan. In 1962, as it continued to grow, the company changed its name to Maule Aircraft Corporation. With its STOL capabilities, float and ski options, stability, ease of handling, roomy interior and economical operation, the aircraft was a success with pilots internationally.

Left: This early Maule advertising brochure is from the plant facility in Michigan.

The Maule Family

In 1968, the Maule family moved to Moultrie, Georgia and set up shop at a former Army Air Force training field, Spence Field. They once again bought land, this time adjacent to the factory site, and designed and built another home. The lodge-style home faces the Maule Pond, which serves as a water runway for the float planes.

B.D. passed away in 1995 and June became president of the company. At the time of his passing, B.D. Maule was the last founder-owner still producing aircraft anywhere in the world.

Through the years, a number of celebrities have purchased Maules including country singer Alan Jackson and NASCAR driver Bill Elliott. Other notable customers have included the Civil Air Patrol, the United States Border Patrol, foreign governments and several law enforcement agencies. Maules are particularly popular with charter operators and bush pilots in Alaska, which alone accounts for almost a fifth of the production. Because of their unique flight characteristics, Maule planes were chosen for movies and television including: *Cannonball Run, Gone Fishin', Speed 2* and *Survivor: The Amazon.*

Maule Air ultimately produced 18 standard models of the STOL aircraft: 16 with piston engines and 2 with turbine engines. In 2003 Maule Air introduced the M-9-230 at the EAA Oshkosh AirVenture and became the first U.S. aircraft original equipment manufacturer (OEM) to utilize the SMA SR305 Jet A powered diesel engine. The M-9-230 serves as either a five-seat passenger plane or a two-seat cargo hauler. In July 2006 Maule

(continued on page 176)

The MAULE M-4

HAS MANY OF THE FINEST FEATURES USUALLY FOUND ONLY IN AIRCRAFT COSTING HUNDREDS OF DOLLARS MORE . . . GET THE FACTS AND A DEMONSTRATION FROM YOUR DEALER TODAY!

Above: Three M-4s stand ready for delivery from the Michigan plant. Note the wheel fairings, an unusual feature in postwar private aircraft.

The Maule Family

Right: A Maule M-6. Floats expand the versatility of any aircraft.

M. Steiner Archives

173

The Bell Bomber Plant

The headline virtually screamed off the January 24, 1942 Atlanta Constitution front page: "$15,000,000 Army Bomber Plant In Cobb County." This plant would ultimately build 665 of the nearly 4,000 B-29 Superfortress Bombers.

The construction of the bomber plant exemplified America's incredible ability to quickly do the seemingly impossible during World War II. Even with shortages of labor, materials, and transportation, the plant was completed in less than one year. Construction began within thirty days of the announcement, and the first plane was rolled out in November of 1943. At its peak, employment at the plant was over 28,000. More than a third of the employees were women ("Rosie the Riveter"), and more than 2,000 were African Americans. When construction began, Marietta was home to 9,000 people, but rapidly grew to over 30,000. When it opened, the building was the second largest building in the world under one roof. The railroad line supplying materials ran right through the building.

The concept for the B-29 dates back to 1938. With Charles Lindbergh's active involvement in long-range planning, military strategists identified a need for an aircraft that could reach all of a German-occupied Europe from either Africa or the Azores. It was anticipated that England might fall and not be available for Allied bomber bases. At the time, the war in the Pacific was not fully anticipated. England did not fall, but the range of the B-29 made it the ideal bomber aircraft for the bombing of Japan from American-occupied Pacific islands.

The Museum of Aviation at Robins AFB displays a completely restored Bell-built B-29, nicknamed *Bonnie Lee*. Other B-29s on display are the *Sweet Eloise*, a Boeing Wichita product, at the Dobbins Air

Reserve Base in Marietta and *Dark Slide* located at the Georgia Veterans Memorial State Park near Cordele. The Dobbins B-29 was restored in 1995-96 by a cooperative of State Technical Colleges. Currently, the Cordele relic has not been restored and is not in covered space.

The Bell "Ol' Bummer Plant," as it was known locally, operated until 1945. Owned by the U.S. government, and designated Air Force Plant #6, it would stand idle for six years and be reopened by the Lockheed Aircraft Corporation, Georgia Division, in 1951.

Facing Page, Top: The sprawling Bell Bomber plant, circa 1943. Note the B-29s on the tarmac.

M. Steiner Archives

Right, Top: Employees put finishing touches on the nose section of a B-29 at the Bell Bomber plant, circa 1944.

The Atlanta History Center

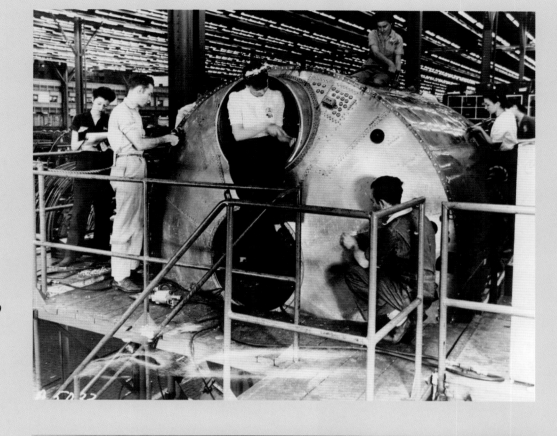

Right, Bottom: Female employees inspect plastic domes for B-29 aircraft at the Bell Bomber plant, circa 1944.

The Atlanta History Center

Facing Page, Bottom: A B-29 test crew loads for pre-flight testing at the Bell Bomber plant in Marietta, circa 1944.

The Atlanta History Center

(continued from page 173) announced production of a turbocharged, diesel-powered M-7. With lower fuel consumption, the new power plant will expand the remarkable Maule performance to higher altitudes and greater range.

A large percentage of Maule employees are family members including in-laws and fourth generation descendants. B.D. was inducted into the OX-5 Hall of Fame in 1994. Both B.D. and June Maule were inducted into the Michigan Aviation Hall of Fame. In 1992 B.D. was inducted into the Georgia Aviation Hall of Fame, and June followed seven years later. The National Aeronautic Association, the International 99s, and Women in Aviation International Pioneer Hall of Fame have all honored June.

Above: The M-5 first flew in 1972 and received the FAA Production Certificate on December 28, 1973. The wheel farings were gone and the long swept-back tail introduced.

M. Steiner Archives

 # LOCKHEED-GEORGIA DIVISION

Lockheed-Georgia

Lockheed Martin

The Lockheed Corporation traces its history back to 1913 in California, where the Loughead brothers, Malcolm and Allan, designed and built their first aircraft. It was a floatplane flown in a charter-like operation. Over time,

Lockheed in California became legendary for high-performance aircraft. Its design group, the "Skunk Works," has repeatedly created landmark designs that often presented a quantum jump in performance.

Lockheed first came to Georgia in 1951. The Korean Conflict prompted the U.S. Air Force to ask Lockheed to reopen the government-owned "Bell Bomber" plant in Marietta. The plant was reopened in

January 1951, after sitting idle since the end of World War II. Its first order of business was to modify 120 cocooned B-29s and ready them for operations in Korea. The first B-29 arrived at Marietta in April of 1951 to be processed.

Later, a production line was put in place to produce Boeing B-47 Stratojet bombers. Nearly 400 Stratojets were produced by Lockheed from 1953 through 1957. The company then moved production of two new Lockheed-designed aircraft to Marietta. The C-140 JetStar executive/corporate aircraft and the C-130 Hercules turboprop military transport each had prototypes built and flying in Burbank, California. These were the first true Lockheed products that would be produced by Lockheed's Georgia Division.

Mission-designed transports came on the scene only after the end of World War II. These provided larger volume, larger overall dimensions, reinforced floors, ramps and large openings such as clam-shell doors. High-wing aircraft became standard, allowing close-to-the-ground and truck-height loading levels. The first mission-designed cargo aircraft in widespread Air Force use was the Fairchild C-119 Flying Boxcar. The Air Force issued a Request for Proposals (RFP) in February of 1951. The RFP was issued to Boeing, Douglas, Lockheed and Fairchild, and proposals were to be submitted in April. In July, Lockheed was awarded a contract for two prototypes.

C-130 Hercules

The first YC-130A prototype made its maiden flight on August 23, 1954, flying from the Burbank, California plant directly to Edwards AFB for flight testing. This was somewhat unusual and a show of faith by Lockheed. First flights typically return to their takeoff site. It would soon be joined by the second prototype to successfully complete all testing and exceed almost all expectations of its design points. A team from Lockheed-Georgia was onsite in Burbank for the building of both prototypes, a strategy that helped save time in setting up the production line in Marietta. Less than eight months after the first prototype was completed, the first production aircraft flew on

April 7, 1955 and deliveries began in December 1956.

Approximately 219 "A" Models were delivered. The C-130A is easily identified by the three-bladed propellers and a blunt nose. Two of these aircraft were specifically built with removable drone launching and directing capability, an early version of today's unmanned air vehicles (UAVs). One unusual use of C-130A aircraft was formation of a four-ship flight demonstration team. Known as the "Four Horsemen," they were part of the 463rd Troop Carrier Wing and performed at numerous air shows.

The C-130 may be the best example of an evolutionary design in aviation history. The C-130B entered service in June 1959. With distinctive four-bladed propellers, it featured more powerful, Allison turbo-props, larger fuel capacity, and stronger landing gear. Ultimately, 134 "B" models were delivered, six of which were modified to perform "mid-air snatch" recovery of capsules from classified Air Force satellites. This would be just one of many unique mission modifications to the Hercules line.

In this same timeframe, some Air Force C-130As were being converted into gunships. Equipped with side-firing Vulcan cannons, sophisticated electronics (including forward looking infrared [FLIR]) and low-light television, these were designated AC-130s – the "A" for attack.

For a period of time, a number of original C-130s were modified with wheel/ski combinations for arctic use and were designated C-130Ds. Many of these were used to supply the Distant Early Warning (DEW) line stations. These also carried jet-assisted takeoff (JATO) capability. JATO was a grouping of small, solid rocket engines (bottles), mounted in such a fashion to boost the aircraft on takeoff. A retired "D" model is on display at the Museum of Aviation at Robins Air Force Base.

Perhaps no aircraft has served as many roles as the Hercules. Many, like the Boeing C-135, would have an additional designation for an alternative use, such as KC-135, for the tanker version of that aircraft. The C-130 has had many such special designations. One reference cites fifty major variants with a number of one-off versions.

Left: Lockheed's C-130A was the first U.S. production propjet. The distinctive three-bladed prop and blunt nose define the aircraft.

Below: An early C-130A takes off on an evaluation flight. The Lockheed plant and Kennesaw Mountain are in the background.

M. Steiner Archives

The C-130 is the aircraft type with the longest production run in aviation history. On November 30, 2006, the 2,300th Hercules rolled out of the Lockheed Martin plant in Marietta. The grey KC-130J Marine tanker was greeted by military officers, elected officials, members of the press and a crowd of Lockheed workers, all there to celebrate the first airplane in history to be in continuous production for fifty years.

In September of 2006 defense funding approved 14 additional C-130Js, with 23 more authorized by contract. On December 10, 2006 four additional aircraft were ordered under the War on Terror funding, bringing the total on-order to 186. The J offers 40% improvement in range and altitude and is easily identified by its six-bladed propellers. Simply stated, this latest version climbs faster and higher, flies farther at a higher cruise speed, and takes off and lands in a shorter distance than any prior model.

C-140 JetStar

The JetStar story is entirely different from the Hercules. There was no military RFP for the JetStar, which was a private venture designed to the specifications of Kelly Johnson and his "Skunk Works" team. Johnson announced that the first prototype would fly eight months after the final design, and it did to the day on September 4, 1957. This is considered to be the first flight of any business jet.

The two prototypes were powered by two French-built Orpheous jet engines mounted on the rear of the fuselage, a design that resulted in a very quiet cabin. When Lockheed was unable to reach a licensing agreement for the engines, the design was modified in 1959 to utilize four Pratt & Whitney jets. Production began in mid-1960 at the Lockheed-Georgia plant with first customer deliveries in 1961. All production JetStars were powered by four engines, thereby becoming the only civilian jet then meeting government requirements for extended, over-water flights.

In the meantime, a government specification was issued that was satisfied by the JetStar. Sixteen aircraft were ordered by the U.S. Air Force with first deliveries in 1962. Five were utilized for Flight Inspection purposes (Flight Checks) and designated C-140A. The other eleven were designated C-140B and became personnel transports. Six of those personnel transports were assigned to VIP usage and carried United States of America livery and the VC-140B designation. Four U.S. Presidents used a VC-140B as *Air Force One* including Presidents Nixon, Ford, Carter and Reagan. Other countries, including Canada and Germany, have also used VC-140B JetStars for their heads of government.

Production ended in mid-1973 after 164 JetStars were built. Noise regulations and high fuel costs motivated a modification program. With newer engines and different, larger fuel tanks, the modified JetStar went into production in 1976. The modifications were so successful that 40 new JetStar IIs were also produced. Both programs ended in late 1979. In total, 204 JetStars were produced.

C-141 Starlifter

The first official act of newly inaugurated President, John F. Kennedy, was to sign an order directing the development of an all-jet military transport. The resulting Air Force specification required low-altitude drops of troops and supplies anywhere in the world, have a range of 3,500 nautical miles and be able to carry a 60,000 pound load. The result was Lockheed's C-141 Starlifter. The first flight was on December 17, 1963, the 60th anniversary of the Wright Brothers' first powered flight.

Above: Touted as being the "world's fastest fanjet airlifter," the C-141 became the big brother to the C-130 Hercules. The C-141 Starlifter was retired from active service on May 5, 2006.

M. Steiner Archives

Interchangeable interiors for the Starlifter included roller floors for palletized cargo, smooth floors for vehicles, rear facing passenger modules and side mounted canvas paratrooper seats. A total of 285 C-141As were produced from 1964 through February 1968. All were Air Force versions, except one that was developed for NASA as a high-altitude observatory.

It was quickly discovered that a typical C-141 load ran out of volume before exceeding weight restrictions. The Air Force and Lockheed then specified a stretched version, the C-141B, with an additional 23 feet of cabin space. This move essentially increased the fleet capability by 30% at far less cost than building that number of additional aircraft. Aerial refueling capability was also added to extend the range without landing. Thirteen of the "B" models were also equipped for Special Operations Low Level (SOLL) use. The first flight of a C-141B was on March 24, 1977, with the last delivery on June 29, 1982. These aircraft were capable of lifting 91,000 pounds, 50% more than the original directive.

After nearly 25 years of operation, 63 of the "B" models were given avionics upgrades and designated C-141C. The conversions, completed on all 63 aircraft by 2001, included glass cockpit, Global Positioning System and electronic defense systems.

The C-141 maintenance facility was located at Robins Air Force Base. When the fleet was retired in May of 2006, examples were placed in a number of air museums. The "Hanoi Taxi," which brought many American POWs back from North Vietnam, was retired to the U.S. Air Force Museum at

Wright Patterson AFB near Dayton, Ohio. Another example was placed at the Museum of Aviation at Robins AFB in Warner Robins, Georgia.

C-5 Galaxy

In 1962 talks began both at the Pentagon and in Congress about the possible need for an additional military transport. This aircraft would be able to handle the oversized cargo that could not be carried by either the C-130 or the C-141. By Pentagon estimates, this accounted for one-third of the equipment needed by our ground forces. It would be May 1964 before the Air Force

approached their three largest aircraft suppliers requesting design concepts for a large transport capable of carrying almost anything in the military inventory. Boeing was already pushing their 747 design, Douglas was desperate for a new contract and Lockheed-Georgia believed that their C-141 production would be ending soon. Based on the industry's input, a formal RFP was issued in December of 1964, with response required in April 1965. Lockheed was awarded the contract in October of 1965.

Above: Lockheed issued First Flight Covers for the C-5A Galaxy flight on June 30, 1968. Each envelope held a card containing essential information about the giant transport.

Lockheed's design drew heavily on both the C-130 and the C-141. The high T-tail, swept wings and engine pylons are large-scale versions of the C-141. Added wheels brought the total to 28, allowing the C-5 to support almost 770,000 pounds of aircraft and 270,000 pounds of cargo. Cargo capability ranges from 36 standard pallets up to a 74-ton mobile scissors bridge. With doors at each end, simultaneous loading and unloading can occur and the aircraft "kneels" to convenient height with ramps for driving on and off. The net result is minimized ground time.

Right: Lockheed-Georgia employees are elated as their first C-5A takes to the skies over Marietta.

M. Steiner Archives

Construction of the prototype began in August 1966, with

rollout of the first C-5A on March 2, 1968. The first flight on June 30, 1968 had all the drama and media attention of the Academy Awards. The C-5A was accepted by the Air Force in late 1969, with the first operational aircraft delivered to the Air Mobility Command at Charleston AFB, South Carolina in June 1970. Eventually, 76 C-5As were delivered. Equipped for aerial refueling, a C-5's range is limited only by its crew's endurance. All C-5 aircraft are operated by USAF crews.

The C-5B Galaxy incorporated over a hundred systems modifications, primarily to improve reliability and maintainability. The first C-5B flew on September 10, 1985. Sixty C-5Bs were produced from 1986 to April 1989. Two specially-equipped C-5Cs were built for NASA, primarily to carry satellites and other special equipment. Both are heavily modified A models, with oversize cargo space.

Emulating the ongoing success of the C-130 evolution, the latest C-5 Galaxy, the C-5M, was rolled out on May 16, 2006 at the Lockheed Martin plant in Marietta. The "M" is for modernized. New 21st century engines with 22% more power translates into 30% reduction in takeoff roll, 38% increase in climb rate, lower fuel consumption and quieter operation. New avionics and an all-glass, flat-panel cockpit provide all-weather capability. This modernization extends the life of this fleet beyond 2040.

Above: Today, major corporations collectively design and build advanced technology aircraft. The team of Lockheed, General Dynamics and Boeing developed the F-22. This decal reflects the partnership from early in the development process.

Above: Two prototypes (YF-22) were constructed for a fly-off competition.

F-22 Raptor

The U.S. Air Force issued an understated but landmark press release on December 8, 2006. Headed, "F-15 Demo Team Transitions To F-22 Demo Team," the release states in part, "Because there are now two full squadrons operating the Raptor and only one squadron to fly the F-15…it only makes sense to embrace the new aircraft and highlight its capabilities worldwide." With that pronouncement, the Raptor became mainstream Air Force and the first new Air Force fighter in thirty years.

In a dramatic change of pace for Lockheed-Georgia, the company decided to produce the F-22 Raptor in Marietta, Georgia. Although Lockheed had

Right: First flight doesn't take place until after years of design and competition.

produced a number of landmark fighter aircraft in the past, all were built in West Coast plants. Among those were the P-38 Lightning, the P-80 Shooting Star, the F-104 Starfighter, and the F-117 Stealth fighter. The F-22 is the first Lockheed fighter to be built in Georgia.

Although the F-22 Raptor is regarded as a new aircraft, its history actually goes back well over twenty years. The basic design points include stealth technology, supercruise capability and an advanced electronic envelope. Originally designated the F/A-22, the aircraft was officially re-designated the F-22A in December 2005. The first production aircraft were delivered to Nellis AFB in Nevada, where eight instructors developed the training program. Additional aircraft were assigned to Tyndall AFB in Florida and Edwards AFB in California. The 43rd Fighter Squadron at Tyndall took delivery of 18 operational Raptors.

Today, at a single site in Marietta, Georgia, Lockheed-Georgia can stake its claim to producing the world's most advanced manned aircraft, the world's largest production transport and the world's longest production run of any type of aircraft.

Right: The basic shape of the airframe can be seen on the production line at Marietta.

M. Steiner Archives

183

THRUSH AIRCRAFT, INC.

There are currently three major agricultural aircraft manufacturers in America. One, Thrush Aircraft, Inc., is located at the Southwest Georgia Regional Airport in Albany. Their 227,000-square-foot manufacturing facility was built in 1965 by Rockwell International.

Prior to coming to Georgia, the Rockwell International Corporation was attempting to build an aviation conglomerate. They hoped to accomplish this by acquiring design and manufacturing rights to existing aircraft, primarily from smaller manufacturers. In October of 1960 Rockwell purchased the Aero Design and Engineering Company of Oklahoma, which designed and manufactured the Aero Commander product line, known primarily for its high-wing, twin-engine general aviation aircraft. The newest development of the Rockwell Aero Commander line was the Aero Commander 1121 Jet Commander. This early business jet first flew on January 2, 1963 and began shipping to customers in 1965.

When Rockwell purchased North American Aviation in 1967, they were faced with the dilemma of owning two different business jets, the Jet Commander and the North American Sabreliner. Rockwell chose to sell the Jet Commander designs and manufacturing rights to Israel Aircraft Industries, Ltd. (IAI). Among the other aircraft acquired was the Meyers 200D, a four-place, all-metal, low-wing speedster with fully retractable landing gear. It was the fastest, non-turbocharged, production single-engine, general aviation plane ever built. The airframe is so rugged that no Airworthiness Directives (ADs) have been issued for this type.

Al Meyers, the designer, had a small plant where aircraft were basically hand-built with no real production tooling. Approximately thirty-three 200Ds had been built from

Above: A Thrush doing what it was made to do: put down an accurate spray over a field.

Thrush Aircraft, Inc.

Below: The busy production floor at Thrush Aircraft.

Thrush Aircraft, Inc.

1953 through 1965, when Rockwell's Aero Commander Division purchased the design and manufacturing rights. Marketing the plane as the Aero Commander 200D, eighty-three aircraft were built and sold. Unfortunately, the aircraft were so expensive to build that Rockwell later sold the design and manufacturing rights to a Detroit company, the Interceptor Corp.

Looking for yet another aircraft type, Rockwell noticed designer Leland Snow's Olney, Texas agricultural aircraft company, then named Snow Aeronautical and now known as Rockwell Standard. Rockwell decided to move the production to Albany around 1970. This agricultural plane was marketed as the Ag Commander S-2, formerly the Snow S-2.

In March of 1970, Rockwell introduced the Rockwell Thrush Commander. One of the most successful agricultural aircraft in the world, it is a single-engine, single-seat, low-wing monoplane in tail dragger configuration. Originally, the aircraft was piston-powered with a radial engine. Later production was turboprop powered.

The Ayres Corp. purchased the entire Albany operation on November 23, 1977, when Rockwell decided to exit the general aviation market. Fred Ayres, who lived in Albany, had been Rockwell's top dealer, and his company was already performing Thrush rebuilds and turboprop conversions. After the purchase, the Ayers Corp. aggressively sought contract work from major aerospace companies. Hush kits for Douglas DC-9s and Boeing B-737s, thrust reverser rebuilds, and parts kits were among their contracts.

Thrush Aircraft, Inc. bought the facilities, the aircraft and the designs of the bankrupt Ayres, Corp. on June 30, 2003. The Thrush team has over thirty years experience in designing, manufacturing and installing aerial spray systems, in addition to aircraft manufacturing. Some of the current Thrush employees have actually been at this site since the Rockwell startup in 1965. Today, Thrush continues to produce what is considered the most reliable agricultural aircraft in the world.

Below: Thrush has refined the ability to "load and go" without even shutting down.

Thrush Aircraft, Inc.

AIRCRAFT MANUFACTURING & DEVELOPMENT CO. (AMD)

Like Maule Air, Inc., Aircraft Manufacturing & Development Co. (AMD) in Eastman is a reflection of the strong individual who designed the aircraft and the small, dedicated group of people that produce and sell them. AMD is the end result of the designs of Chris Heintz. Following his tour in the French Air Force, he worked on the Concorde development team at Aerospatiale. He later served as chief engineer with the French light aircraft manufacturer, Avions Robin, designing 2- and 4-seat, all-metal production aircraft.

On his own time, Heintz designed a simple, two-seat, all-metal home-built aircraft. Simplicity was his standard, due in large part to his self-confessed limited construction skills. His prototype flew in 1969, and he offered the plans and manuals for his plane, the Zenith, to the growing home-built market. A non-compete clause in his Avions Robin contract led Heintz and his family to move to Toronto, Canada in 1973, where he joined deHavilland of Canada and worked with empennage (tail assembly) development for the Dash 7 airliner.

In 1974, Chris Heintz formed Zenair, Ltd. and produced Zenith home-built kits in his garage. The exclusive rights to manufacture and market his most popular kits, the STOL CH701 and the Zodiac CH601, were granted to the Zenith Aircraft Company of Mexico, Missouri in 1992. The current president of Zenith Aircraft is Chris Heintz's son, Sebastian Heintz.

For more than 20 years, Chris Heintz's name has been synonymous with the very best kitplane designs, with more than a dozen all-metal designs to date. These designs have earned him numerous international awards. In 1995, the Federation Aeronautique Internationale (FAI) honored Zenair with the Honorary Group Diploma for "greatly contributing to the advancement of design of light aircraft." The Experimental Aviation Association (EAA) inducted Chris into the EAA Hall of Fame in 1999, and the Light Aircraft Manufacturing Association (LAMA) presented him the Outstanding Individual award in 2001.

It was only logical that a ready-to-fly, manufactured version of the Zodiac would eventually be produced. The first such productions took place in Canada, Europe and South America. AMD was established in Eastman, Georgia in 1997 to produce the Alarus, which is primarily a flight school training aircraft. Eastman was selected in large part to take advantage of the flow of trained and qualified graduates at the nearby Georgia Aviation and Technical College. Another draw was Eastman's Heart of Georgia Regional airport, which features every advantage of a major airport but with light traffic.

186

In addition, Georgia offered economic incentives that made the decision to come to Georgia an easy one for AMD.

Zodiac production at AMD began in 2005, in compliance with the new FAA Light Sport Aircraft (LSA) regulations. The Zodiac XL (VFR version) and Zodiac Xli (IFR version) are typically utilized by pilots with sport or recreational certification, which does not require a medical. Aircraft complying with the LSA standard/classification will have a maximum weight of 1,320 pounds, a maximum speed of 138 MPH, one or two seats, single-engine, fixed gear, and will be FAA registered (N-number). These aircraft may be used legally for sport and recreation, flight training and rental.

The AMD Zodiac models are available only as a manufactured, ready to fly airplane for those customers who do not want to assemble their own aircraft. Currently, the Zodiac is the only LSA powered by a standard aircraft engine (Continental O-200) rather than the Rotax. This allows maintenance at almost any airport. Zodiac features a forward-hinged canopy in place of traditional doors, has a 27-foot wingspan and is 20 feet long.

An AMD (Aircraft Manufacturing and Development) Zodiac over South Georgia. The AMD plant in Eastman produces the Zodiac and Alarus. Both aircraft feature the latest in high-tech materials and methods of construction.

Aircraft Manufacturing and Development (AMD)

AMD's other Heintz-designed aircraft, the Alarus, was type certified in 1996. Although not specifically designed to replace the most common general aviation trainer, the Cessna 150/152, the Alarus represents a significant improvement over the vast training fleets of the flight schools. Most existing training aircraft are 30 years old, expensive to operate and maintain, and do not offer the latest cockpit and panel design. AMD also developed and offers a companion simulator that replicates the standard Alarus cockpit design.

The Alarus and the Zodiac are both two-seat, low-wing aircraft. The LSA category did not exist when Chris Heintz designed the Zenith, predecessor of the Zodiac. In fact, he served in an advisory capacity to the FAA in drafting the definition of an LSA.

Airframes and other components are manufactured in Canada and shipped to AMD in Eastman for assembly and completion. AMDs 28,000-square-foot plant is staffed with 12 to 15 personnel who produce a total of 36 to 40 aircraft a year. After Chris Heintz retired, he was succeeded by his son, Mathieu Heintz.

"What Chris Heintz created was the perfect flight school trainer" read the introduction to the flight test report in the November/December 2003 AutoPilot. *The author of the very positive report concluded with, "the Alarus is a fun little airplane."*

Aircraft Manufacturing and Development (AMD)

Greenland Expedition Society 1981–1992

After the United States entered World War II, the responsibility for getting men and equipment to Europe fell to Major General "Hap" Arnold, Chief of the Army Air Force. The most economical method would have been to load planes onto freighters and ship them to England, but German U-Boats were sinking more than one half million tons of allied tankers and freighters a month. The solution was to fly combat-ready fighters, escorted by B-17 bombers, to England via Labrador, Greenland and Iceland. It was a difficult journey with little margin for error at any time, but it was especially treacherous during wartime.

Operation Bolero, as it was code-named, began early in 1942. The very first flight of one B-17 mother ship and four P-38s was commanded by Paul Tibbets, better known as the pilot of the *Enola Gay*, the B-29 that dropped the first atomic bomb. In July of that same year, two B-17s and six P-38s followed the same path with considerably less luck. Weather and communications problems resulted in all eight planes crash landing on Greenland's icecap. None of the crew members were seriously hurt and all were evacuated safely, but the airplanes remained behind.

In the summer of 1977, Pat Epps, President of Epps Aviation Services, Atlanta, Georgia and his architect friend, Richard Taylor, ferried a twin-engine Piper Aztec from Dekalb Peachtree Airport to Paris, France for the Paris Air Show. Their route was similar to that of the Operation Bolero pilots, and one of their stops was Greenland. At a chance encounter with some Danish pilots, they learned the story of the "Lost Squadron" and thought that maybe someday they would fly over the icecap and see if they could spot the tails sticking out of the snow.

The following year, Epps received a phone call from Russell Rajani, who wanted to rent hangar space to restore World War II aircraft. Rajani and his partner, Roy Degan, had been granted salvage rights by the Danish Government to excavate the missing B-17s and P-38s. Epps acknowledged knowing about Operation Bolero, but his business catered to the corporate jet business and they had no space to rent. In April of 1981, a brand new Lear Jet taxied to a stop in front of the Epps terminal and Epps greeted the owner, Charlie Gay, as he deplaned. Gay thanked him but said that if he could have any plane in the world, he would rather have a P-38. Epps called Russell Rajani to see if he still had the rights to salvage and then called Richard Taylor to tell him that he had a buyer for one of the P-38s. They would be partnering with Rajani and Degan to recover the lost planes. The Greenland Expedition Society was born.

Believing that all they had to do was sweep some snow and ice off the wings, repair the propellers and perform some basic service work, the four adventurers left for Greenland's icecap with only a four-man tent, some sleeping bags, rented magnetometers and a shovel. They reached what they assumed to be the crash sight by flying an Aztec to Sondre Stromfjord, Greenland and renting a ski-equipped Cessna 185 with pilot.

There were no airplanes visible at the site. With photographs taken in 1942 as a reference, they tried to determine positions by sighting mountains in the shots, but learned that they would need a lot more than photographs.

The second 1981 excursion left Atlanta in October with more equipment and one more person, Norman Vaughn. Vaughn, a hearty sixty-six year old from Alaska, was

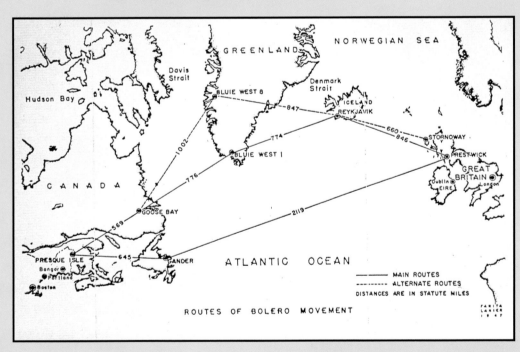

a veteran of the Byrd expedition to Antarctica in 1928, but most importantly, he was on the salvage trip to the Greenland crash sight in 1942. He was the last person to see the airplanes. If nothing else, Vaughn would be able to put them in the best location to find the squadron. However, weather failed to cooperate, and the mission never got past Sondre Stromfjord.

Bickering, arguing and an eventual lawsuit ended the relationship between Rajani-Degan and the Greenland Expedition Society, and although Rajani tried again over the next five years, he never reached the planes. In April 1986, Taylor successfully petitioned the Danish Government to transfer the salvage rights from Rajani. The Greenland Expedition Society had officially obtained a three-year right to salvage.

The third expedition was launched that summer and to fund the project, Epps came up with the idea of selling rights to would-be adventurers who would pay to make the trip and work for free. The trips were sold for $5,000 each and they raised $35,000. The balance was paid by Epps and Taylor. The key to the success of this trip was sub-surface radar. Its electromagnetic energy would penetrate the snow and reveal the location of the airplanes. Believing the targets to be no more than eighty feet below the surface, they used an antenna capable of only reaching one-hundred, twenty-five feet. The expedition ended as had all the others before it, empty handed. Discouraged, the GES team returned to Atlanta.

In the spring of 1988, Epps attended a function honoring the achievements of his father, Ben T. Epps, and met Dr. Dan Callahan. Callahan personally contributed to the 1988 expedition and also organized a consortium of other doctors willing to contribute. Another contributor was Charlie Gay, the man who triggered the inception of The Greenland Expedition Society back in 1981. The objective for the 1988 expedition was to locate the squadron, determine the depth and bring back proof. This time, they used sub-surface radar of very low frequency and found and marked all eight airplanes. The depth was determined to be two-hundred, fifty feet below the surface. A probe was sent down and actually touched the wing of a B-17, but the auger equipment was still not long enough to reach any surface area. They would have to come back again, however, they had succeeded in finding the "Lost Squadron."

Don Brooks of Douglas, Georgia not only contributed financially to the 1989 expedition, but also invented the melt-down generator and provided a ski-equipped DC-3 to ferry people and equipment to the icecap. The melt-down generator was a 36-inch copper tubing wrapped cylinder with hot water running through it to melt the ice. The system worked well, but it tended to stray off course once it hit the ice field. It needed one more piece, a guiding device, to work perfectly. This last piece was included in the 1990 Expedition.

In 1990, all equipment worked well and the GES reached one of the B-17s. It was first thought that the big bomber was in fair condition, but after getting a closer look it proved not worth salvaging. Attention turned to the P-38s and at least one was salvageable, but it would take one more trip to the icecap. In 1992, a final expedition began, funded primarily by Kentuckian Roy Shoffner for all rights to the recovered aircraft. Extracted from where it had landed fifty years earlier, the P-38 dubbed *Glacier Girl* made the journey from two-hundred, fifty feet below the Greenland icecap to Middlesboro, Kentucky. Her new owner, Schoffner, painstakingly restored her and, in October 2003, returned her to the sky.

African American Aviators *in Georgia*

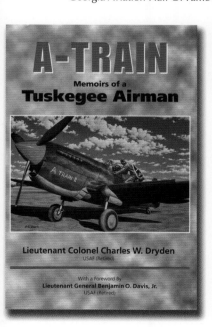

African Americans in Georgia have contributed to aviation from the very early days of the industry, producing some "firsts" of their own. Barred from taking flying lessons, Eugene Jacques Bullard taught himself to fly then moved to France to become involved in World War I. Already an accomplished pilot yet unaccustomed to the degree of discrimination in the Deep South, Charles W. "A-Train" Dryden answered the call during World War II. He signed up for training at Moton Field in Alabama and graduated in the second class of the original Tuskegee Airmen. Delta's first African American pilot was Samuel Louis Graddy in 1979. In January, 2001 Dana Nelson earned the distinction of being Delta's first female African American pilot.

The remarkable story of Eugene Jacques Bullard is recounted in Chapter Two of this book. This section honors several African American pilots who have made their mark on aviation in Georgia. Along with the many African Americans who have served the field of aviation in other roles, they have inspired future generations to follow in their footsteps.

LT. COLONEL CHARLES W. DRYDEN

Charles "Chuck" Dryden was an original member of the renowned Tuskegee Airmen. "A-Train" was his P-40 nickname. Dryden was commissioned on April 29, 1942 as a second lieutenant in a class of only three graduates and flew with both the famed 99th Pursuit Squadron and the 332nd Fighter Group, which served in North Africa, Sicily and Italy. Theirs was a tight-knit squadron of dedicated, determined young enlisted men who became America's first black military airmen at a time when prejudice and policy greatly limited their equal opportunities. A-Train played a pivotal role in convincing leadership that blacks were no less intelligent, skilled, courageous and patriotic than any other Americans.

On June 9, 1943, Lt. Dryden led a formation of six pilots that engaged enemy fighter aircraft in aerial combat over Pantelleria, Sicily. It was the first time in aviation history that black American pilots of the U.S. Army Air Forces engaged aircraft in combat.

After WWII, Dryden taught at Howard University as a professor of air science. He retired in 1962 as a command pilot with 4,000 hours flying time.

Born in New York City in 1920, to Jamaican parents, Dryden graduated from Peter Stuyvesant High School, earned a BA in Political Science from Hofstra University and an MA in Public Law and Government from Columbia University. In 1996 he was awarded an honorary degree of Doctor of Humane Letters by Hofstra University.

A career move brought Dryden to Atlanta in June of 1975. In 1978 he helped found the Atlanta Chapter of Tuskegee Airmen, Inc. (ACTAI) and served as president, vice president and national convention committee

Above: An all the more seasoned Lt. Colonel Charles "Chuck" Dryden.

Georgia Aviation Hall Of Fame

194

chairman. His moving autobiography, *A-Train: Memoirs of a Tuskegee Airman*, was published by the University of Alabama Press in 1997. In his memoirs, Dryden wrote of the transition from a rigidly segregated U.S. Army to an Air Force with racial policies that, in 1962, were far in advance of the country at large.

He was designated an Outstanding Georgia Citizen by the Secretary of State in 1997 and the next year was inducted into the Georgia Aviation Hall of Fame. His name can also be found among the distinguished members of the Honorable Orders of the Daedalians, the Kentucky Colonels and the Palmetto Gentlemen of South Carolina.

JULIUS ALEXANDER

Julius Alexander is a pioneer in aviation education. Growing up in the University Homes Housing Project of Atlanta in the mid-1940s, he was never far from aviation. The world was at war and Georgia was a primary location for flight training. Alexander remembers there wasn't a day that he didn't see squadrons of military aircraft flying overhead. Cementing his interest was his older brother who built and flew model airplanes. After watching the film *God is My Co-Pilot*, the story of Brig. General Robert L. Scott, he wanted nothing more than to become a fighter pilot. Instead, he devoted his 36-year career to flight instruction, helping thousands of young people fulfill their dreams to fly. Passionate about airplanes, he initiated aviation courses in Atlanta's high schools and since 1980 has helped to inspire young African Americans through the not-for-profit program, Aviation Career Enrichment (ACE).

Initially located in a trailer at Fulton County Airport, ACE specializes in teaching teenagers to fly. A dozen children with a genuine interest in pursuing a career in aviation but without the financial means to realize their dreams were the first ACE students. The program quickly expanded into the old control tower, and by 2007 ACE had secured additional offices and airplanes for

Below: Julius Alexander, 1964. The new private pilot flew a Cessna 182.

Julius Alexander

computer training and instruction. Graduates of the program have gone on to careers in both military and commercial aviation, and many return to ACE as instructors in their spare time.

After graduating Morehouse in 1959 with degrees in English and Secondary Education, Alexander taught English – and later Aviation – at Price, O'Keefe, Grady, Dykes and Washington High Schools. In 1965 he set up a Civil Air Patrol squadron at Price High School, the first CAP unit in any school in the Atlanta public school system. He used flight training curriculum for improving academic skills in other areas. He taught that aerodynamics is nothing but physics; navigation is geometry, geography and trigonometry; and communications is language skills.

In the mid-1970s, Alexander left teaching for a position in public relations at Lockheed, Georgia, where he remained for 23 years. As assistant to the director and then senior public relations coordinator, Alexander wrote articles that deciphered the technical side of the company's endeavors into non-technical language. He traveled extensively; wrote for Lockheed's Georgia employee newsletter, *The Southern Star*; and pursued photography, particularly aerial photography. But he missed the interaction with his students.

In 1977 Alexander returned to education when he became involved with two different programs. The federal program CETA (Comprehensive Employment Training Act) offered youngsters a summer job and a chance to fly while earning the minimum wage. A second aviation education program was sponsored by the National Alliance of Business. Both programs were successful but only a few of the children involved had genuine interest in aviation as a career. The all-volunteer ACE program sprang from these two experiences.

CAPTAIN JOHN BAILEY
John Bailey considered his time in the U.S. Air Force the best flying in the world. During his stint in Vietnam, he flew DC-3s and "Electronic Goons" (EC-47s) and received the Distinguished Flying Cross for his efforts. Upon completing his military career, Bailey flew for Delta Air Lines and became the first African American to fly the MD-88 and the Boeing 767-400.

Below: John Bailey felt U.S. Air Force flying was the best in the world.

John Bailey

Bailey retired from Delta in November 2003 and turned his attention to reaching out to aspiring aviation-career-oriented youngsters through Delta-supported programs. Among those programs were OBAP (Organization of Black Airline Pilots) – which Bailey helped create – Dream Flight and Flight Line. Through Flight Line, Delta provides 15 hours of free lessons, 30 hours of ground school and 15 hours of flight training for the top 10 students from ACE Camp. For

Dream Flight, Delta provided Bailey with a Boeing 757 to fly 150 children to the National Air & Space Museum in Washington, D.C. Dream Flight/ Dream Jamboree exposes children to all things aviation and encourages them to consider aviation as a career. In his words, "children are the future of aviation."

GEORGES "PACO" SUMNER

When he was just 11 years old, French-speaking Georges Sumner left Haiti and arrived in the family's new hometown of New York City on December 29, 1957. It was his first airplane ride. From the moment the pilot brought him into the cockpit, Georges was hooked on flying. He started building model airplanes and had constructed 115 by the time he graduated 8th grade. With his teacher Mrs. Day's encouragement, Sumner was accepted into the Aviation High School in Queens, New York in 1963. He began flying lessons in January 1964 and soloed in June the same year. In April 1965, he received his pilot's license and by 1967 he had obtained his instructor's license.

In 1968, at the age of 22, Sumner began flying for Northeast Airlines, the second black pilot hired in commercial aviation. He had overcome a number of obstacles to reach his dream, including discrimination and learning English.

When Northeast merged with Delta Air Lines in 1972, Sumner moved to Atlanta. By 1974 the industry was facing a fuel crisis and very little hiring was taking place, with the exception of Eastern, who continued to thrive by serving the leisure markets. During the period 1972-1978, Eastern hired close to 55 black pilots – the most of any airline in the country. Sumner left Delta for Eastern and was the sixth black pilot hired by the airline. He became actively involved in recruiting pilots for the company.

Georges Sumner worked tirelessly alongside other concerned individuals to end discrimination in the airline industry. He founded Flying Mentors, an organization committed to teaching flying and inspiring young African Americans to enter the field of aviation.

JAMAIL LARKINS

Augusta-born Jamail Larkins represents the next generation of African American aviators. Larkins began his flying career at the age of 10 when his father bought him a computer flight simulator. When he was 12 years old he flew his first flight with the Experimental Aircraft Association (EAA) Young Eagles Program. He became one of the youngest American pilots when he soloed a powered aircraft in Canada at the age of 14. Unlike the U.S., Canada allows pilots as young as 14 to fly solo. The day after his 16th birthday Larkins became the first and youngest student pilot in the United States to solo in a Cirrus SR20.

An Evans High School honor student, Tae Kwan Do black belt and aerobatic pilot, Larkins has continually been led by his own self-motivation and intellect. He has been recognized as an Outstanding Young Eagle and an Outstanding Camper at Space Camp in Titusville, Florida. He received a Certificate of Special Recognition for Aviation Education from the U.S. Congress in 2004. As a national spokesperson for EAA's Young Eagles Program, Larkins has made appearances at more than 20 air shows and conventions a year and served as a columnist for aviation publications. He has trained in several different kinds of airline simulators including the Boeing 777, 767 and 757 and the McDonnell Douglas Super MD-80. He is a graduate of Embry-Riddle Aeronautical University in Florida.

In addition to representing the EAA, Larkins was also national spokesperson for Careers in Aviation, a non-profit organization that exposes young people to opportunities in the field of aviation and encourages their participation. Larkins also acts as an official representative of the FAA in his capacity as Ambassador for Aviation & Space Education. This role provides Larkins an opportunity to promote aviation as a career choice for the nation's youth and to highlight the benefits of aviation to mainstream America.

Facing Page: Jamail Larkins standing with his aerobatic Christen Eagle II.

Jamail Larkins

Georgia's Next Century Of Flight

Looking Forward
By Dave Hirschman
Aviation Writer

Kids overrun the grassy park at the foot of DeKalb Peachtree Airport's control tower, chasing each other on the playground and sitting with their parents on the cement observation deck. The vibrancy and variety of Georgia's first century of aviation are all around them. Directly ahead, students practice touch-and-go landings on the busy parallel runways; vintage biplanes take passengers on scenic jaunts around Stone Mountain; private pilots carry medical patients on mercy missions; fledgling air taxi services connect passengers that may have hailed them on the Internet; and luxurious Gulfstream corporate jets whisk executives to far-off destinations.

Scuplture: Larry Gross

Photograph: Mike Green

Photocomposite: Sue Mabry

All of the people – and all of the aircraft – have deep Georgia ties: the Alarus trainer, designed for ruggedness and economy, was built in Eastman. Biplanes from the 1930s were lovingly restored by Atlanta craftsmen. The stubby, single-engine Maule utility plane, performing its charity for Angel Flight of Georgia, was built in Moultrie. The ImagineAir taxi service was founded by a group of Georgia Tech grads. And the gleaming Gulfstream jet emerged from the cacophonous aircraft plant in coastal Savannah.

Higher in the sky, there are many more Georgia stories. A Georgia-built C-5 Galaxy transport lumbers overhead on its way to nearby Dobbins Air Reserve Base. The hulking jet is on a homecoming of sorts. It was built at the Lockheed Martin facility there 30 years ago, and it's undergoing a series of upgrades designed to keep it flying another 40 years. The same factory is also giving life to the world's most technologically advanced F-22A Raptor fighters. The ghostly gray-colored planes regularly streak by, shadowed by F-16 chase planes on supersonic test flights that take them from east Tennessee to northern Alabama in minutes. The factory's skilled workers also produce stubby C-130J Hercules transports, as they have since 1954, on the world's longest continuously running production line.

Look even higher in the sky over PDK at a steady stream of airliners climbing and accelerating as they pass 10,000 feet in altitude. Heavily laden Delta Air Lines jets leaving Hartsfield-Jackson International Airport – the world's busiest – are bound for locales as distant as Europe, Alaska and Hawaii. A parade of green-tailed AirTran jets plies the same airspace, gaining altitude as they race toward nearer, domestic cities.

When the Atlanta Airport was founded on an abandoned auto racetrack south of the city, no one could have foreseen how important it would one day be. The airport's five parallel runways allow upwards of 140 arriving planes to land each hour. And the most recent of the runways – a two-mile, $1.2 billion, three-foot-thick slab that stretches over 16 lanes of Interstate 285 – is an engineering marvel. It's the longest runway/tunnel in the world.

Jets bound for Hartsfield are clearly visible to the children at PDK as the planes arrive from the east. A baby blue Korean Airlines 747 seems to be traveling at an impossibly slow speed as it hangs in the air over Stone Mountain. It is followed by a South African Airways A340 about to finish its daily trek from Johannesburg, South Africa. The city's international air connections helped it win the 1996 Olympics, and Atlanta has become a headquarters for some of the world's largest corporations because key workers can reach so many non-stop destinations.

The incredibly complex choreography in the skies over Georgia is almost taken for granted by the state's citizens. But the pace of aerial innovation throughout the state is quickening. Thrush Aircraft in rural Albany has updated its turbine agricultural aircraft, and its highly capable planes are sold around the world as aerial applicators and tankers for fighting fires. Air taxi companies recently founded with a fleet of single-engine Cirrus SR-22s are set to expand into "very light jets." That exciting new category is just now making its way to the market in commercially significant numbers – and the planes seem to have the potential to radically change the face of business and personal travel.

Georgia is an innovator in that category, too. Former textile workers in Columbus make precision parts for the Cessna Mustang, among the most capable of the VLJs and the first to be fully FAA-certified. Cessna workers in Columbus build control surfaces for the Mustang, as well as propellers and substructures for other Cessna planes. From Columbus, the parts are shipped to Wichita for final assembly.

Fractional ownership groups such as AirShares Elite, founded and pioneered by Atlanta entrepreneurs, are altering aircraft ownership and personal flying. AirShares saw the advantages some businesses were gaining through fractional jet ownership and applied the same principles to single-engine aircraft ownership for individuals.

The FAA's new Light Sport Aircraft category holds out the promise of simplifying flying for hobbyists, lowering costs and eliminating other barriers to entry.

What kind of future awaits the people who enter the aviation industry this way? Limitations don't seem to exist. Even within our state's borders, pilots can learn to fly planes ranging from agricultural aircraft that work a few feet off the ground to Boeing 777s that connect distant continents. Georgians restore antique Piper Cubs in basements and garages, and they assemble the world's most lethal military fighters on some of the industry's most sophisticated production lines. Some among us maintain airliners to reliability and safety standards that would have seemed unimaginable at the outset of the last century.

As much as our body of aviation knowledge has grown, we're only at the beginning of some of the most promising aviation endeavors. Students at the Georgia Aviation and Technical College in Eastman are exploring new materials that promise to make future aircraft lighter, stronger and safer than any that have come before, and they're learning new methods for air traffic control. At Georgia Tech, an enterprising group of engineering students is testing a hydrogen-powered Unmanned Aerial Vehicle they hope to someday fly across the Atlantic. Gulfstream is pioneering commercial use of "synthetic vision" – technology that allows pilots to literally see through clouds as they approach airports in poor weather.

Yes, there are threats to our aviation future as well. Delta Air Lines, once the state's largest private employer, entered Chapter 11 bankruptcy court protection after more than seven decades as an industry leader. The fate of the proud, Atlanta-based carrier and its 45,000 employees is uncertain as the company faces hostile takeover attempts and severe competition from a new breed of low-cost competitors. Airliners became terror weapons in 2001, and there's a real chance that U.S. passengers will be targeted again. The price and availability of fuel is an acute concern, aircraft noise and emissions must be reduced, and burdensome regulations sometimes seem to threaten the very industry they were supposed to protect.

But the obstacles seem minor compared to the far more daunting challenges our ancestors faced a century ago. Long-settled aerodynamic principles were mysteries to them. Durable, lightweight materials were unavailable to them, and the process of sharing the information they did have was cumbersome and time consuming at best. If Ben Epps could see the same sights as kids at PDK on any sunny weekend, he'd recognize and be gratified by the fact that his dreams of flight haven't just been realized – they've been far surpassed. He and other pioneers of his generation might congratulate us on some of the discoveries and advances we've made, and they would likely applaud our curiosity and creativity. But they would certainly recognize that there is much more work to be done.

The kids at the park need inspiration. The body of knowledge and tools they stand to inherit are tremendous, but those gifts are only a starting point. The future is theirs to determine. Will our Raptor fighter someday seem as anachronistic to them as the 1907 Epps Flyer looks to our eyes?

Let's hope so.

What's Next For Aviation Education?
By Dr. Deborah J. Huffman
Fernbank Science Center, Aeronautics Instructor
NASA Network of Educator Astronaut Teachers

Aviation has come a long way in the last one hundred years. Nearly fifteen per cent of the gross domestic product of the United States and approximately 11,000,000 jobs are currently generated in the aerospace industry, leading our country's economy in net exports. The industry contributes directly to economic and national security through military, space, air transport, and information technology applications.

How did we progress so far in such a short period of time? How will we prepare for the next hundred years? The aviation pioneers were inspired to apply their knowledge and skills toward flying machines and building a huge, dynamic industry around them. What is Georgia doing to help inspire the next generation of aerospace workers? How important is education in attracting new aviation-related industries to Georgia?

Many highly skilled aerospace workers will be retiring by the year 2008. American students currently rank near the bottom, in mathematics and science test performance, compared to students in leading industrialized countries of the world. The stability of these highly skilled jobs and global competitiveness requires coordinated federal policies to sustain and expand the science, mathematics, engineering, and manufacturing workforce. In response to this, the United States Congress established an Interagency Aerospace Revitalization Task Force to develop a strategy for workforce development in the aerospace industry.

Georgia's Governor Sonny Perdue recognizes the need to build the state's science and technology infrastructure and has created an Aerospace Innovation Center. The objective behind the center is to grow long-term economic opportunities for Georgians and to attract new companies to the state. The Georgia Department of Education has revised the curriculum to make it more rigorous so that more students will be prepared for AP (Airframe and Powerplant mechanic) courses and college. Most importantly, our students will be more competitive nationally and internationally.

The new Georgia curriculum is based on Georgia Performance Standards in several different Peach State Pathways. The Career Technology and Agricultural Education division has developed pathways around a series of career clusters, including Architecture, Construction and Transportation. This specifically addresses the aerospace industry through two different pathways, Flight Operations and Aircraft Support. Once approved, any high school in Georgia can offer the courses in either or both pathways to their students.

Flight Operations:

1st Year - Fundamentals of Aviation: Students will build a solid knowledge base in the history of aviation, the principles of flight and navigation, the aerospace community and aviation meteorology. Classroom and laboratory activities assure a thorough understanding of the aviation environment. The course will help students make an informed pathway decision upon completion. Leadership development activities through the Civil Air Patrol (CAP), the Experimental Aircraft Association (EAA) and industry mentorship will prepare students with a competitive edge for the global marketplace.

2nd Year - Navigation and Communication: Navigation and Communication are essential to the safe operation of aircraft within the airspace system. This course provides a foundation that enables the student to apply the basics of aircraft navigation and utilize efficient communication methods for safe aircraft operations.

3rd Year - Aviation Meteorology: Atmospheric dynamics and concepts are addressed to build a meteorological foundation that will enable students to understand environmental variables that create and change the Earth's weather. Meteorological techniques will be used in analyzing, charting, and forecasting weather patterns, and students will apply learned skills to the aeronautical needs and procedures of the air transportation industry.

4th Year - Aeroscholars Aircraft Ground School: Aeroscholars Aviation Ground School is the final course of a four-year term of study. Upon successful completion of this course the student will be prepared to take the Federal Aviation Administration (FAA) Private Pilot Written Exam.

Aircraft Support:

1st Year - Fundamentals of Aviation

2nd Year - Aviation Maintenance I: Aviation Maintenance I is the second course of a four-year term of study. Students will build a solid knowledge base in the basics of aircraft maintenance, performance and design. Classroom and laboratory activities assure a thorough understanding of the aviation environment.

3rd Year - Aviation Maintenance II: Aviation Maintenance II is the third course of a four-year term of study. Students continue to build and expand their solid knowledge base in the basics of aircraft maintenance, performance and design. Classroom and laboratory activities assure a thorough understanding of the aviation environment.

4th Year - Aviation Maintenance III: Aviation Maintenance III is the fourth course of a four-year term of study. Students continue to build and expand their knowledge base in the basics of aircraft maintenance, and focus on aircraft engines, overhaul and inspection procedures.

The next hundred years of aviation will be a challenge, and Georgians who understand how important this industry is to our state will also recognize our need to inspire, educate and train young people to meet that challenge. Peach State Pathways will be clearly linked to post secondary programs and opportunities including technical colleges, college and university programs, internships, apprenticeships, on-the-job training, industry-sponsored training, and military service. There are plans to articulate many of the courses with college credits so that the student can have a head start on employment. These measures clearly demonstrate the dedication of Georgia leaders and educators to guide young people into rewarding and meaningful futures in aviation through personal career preparation, and at the same time, to keep and attract new aerospace industries to our state.

Lt. Governor Casey Cagle

State of Georgia, Department
of the Lt. Governor

Roadmap for the Future

A Message From Lt. Governor Casey Cagle

Georgia's next 100 years of flight will take the industry and our highly-skilled aerospace workforce to new heights. As Lieutenant Governor, I am committed to helping prepare this future workforce by creating an education system that produces a new generation of Georgians that are competitive, technologically advanced, and dedicated.

As home to the world leader in business aviation, Gulfstream Aerospace sets a pace and example all of us can follow. Through Georgia's partnership with the National Aerospace Development Center and opening the Georgia Aerospace Innovation Center, we will continue to be a leader in the aerospace field.

The Aerospace Innovation Center creates the bridge between a focused education and an exciting career in the aerospace industry. Whether through the creation of new technology companies to support the technology insertion needs of the industry, supporting the development of our aerospace supply chain, or by providing workers aerospace educational opportunities, the Aerospace Innovation Center is the "One-Stop-Shop" to position our state for the next 100 years of innovation and growth.

It is my goal to improve education by developing highly focused career academies – some which may focus on aerospace needs – which will be a perfect complement to Georgia's highly-acclaimed QuickStart job training programs. If our state remains committed to the long-term needs of prospering, highly-demanding industries like aerospace, we will achieve great success.

We are excited that the book you hold in your hands is not just a chronicle of Georgia's amazing accomplishments, but also a roadmap to the future. The lessons we have learned as pioneers are being translated into action plans for our future. Welcome aboard!

ACKNOWLEDGEMENTS

Aerospace Innovation Center

Ag-Air Update, Bill Lavender

Ag-Flight, Inc., Billy Howell

Aircraft Manufacturing & Development Co. (AMD), Chris Heintz, John Degonia

AirTran Airways, Jodi Kemp

Beth Alligood

Alan Armstrong, aviation attorney, author and publisher

Association County Commissioners of Georgia

Atlanta-Fulton County Public Library

Atlanta History Center, Betsy Rix, Gordon Jones

Atlantic Southeast Airlines, Mary Bruce

Bainbridge College, Gilbert H. Gregg Library

Bainbridge Post Searchlight, Barbara Parsons, Sam Griffin

Blackshear, Charlie, formerly w/Darr Tech

Bill Blankenship, Fort Mountain Preservation Services

Ken Breeden, former Commissioner, Georgia Department of Technical and Adult Education

Office of Lt. Governor Casey Cagle, Elizabeth Dewberry, Jailene Hunter, Brad Alexander

Bonne Cella, author

Steve Champness, *Trade-A-Plane* magazine

Cornell University, Division of Rare and Manuscript Collections, Kroch Library, Patrick J. Stevens, Coordinator of Reference

Decatur County Historical Society, Lt. Col. Kathryn Lillethun, USAF (Ret)

Delta Air Lines Gold Wings

Delta Air Transport Heritage Museum, Marie Force, Archives Manager

Dougherty County Public Library – Genealogy/Reference

Ellen Payne Odom Genealogy Library, Irene Godwin, Ann Glass, Catherine Bryant

Epps Aviation, Pat Epps, Elaine Persons

Family Business Institute, Don Schwerzler

Fernbank Science Center, Dr. Deborah J. Huffman

Fort Stewart Museum, Walter W. "Buck" Meeks, III

Georgia Agrirama, John Johnson

Georgia Aviation Hall of Fame "Mac" McWhorter, Vanessa Haun, Office Director, Chris Jernigan, Archivist

Georgia Civil Air Patrol, Paige Joiner, Statewide Public Affairs Officer

Georgia Department of Economic Development, Susan Barnett, Senior Research Specialist, Division of Policy & Research

Georgia Department of Transportation, Ed Ratigan, Aviation Programs

Georgia Southern University Library, Loretta Brandon, Delma Presley, PhD

Johnny Gresham, Georgia Department of Transportation Board

Georgia Henderson, Marketing Director, City of Douglas

Vic Hewes

Hill Aircraft & Leasing Corp, Guy Hill, Jr., Larry Westbrook, Diana Ries

Frank Hulse, IV

International Association of Machinists (Miami), Rick Iacino

T. M. Jackson, Leslie Jackson

Jakin Centennial Committee

Don Johnson

Liberty Belle Foundation, Don Brooks

City of Louisville

Howie Lowden, the Admiral John H. Towers Memorial Committee

Lowe Aviation Company, Henry Lowe

Lowndes County Historical Society, Renate Milner

Maule Air, Inc., June Maule, Barbara Maule, Vanessa Harris, Shirley Maule, Brent Maule

Tom Millin

Moultrie-Colquitt County Public Library, Johnnie Reynolds

Museum of Aviation at Robins AFB, Dudley Bluhm

National Aerospace Development Center, Troy Thrash

National Air and Space Museum, Smithsonian Institution, Tom D. Crouch, Senior Curator, Aeronautics; Kate Igoe, Permissions Archivist; Allan Janus, Archives Reference Desk

National Aviation Hall of Fame, Cecelia John

Jerry Newton

Mike O'Connor

RAF Albany Committee

Retired Eastern Pilots Association (REPA), Jim Holder, Jerry Frost

Governor Carl Sanders, Doris M. Barnes, Troutman Sanders

M. L. Shettle, author

South Georgia Technical College Library, Jerry Stovall

Taylor Multimedia, Roxanne Taylor

The Admiral John H. Towers Memorial Committee, Howie Lowden

The AutoPILOT magazine, Brenda Tran, Publisher

The Warren Featherbone Foundation, Charles E. "Gus" Whalen

Thomas County Historical Society Museum of History, Ann Harrison, Melissa Sanford, Cynthia Nickerson

Thrush Aircraft, Inc., Eric Rojek

Tifton Gazette, Flo Rankin

Tifton-Tift County Public Library

United Parcel Service/UPS Airlines, Jackie Blair

Veterans Memorial State Park

Virginia Military Academy, Mary Laura Kludy, Archives and Records Management Assistant

Wings & Things, Leonard Harris

Peg Woodruff

World Airways, Steve Forsyth

ORGANIZATIONS

ANGEL FLIGHT OF GEORGIA, INC.

Angel Flight of Georgia is the original volunteer pilot organization east of the Rockies and has served Georgia, Alabama, Mississippi, Tennessee, and the Carolinas since 1983. Jim Shafer, a hospital broker and private pilot, organized Angel Flight of Georgia by recruiting 15 pilot friends to respond to the needs of the community. Angel Flight incorporated in Georgia in 1984 and remains an independent charity located at the Dekalb Peachtree Airport (PDK) in Atlanta.

The Angel Flight of Georgia philosophy is that distance should never stand in the way of receiving necessary medical care. Volunteer pilots stand ready to fly patients to locations where they can receive critical care and sometimes lifesaving treatment. There is no charge for the flight.

Angel Flight also serves as a resource for disaster relief efforts and played a significant role during the 9/11 tragedy. Since 2000 the organization's missions have increased from hundreds to thousands per year, all made possible by the generous contributors of pilots and other financial supporters.

THE ATLANTA AERO CLUB

In the 1920s a number of aviation enthusiasts in the Atlanta area banded together to form the Atlanta Aero Club with Jesse Draper as first club president. The group recognized the potential of 300 acres of fairly level land on the old Camp Gordon property (currently PDK Airport). Throughout the 1920s and '30s – largely through the efforts of Draper – the group was instrumental in raising public interest in building an airport on the site.

The goals of the Aero Club are to provide a forum for matters affecting both commercial and general aviation in the Atlanta area; to recognize and award those individuals and entities making the greatest contribution to furthering aviation in the Atlanta area; to communicate and disseminate information affecting aviation; and to promote aviation and recognize its importance to the Metro area and to all of Georgia. Ultimately, the Aero Club serves as a platform for members to discuss aviation-related issues.

THE CIVIL AIR PATROL

The Civil Air Patrol (CAP) was founded one week before Japan's attack on Pearl Harbor in December, 1941. Over 150,000 concerned citizens formed the organization to provide defense of the U.S. coastline. In 1946, President Harry Truman established the CAP as a federally chartered, benevolent civilian corporation. In the spring of 1948, Congress passed a law which made the CAP an auxiliary of the new U.S. Air Force.

The CAP is charged with three primary missions: to promote aviation and aerospace education; to provide cadet programs in support of the nation's youth and preparing them for successful adult lives; and emergency services. The Georgia Wing consists of six groups that are spread throughout the state which participate in activities such as aerospace education workshops and conferences, inland search and rescue, aerial reconnaissance for homeland security, disaster relief and transport of medical materials. Georgia Wing Headquarters is based at Dobbins Air Force Base.

CAP chapters can be found in middle schools, high schools, colleges and universities throughout the state. Among the various programs targeted at Georgia's youth is Aviation Awareness Day where young people are exposed to careers in aviation, and where the value of mathematics, science and technology are stressed.

THE COMMEMORATIVE AIR FORCE

The Commemorative Air Force (CAF, formerly The Confederate Air Force) is a patriotic organization dedicated to the preservation of the world's greatest classic combat aircraft. The idea for the organization originated in 1951, when former World War II Army Air Corps flight instructor, Lloyd Nolen, purchased a surplus Curtiss P-40 Warhawk. The CAF is the 16th largest Air Force and owns more World War II aircraft than any other organization or individual. The CAF is a non-profit corporation and all donations are tax deductible.

The Dixie Wing of the CAF first met in 1986 to start a unit in the Atlanta area. It has since displayed its collection of vintage World War II aircraft in numerous air shows throughout the Southeast. Over 250 Colonels participate in maintenance and restoration activities in the Atlanta area. The Dixie Wing also has developed a Historical Aviation Educational Program geared to meet the curriculum subject matter for 6th to 12th grade students. Through field trips and hands-on experience, Cadets learn about U.S. World War II heritage, aircraft maintenance, leadership skills and teamwork.

THE EXPERIMENTAL AIRCRAFT ASSOCIATION (EAA)

The Experimental Aircraft Association (EAA) was founded in 1953 by Paul H. Poberezny and a group of like-minded individuals from Milwaukee, Wisconsin. Intent on building their own airplanes, either from kits or sets of plans, these aircraft display an "EXPERIMENTAL" placard usually on the door or cockpit. In the half-century since its founding, EAA has grown into a diverse, international group representing virtually the entire spectrum of recreational aviation. It is best known for its annual fly-in convention in Oshkosh, Wis., which welcomes more than 10,000 aircraft for a weeklong celebration of flight each summer. EAA communicates through its publications, its chapter network, websites and other programs. The EAA Young Eagles program targets youth ages 8-17 and is the largest youth aviation program ever created. EAA Air Academy Camps range from introductory courses in aviation to advanced, total immersion experiences. Scholarships are also available. There are more than 20 EAA chapters in the state of Georgia, and nearly 1,000 worldwide.

GEORGIA BUSINESS AVIATION ASSOCIATION

The Georgia Business Aviation Association (GBAA) was formed to promote the aviation interest of companies operating aircraft in the state of Georgia. The organization fosters the highest degree of operational efficiency and safety and serves as a platform for members to exchange ideas on operational matters. The group also works to enlighten government and airport authorities on behalf of members' concerns and to promote better relations with regulatory and other agencies.

The goal of these activities is to raise awareness about the importance of business aviation to the economy of the state.

GEORGIA DEPARTMENT OF TRANSPORTATION AVIATION PROGRAMS

The State of Georgia initiated an aviation program during Governor Carl Sanders' tenure in the mid-1960s. An office of Aviation Development was formed within the Department of Industry and Trade. Governor Sanders was a strong advocate of economic development and aviation's role in that development for Georgia. During his term, he led the nation in airport construction with emphasis given to smaller general aviation airports throughout the state.

Shortly after his inauguration in 1971, Jimmy Carter reorganized state government thus forming the Department of Transportation (DOT) which augmented the State Highway Department into a multimodal transportation arm of state government. An office of Aeronautic and Public transportation was formed within the DOT with responsibility for airport construction programs. The two separate aviation activities within the DOT were merged in 1974 and renamed the Bureau of Aeronautics.

The Bureau of Aeronautics became a fully functioning aviation office with planning, construction, licensing and aeronautical publications responsibilities. The Bureau remained as organized until 1992 when the Office of Intermodal Programs was formed within the DOT. The reorganization combined all forms of transportation except highways into one office. The Bureau of Aeronautics was organizationally unchanged and renamed Aviation Programs, which is the current title.

THE ORGANIZATION OF BLACK AIRLINE PILOTS (OBAP)

Established in 1976 by black Eastern Air Lines pilot Benjamin Thomas, the Organization of Black Airline Pilots (OBAP) serves to enhance and advance the participation of blacks and other minorities in the aviation industry, especially pilots. The organization also places a high priority on preparing young people to pursue careers in aviation.

High among OBAP's goals is motivating black youth to complete higher education and to encourage these youth to participate in aviation. The organization also provides a network in which black pilots can communicate with and mentor one another. Since its inception, OBAP has worked tirelessly toward increasing the number of black pilots hired by the airlines. Working in cooperation with several airlines, government agencies and private organizations, OBAP has 3 basic programs: The Aviation Career Enrichment (ACE) Program, the Professional Pilot Development Program (PPDP), and the Type Rating Scholarship Program.

SILVER WINGS FRATERNITY

The Silver Wings Fraternity is an international fraternal order of pilots who soloed over 25 years ago. Membership is open to men and women of all nations. The purpose of the organization is to support a spirit of camaraderie among members and to recognize the aviation accomplishments of its members. Silver Wings strives to encourage and promote interest in the advancement of aviation, including youth challenge programs.

The late Captain Bill Winn, a retired Eastern Air Lines captain, started the Georgia chapter of the Silver Wings Fraternity in the 1970s. There are approximately 170 members in Georgia with a wide range of aviation-related backgrounds.

THE GEORGIA AVIATION HALL OF FAME is the only exclusively aviation-related organization chartered by the General Assembly of the State of Georgia. In recognition of its importance to the State, the Georgia Legislature passed House Bill 110 creating the organization, which was formally signed into law by Governor Joe Frank Harris on April 19, 1989. The Georgia Aviation Hall of Fame is established in the Museum of Aviation at Robins Air Force Base, Georgia, which is one of the fastest growing military aviation museums in the Southeastern United States.

It is dedicated to the preservation of aviation greats. Among the purposes established for the organization by the General Assembly are:

- To promote and encourage the growth and public support of aviation within the State of Georgia.
- To honor aviation leaders, living or dead, who by extraordinary achievement or service have made outstanding and lasting contributions to aviation in Georgia.
- To perpetuate the memory of such persons and record their contributions and achievements by suitable memorials that shall be located in the Museum of Aviation at Warner Robins in Houston County, Georgia.
- To promote a better sense of appreciation of the origins and growth of aviation and the part aviation has played in the changing aspect of our State.
- To receive and maintain funds for charitable, scientific, literacy and educational purposes.
- To cooperate with other recognized organizations in promoting aviation throughout the State of Georgia.
- To be the repository of Georgia Aviation History with the establishment of a library and archives research center for schools and the public.

AVIATION MUSEUMS IN GEORGIA

DELTA AIR TRANSPORT HERITAGE MUSEUM, Atlanta
The Delta Air Transport Heritage Museum collects preserves and presents the history of Delta Air Lines.
www.deltamuseum.org

MIGHTY EIGHTH AIR FORCE MUSEUM, Savannah
The Mighty Eighth Air Force Museum honors the more than 350,000 members of the 8th Air Force.
www.mightyeighth.org

MUSEUM OF AVIATION AT WARNER ROBINS, Warner Robins
The Museum of Aviation is the second largest museum in the United States Air Force.
www.museumofaviation.org

VETERANS MEMORIAL STATE PARK, Cordele
Established as a memorial to U.S. veterans, the Georgia Veterans State Park features a museum with aircraft and other military exhibits.
www.gastateparks.org/info/georgiavet/